THE NEW CAITHNESS BOOK

PUBLICATIONS EDITED BY DONALD OMAND

The Caithness Book	Inverness	1972
The Moray Book	Edinburgh	1976
Red Deer Management	Edinburgh	1981
The Sutherland Book	Golspie	1982
The Ross and Cromarty Book	Golspie	1984
The Grampian Book	Golspie	1987

OTHER PUBLICATIONS

The Caithness Flagstone Industry (with J. D. Porter)	Aberdeen	1981
A Kaitness Kist (with J. P. Campbell)	Thurso	1984
A Northern "Outlook" (forthcoming)		

THE NEW CAITHNESS BOOK

Edited by

DONALD OMAND

NORTH OF SCOTLAND NEWSPAPERS

Home of the
John O'Groat Journal and Caithness Courier
42 UNION STREET, WICK, CAITHNESS, SCOTLAND

First published 1989. The year of the Quatercentenary of the Royal Burgh of Wick

North of Scotland Newspapers

First published 1989. Reprinted 1992

*Published and Photocomposed by North of Scotland Newspapers, Wick,
Caithness, Scotland.*

Printed by Highland News Group Limited, Inverness, Scotland
© Copywright of the articles in this book rest with the individual authors. 1989
© Copyright North of Scotland Newspapers, Wick, Caithness, Scotland. 1989
ISBN 1 871704 00 6

ACKNOWLEDGEMENTS

We wish to acknowledge, with gratitude, the help given by Mr. D. M. Walker, with Chapter 13, to Aberdeen Art Gallery and Museums for Plate 56, to Mrs. Tait, Thurso for Plate 57, to the United Kingdom Atomic Energy Authority for Plates 58 and 59, to the Historic Buildings Division, Historic Buildings and Monuments Directorate for Plates 28, 29, 34, 35, 36 (Crown Copyright), to the Royal Commission on Ancient and Historic Buildings of Scotland (Crown Copyright) for Plate 33 and to Highland Regional Council for Plate 16.

We are indebted to Dr. C. Gillen, University of Aberdeen for drawing most of the figures and to Mrs. J. Mowat, Halkirk, for invaluable secretarial assistance.

THE NEW CAITHNESS BOOK CONTRIBUTORS

Mr. D. Omand	Centre for Continuing Education, University of Aberdeen
Mr. L. Masters	Dept. of Adult and Continuing Education University of Glasgow
Mr. L. Myatt	Head of Department of Engineering and Building Thurso Technical College
Dr. C. Swanson	Archaeological Adviser, Planning Department Strathclyde Regional Council
Mr. R. Gourlay	Regional Archaeologist, Highland Regional Council
Dr. C. Batey	Lecturer in Medieval Archaeology, University College, London
Mr. J. Miller	Freelance Writer
Dr. D. Waugh	Teacher, Edinburgh
Mr. D. Miller	Farmer, Wick
Mrs E. Beaton	Inspector, Historic Buildings Division, Scottish Development Department
Mr G. Watson	Engineer, U.K.A.E.A., Dounreay
Mr. D. Young	Managing Director, Perth

THE NEW CAITHNESS BOOK

Introduction   D. Omand

SECTION ONE

	Chapter	Contributor	Page
1.	The Physical Background	D. Omand	17
2.	The Early Settlers	L. Masters	25
3.	Stone Rows and Stone Circles	L. Myatt	40
4.	The Brochs	C. Swanson	47
5.	The Picts	R. Gourlay	56
6.	Viking and Late Norse Caithness	C. Batey	67
7.	The Middle Ages	J. Miller	78
8.	From Reformation to Improvement	J. Miller	91
9.	Modern Times	J. Miller	104

SECTION TWO

10.	Settlements	D. Omand	118
11.	Place Names	D. Waugh	141
12.	Castles	D. Miller	156
13.	Buildings in Town and Country: the 18th and 19th centuries	E. Beaton	170
14.	Communications	G. Watson	180
15.	Famous People	D. Omand	187
16.	Tales and Legends	D. Omand	198
17.	Dialect	D. Young	208

List of Figures

FIGURE.		PAGE
1	Parishes and Settlements of Caithness	15
2	Distribution of Chambered Tombs in Caithness (after Henshall, with additions)	27
3	Plans of (1) Cnoc Freiceadain; (2) Na Tri Shean; (3) South Yarrows North; (4) South Yarrows South; (5) Garrywhin (after Henshall)	32
4	Plans of (1) Tulach an t-Sionnaich; (2) Tulloch of Assery A; (3) Tulloch of Assery B; (4) Camster Long; (5) Camster Round after Corcoran (1-3); Masters (4); Henshall (5)	34
5	Distribution of Standing Stones in Caithness	42
6	Distribution of Brochs in Caithness	49
7	Nybster Broch, Caithness	51
8	Broch and Aisled Dwellings or 'wags', South Yarrows, Caithness	57
9	Class 1 Symbol Stone, with ogam inscription, from Keiss Links, Caithness	59
10	Cross-slab, Old Reay churchyard, Caithness	61
11	Incised crosses, Mid-Clyth graveyard (left) and Roadside, Mid-Clyth, Caithness	63
12	Sites referred to in Chapter 5	65
13	Viking and Late Norse Sites in Caithness	68
14	Place-names containing *bólstaðr* — a farm. The distribution of the place-names is a clear indicator of the extent of Scandinavian settlement in Caithness	144
15	Place-Names containing Gaelic *achadh* — a farm. The distribution of these place-names is a clear indicator of the extent of settlement by Gaelic-speaking people in Caithness	145
16	Castles of Caithness	166

List of Plates

Plate No.

1.	Hills and coast of south-east Caithness from Hillhead, near Lybster.	(J. P. Campbell)
2.	The Langwell valley, the Scarabens and Morven.	(J. P. Campbell)
3.	"The Big Rock", a sea stack at Shelligoe, Lybster.	(J. P. Campbell)
4.	The pyramidal stacks of Duncansby cut in the John O'Groats sandstone.	(J. P. Campbell)
5.	The round chambered cairn, with the long cairn in the background at Camster.	(J. P. Campbell)
6.	The interior chamber of the round cairn, Camster.	(J. P. Campbell)
7.	The horned long cairn, Camster showing restored revetment walling and entrance to one of the two chambers.	(J. P. Campbell)
8.	Cnoc Freiceadain cairns, Shebster.	(J. P. Campbell)
9.	Part of Achavanich stone circle.	(C. Myatt)
10.	The best preserved broch in Caithness, at Ousdale, showing walls rising to 3 metres in height.	(J. P. Campbell)
11.	The cross-slab in the old kirkyard, Reay.	(J. P. Campbell)
12.	The commemorative stone, to the Groat family, located in Canisbay church.	(J. P. Campbell)
13.	A Pictish symbol stone, the Ulbster Stone, in Thurso Museum.	(J. P. Campbell)
14.	A Norse rune stone, found at St. Peter's Church, now in Thurso Museum.	(J. P. Campbell)

15.	An early Christian cross carved on a rough boulder at Lybster.	(J. P. Campbell)
16.	Part of the Wag of Forse complex to the south of Lybster.	(Highland Regional Council)
17.	The dark organic layer is kitchen midden material from Norse times. Freswick Bay.	(C. Batey)
18.	The links at Freswick Bay.	(C. Batey)
19.	Dunnet Church, whose oldest parts are probably pre-Reformation. The tower dates from c. 1700.	(J. P. Campbell)
20.	A medieval church, St. Mary's Chapel, Crosskirk, Reay.	(J. P. Campbell)
21.	The 18th century church at Latheron, now the Clan Gunn centre.	(J. P. Campbell)
22.	Canisbay Church, whose oldest parts are pre-Reformation.	(J. P. Campbell)
23.	The old castle of Braal, Halkirk.	(J. P. Campbell)
24.	Dunbeath Castle.	(J. P. Campbell)
25.	Auldwick (Oldwick) castle, possibly the oldest in Caithness.	(J. P. Campbell)
26.	Sinclair and Girnigoe castles, near Wick.	(C. Cordiner 1780)
27.	In the background is the old 16th century Keiss Castle. It was replaced by the 18th/19th century castle in the foreground.	(J. P. Campbell)
28.	The gateway and gate lodge Thurso Castle, probably designed by Donald Leed of Thurso.	(HBD*)
29.	Watten Mains, dated 1762 (with late 19th century canted dormers).	(HBD*)
30.	Plan of Halkirk village.	(J. Henderson 1812)
31.	Plan of Sarclet village.	(J. Henderson 1812)

32.	Plan of Old Thurso.	(J. Henderson 1812)
33.	Plan of Clashcairn, Ramscraigs, Latheron parish. A cruck framed linear dwelling of 19th or even 20th century date.	(RC)
34.	Early 19th century fishery store at Dunbeath harbour.	(HBD)
35.	The harbour at Castlehill, Castletown, which had a wide rectangular quay for handling bulky flagstones exported from local quarries.	(HBD)
36.	Free church at Achimenach, near Reay, dated 1844. A double aisled church with minister's porch projecting on the left. The manse is to the right, behind the trees.	(HBD)
37.	Whaligoe steps, Ulbster.	(J. P. Campbell)
38.	Old grain stores (girnals) at Staxigoe.	(J. P. Campbell)
39.	The early 19th century harbour at Keiss.	(J. P. Campbell)
40.	Pictish symbol stone at Sandside House, Reay.	(J. P. Campbell)
41.	Memorial commemorating the battle of Altimarlach, near Wick, 1680.	(J. P. Campbell)
42.	The old bridge over the River Forss.	(J. P. Campbell)
43.	Stone shelving at the old croft of Achlipster, near Watten.	(J. P. Campbell)
44.	Laid Hay croft museum, Dunbeath.	(J. P. Campbell)
45.	Janet Street, Thurso.	(J. P. Campbell)
46.	Aerial view of Halkirk village with the Thurso River in the background.	(J. P. Campbell)
47.	Lybster Mains, also known as The Ha'.	(J. P. Campbell)
48.	The old Miller Academy, now the library, Thurso.	(J. P. Campbell)
49.	The old bridge at Halkirk, now demolished.	(J. P. Campbell)

50.	View along Bridge Street, Wick.	(J. P. Campbell)
51.	The 19th century grain mill at Castletown.	(J. P. Campbell)
52.	The picturesque mill at Westerdale.	(J. P. Campbell)
53.	Statue of James T. Calder (Caithness historian) at Wick.	(J. P. Campbell)
54.	Statue of Sir John Sinclair, Thurso, with St. Peter's church in the background.	(J. P. Campbell)
55.	Robert Dick's House, Wilson Lane, Thurso.	(J. P. Campbell)
56.	The S.S. Sovereign entering Aberdeen harbour. The vessel began regular visits to Wick in 1836.	(Aberdeen Art Gallery & Museums)
57.	Short-Scian G-ACUU of Aberdeen Airways at Clairdon Airfield c. 1935. The flagstone road led to the hangar.	(Mrs Tait)
58.	The Prototype Fast Reactor (foreground) and Fast Reactor (sphere), Dounreay.	(U.K.A.E.A.)
59.	Computerised fibre optic spectrometer in operation in a chemistry laboratory, Dounreay.	(U.K.A.E.A.)
60.	Norfrost Factory, Castletown with Fred the robot flanked by John Lowe (left) and Danny Sutherland.	(J. P. Campbell)
61.	Glass blowers at work in the Glass Factory, Wick.	(J. P. Campbell)
62.	Part of Reay village.	(J. P. Campbell)
63.	Scrabster, lying in the lee of the cliffs.	(J. P. Campbell)
64.	The wooded dell of Berriedale.	(J. P. Campbell)
65.	John O'Groats, showing the last house and the hotel.	(J. P. Campbell)

*   Historic Buildings Division, Historic Buildings and Monuments Directorate.
** Royal Commission on Ancient and Historic Buildings of Scotland.

INTRODUCTION

Caithness, the most northerly county in mainland Britain, forms a triangle of undulating lowland beyond the hilly lands of Sutherland. With a population exceeding 28,000, it comprises ten parishes, seven of them coastal (Fig. 1). They constitute a landmass of 177,414 hectares (685 square miles). The county's most famous landmark, John O'Groats (Plate 65) named after the Dutchman Jan de Grot, who set up house in the area in the 15th century, is 1410 km (876 miles) from Land's End.

The low-lying nature of much of the Caithness landscape is the result of millions of years of erosion of the ancient rocks, mainly sandstones and flagstones. If the interior of the county to some eyes is rather dull, then compensation can be had from the swaggering intricacies of the 170 km (105 miles) of coastline. Its varied forms include the steep walls of chiselled granite at the Ord, the almost vertical faces of the sandstone and flagstone buttresses and the sweeping elegance of Sandside, Sinclair's and Dunnet Bays. In its detail, too, the iron coast is immensely variegated with trenched geos, awning caves, delicate arches, cavernous gloups, spurred stacks and scattered skerries, offering some of the finest rock scenery in Britain.

The county's interior, a great expanse of peaty wilderness that runs for endless miles to the foothills of the southern hills, will have a very different aspect in years to come when the military conifers mature and march across the russet moor. This moor is a special place: a vast untouched feel it has, bounded by its wide horizons, where the mind, untramelled by the claustrophobic effects of mountains and men, can relax in Nature's ease. The sodden moor too, the highly publicised Flow Country, is home to a great variety of wildlife. This is an environment that is important not just to Caithness but to a much wider world. Its development should have been planned with the utmost care, understanding and sensitivity.

The fissile (easily split) rocks of Caithness have been used by man as far back as The Stone Age to build his impressive houses of the dead, the chambered tombs, that lie like stranded leviathans upon the landscape. For our early peoples the beautifully-bedded sedimentary rocks readily levered apart to provide great monoliths for the stone circles as well as lesser slabs for building their round houses. From these prehistoric times the land yielded its tough but manageable rock for building in a rural tradition that changed remarkably little until modern times.

It was the 19th century that saw the dramatic transformation of the social and economic fabric of the county with the removal of many people from the uplands and valleys to the newly founded settlements of Pulteneytown, Lybster, Halkirk and Castletown. Pulteneytown rapidly raised the status of Wick to herring capital of the world. Through its outlets in Thurso and Castletown the renowned Caithness flag was being shipped to all corners of the globe. Locally, too, the development of the industry led to an astonishing improvement in the quality of the housing. The agricultural revolution, initiated by pioneers like James Traill of Castletown, Sir John Sinclair of Ulbster and General Sinclair of Lybster saw vast acreages of land drained and fields divided by upright flagstone and drystone dykes as well as by the traditional hedgerows. Huge numbers of people were employed on the land and the large farms with their clusters of workers' houses became small hamlets in their own right. Such was the agricultural prosperity of Caithness relative to many of the northern counties that famine was, mercifully, a rare visitor.

The depletion of the herring stocks, the coming of concrete and the First World War ushered out much of the developed prosperity of the preceding century. The county's population fell dramatically from a peak of 41,000 in 1861 to a low ebb of under 23,000 in 1951.

In the mid fifties the economic gloom was lifted as work started on the Atomic Energy Authority's establishment at Dounreay. With a workforce currently over 2,000 (but declining) it is by far the biggest single employer in the northern Highlands and Islands and the fulcrum around which current prosperity in Caithness pivots. With its development the small town of Thurso rapidly expanded, more than trebling its population to over 9000 people and in the process outstripping in size the county town of Wick.

Having largely lost out on the considerable financial spin-off from Scottish oil, Caithness will be hoping that the new road bridge (? and rail link) over the Dornoch Firth will bring further diversity of economic opportunity to the "Lowland beyond the Highlands".

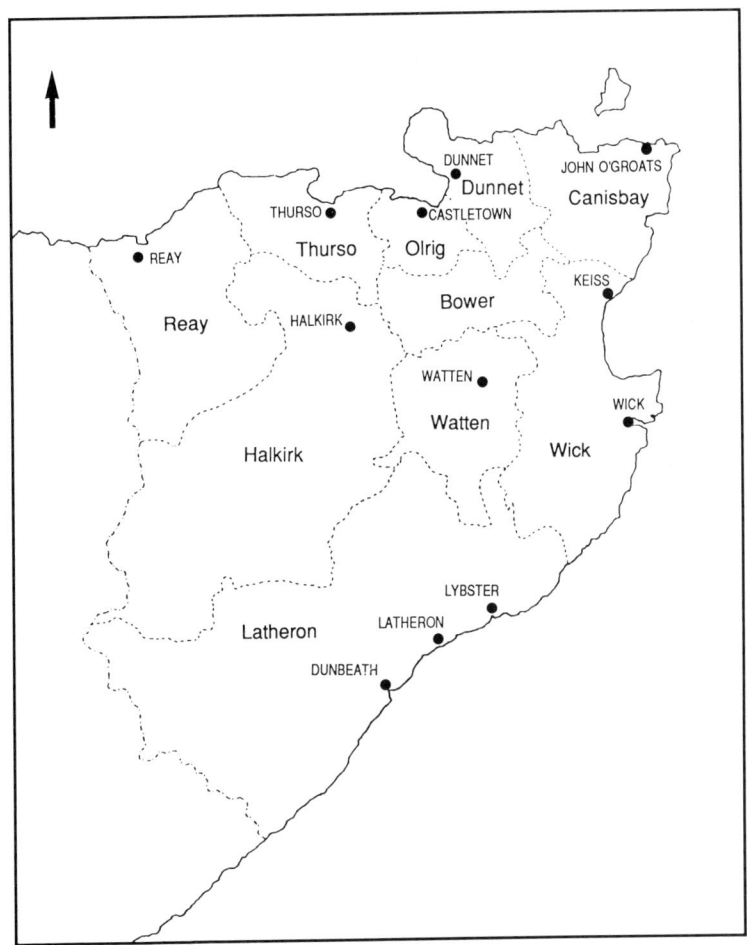

Figure 1. Parishes and Settlements of Caithness

CHAPTER 1

THE PHYSICAL BACKGROUND

Rocks

Travellers entering the interior of Caithness by train, or coming from the south-east or west by road are suddenly aware of a change of landscape; to many it comes as a considerable surprise to find this gently undulating lowland at the very extremity of mainland Britain.

This contrast in landscape between the typical highland scenery of Sutherland and the rolling lowland of Caithness is mostly a reflection of rock type. The general structure of much of lowland Caithness is fairly simple in that it forms part of a basin of sedimentary rocks which extends from the southern shores of the Moray Firth to south Shetland. These rocks of the Old Red Sandstone Series (O.R.S.) are the sandstones and flagstones (containing the famous fossil fishes) derived from sediments deposited in a water-filled basin of varying depth, known to geologists as Lake Orcadie. This O.R.S. series is sub-divided into the Lower, Middle and Upper Old Red Sandstone, all three units being represented in Caithness in a sequence that may be summarised as follows:

TABLE 1.
OLD RED SANDSTONE SERIES IN CAITHNESS

Upper O.R.S.	Dunnet Head Sandstone	Dunnet Head
Middle O.R.S.	John O'Groats Sandstone	Duncansby Head
	Mey Beds	Mey to Castletown
	Spittal Beds	Noss Head; Spittal Quarry
	Wick Beds	North and South Head
Lower O.R.S.	Basement Beds	Ousdale

While the Middle and Upper O.R.S. rocks underlie landscapes of modest elevation, the conglomerates of the lower division give us the highest hill in the county, Morven, 704 m (2313 ft; Plate 1).

Traversing the O.R.S. rocks, at, for example, Dunnet Head and the Thurso area are a number of intruded dykes. Radiometric dating of these intrusions falls within the range 249-268 million years ago during a period known as the Permian.

Although the sedimentary rocks of O.R.S. age are dominant in Caithness, there is quite a diversity of other outcrops. The oldest rocks actually surfacing are the metamorphic Moine schists and granulites which probably date to 800-1000 million years ago. These rocks are found outcropping in the south and west of Caithness, and tend to correspond to low-lying terrain. By contrast, the tough hard quartzite, another metamorphic rock, is identified with the upstanding hills of Scaraben 625 m (2054 ft), Creag Scalabsdale and Cnoc an Eirannaich (Plates 1, 2).

Granite, an igneous rock, is formed from molten material which solidified before it reached the surface and now outcrops because of the prolonged erosion of overlying rocks. Granite is found in the south-east and the west of the county where it marches with Sutherland. Only in the vicinity of Reay does the dark igneous rock, diorite, appear. Of similar chemical composition to it is the tiny outcrop of scyelite, deriving its name from little Loch Scye, located in the heart of Caithness.

ANCIENT LANDSCAPES

Wearing away of the Old Red Sandstone sediments has taken place on a massive scale revealing ancient rock masses which now stand boldly above the adjacent landscape as the quartzite hills of Sal-vaich, Sron Garbh and the Scarabens. The even sky-line at 168 m to 213 m (550 ft to 700 ft), carved in granite, which straddles the Caithness-Sutherland border, also appears to be an old exhumed land surface. It seems likely that while all this erosion was continuing the conglomerate also began to stand out above the rest of the landscape forming the tor-capped hills of Morven, Maiden Pap, Smean and Carn Mor.

RIVERS AND LOCHS

The main rivers show little regard for the underlying rocks: particularly good examples are the Berriedale and Langwell Waters (Plate 2), whose courses in the main are transverse to the underlying structure, probably indicating their superimposition from some ancient surface. Between Watten and Wick the zig-zag course of the Wick River may be attributed to glacial influences. The course of our longest river, the Thurso, is characterised by a series of rectangular bends due to both rock and glacial drift influences. Forss Water has a similar configuration

THE PHYSICAL BACKGROUND

to Thurso River, with north-south and east-west segments. Well-developed terraces have been cut along the major water courses and occur at considerable heights in the Dunbeath, Langwell and Berriedale valleys.

THE COAST

The explosive force which can be generated by storm waves crashing against the coastline is enormous. For example, stones have broken the windows of Dunnet Head lighthouse which is 90 m (300 ft) above the level of the sea and during the persistent gales of 1862 a great sea swept over the north end of Stroma, up cliffs over 60 m (200 ft) in height and rushed in torrents across the land.

The Caithness flagstones, well-jointed rocks, are particularly vulnerable to marine erosion and to cave formation. The roof of a cave may eventually communicate with the surface by means of a vertical shaft known as a "gloup" or blow hole, such as at Latheronwheel, Sarclet, Holborn Head and west Stroma. Certain geos may form by the collapse of the entire cave roof. When two caves on either side of a headland unite a natural arch may form e.g. the Brig O'Trams to the south of Wick, or the Deil's Brig at Holborn Head. The collapse of arches may leave isolated rock stacks. Among the most impressive ones in the British Isles are the pyramids of Duncansby (Plate 4), cut in the well-jointed John O'Groats sandstone. Flat-topped stacks called "cletts" form when the bedding planes of the rocks are nearly horizontal e.g. the cletts at Brough and Holborn Head.

The highest cliffs, towering up to 120 m (400 ft), are cut in Ord granite between Berriedale Ness and the boundary with Sutherland. Near Berriedale, cliffs cut in sandstone rise to 90 m (300 ft) while the highest flagstone cliffs, which exceed 60 m (200 ft), occur immediately to the west of Thurso and between Wick and Thrumster.

The most characteristic feature of the Caithness coastline is the "geo" or "goe", a narrow, steep-walled structurally-controlled inlet. In the upper Old Red Sandstone geos occur as extremely narrow slots traversing the full height of the cliff and are typically excavated in the deeply weathered dykes of Dunnet Head. Geos also occur in the John O'Groats sandstone, but their most spectacular development is found in the Wick and Thurso flagstone series which are cut by sets of well-spaced joints.

Glacial debris still lies in some of the Caithness bays and it is clear that the sea, in these areas at least, is in process of excavating a fossil coastline. The cliffed coastline in part at least, may have formed towards the end of the ice age, as it seems unlikely that the sea stacks could have survived a full glaciation.

GLACIATION
ICE EROSION

In Caithness the bleak Knockfin Heights, which are peat-covered and dotted with lochans, convey the impression that little imprint has been made by ice on this ancient land surface. Similarly, the area straddling the county boundary in the west seems to have suffered no great change of form during the Ice Age. We might say then that the agencies which carved out these old surfaces and cut the deep valleys in the south-east were far more powerful forces in Caithness than the ice sheets and glaciers.

Not being a high, broken, land area ice in Caithness did not produce the dramatic scenic effects that are found over much of the Northern Highlands, but one area of marked ice erosion might occur at Reay where the peculiar knob-like hills are the remnants of a rock mass (perhaps deeply rotted) that was largely swept away by ice.

ICE MOULDING

Journeying through Caithness one cannot fail to notice the large number of long, low, rock ridges that traverse the landscape and frequently run parallel to each other. The features appear to be largely running with the geological strike but have undoubtedly been emphasised by the passage of ice. The Dorrery Hills, near Halkirk, form the only example of a considerable feature which appears to have been cut against the grain of the rocks.

LOCH FORMATION

The lochs of Sarclet, Yarrows, Watenan and Stemster (Achkinloch), Rangag and Bushta (on Dunnet Head) all appear to lie in rock basins which might have been formed by, or at least had their size increased by, ice erosion. The fact that glacial deposits are so thin near Lochs Watten and Calder suggests that they, too, might lie in rock basins. Although lochs such as Calder, Scarmclate, Watten and Heilen lie in long depressions it should not be assumed that these hollows were entirely cut by ice.

GLACIAL DEPOSITION

The low-lying nature of the landscape and the evidence of sections available in the major valleys and along embayments might give the casual observer the impression that Caithness is thickly plastered with glacial deposits. This would be a completely misleading picture. Along the coast the thickest deposits are found at Drumhollistan (near Dounreay), Scrabster, Gills Bay, Wick Bay and at the inlets of Lybster,

THE PHYSICAL BACKGROUND

Latheronwheel, and Dunbeath. At a number of coastal locations the glacial deposits descend to below sea level. In the major valleys of Langwell, Berriedale and Dunbeath the glacial deposits (known as drift) have accumulated to great thicknesses and it seems likely that the smaller valleys were at one time completely infilled with this debris.

Away from the coastal bays and water courses it appears that the drift averages a mere 1 m (3 ft) or so in thickness. On steeper slopes it may be entirely absent e.g. on Ben-a-Chielt. In the south-east of Caithness large areas are free of ice deposits e.g. around the hill of Mid Clyth, Camster, Achkinloch and Smerral, near Latheronwheel. Moreover, it is evident that in many areas peat rests on solid rock e.g. on Dunnet Head and in parts of the Achairn and Shielton Mosses.

ICE MOVEMENTS

Before the major movement of ice came in from the North Sea, it is possible that tongues of ice had crept out from the higher land of Caithness on to the lowland plain. This is suggested by some sections in the ice deposits (at Latheronwheel harbour, for example) where a drift containing no shells is overlain by a shelly one deposited by ice coming in from the North Sea. The shelly deposit is frequently of a blue-grey colour, but varies considerably depending on the colour of the adjacent or underlying rock over which the ice has passed. In winter, as farmers well know, this material can have the consistency of glue and in summer attain the hardness of concrete!

Following the North Sea glaciation, local ice, perhaps at a much later date, was able to extend over some of the area of lowland Caithness formerly occupied by the ice sheet that deposited the shelly drift. Moraines, (mounds consisting of boulders, clay, silt and sand) may be referred to this local glacial episode. Good examples of moraines can be viewed in the Loch Watten area. A large esker system (excavated as a sand/gravel pit) stretches from Dirlot towards the Causewaymire. The only other esker of any size in Caithness occurs at Braemore.

ICE MELTWATER

It appears likely that most of the deep valleys of Caithness, which had become plugged with drift, were largely re-excavated by meltwater as the ice thawed and, as far as can be ascertained, rivers have in the main regained their old courses. Typical examples are the valleys of Berriedale, Langwell and Dunbeath which are flanked by successions of terraces eroded from the drift. However, some modifications to the river courses did take place. For example, the Clyth Burn was obliged to find a new outlet at Occumster as the lowest part of its course was plugged with drift; the burn now tumbles over a series of waterfalls before splashing into the sea over a 24 m (80 ft) cliff. It may be that the small plugged channel immediately to the north of the common outlet of the Berriedale and Langwell Rivers was at one time the independent mouth of the Berriedale River.

Meltwater channels cut in rock can be of impressive depths, the most massive being at the mouth of the Reisgill Burn, Lybster. Here, a zig-zag gorge 0.8 km (1/2 mile) long and 30 m (100 ft) deep has been carved out of the sandstone. Lesser examples occur at Camster, Achorn (a tributary of the Dunbeath River) and at Dirlot on the Thurso River. In the Loch Yarrows/Watenan area meltwater activity seems to have played a role in fashioning the rugged ridge and valley landscape.

ARCTIC CAITHNESS

The Arctic-type climate prevailing in Caithness at the end of the Ice Age was favourable to the production of certain landscape influences, some of which might be summarised as follows:

FEATURES ASSOCIATED WITH PERMANENT FROST

Soil flow (solifluction) is quite common in an Arctic environment where conditions of abundant soil moisture, sparse vegetation cover and repeated freeze-thaw lead to a progressive downhill movement of all grades of material of the soil even on the most gentle slopes. The most conspicuous landscape influence inherited from Arctic times in Caithness has been this sheet solifluction of drift which has given an additional smoothing to the landscape, already well-planed before the Ice Age. Thin deposits of frost-shattered rock can be found scattered throughout Caithness, the thickest accumulations recorded so far being at Ousdale, along the Langwell valley.

In Caithness striking tors (dissected blocks of rock outcrops) occur on the summits of Morven, Smean, and Maiden Pap. The flanks of Morven are completely buried in enormous fallen blocks while the steep conical slopes of Maiden Pap are littered with angular debris. This vast accumulation of shattered blocks suggests that although the tors may have originated before the Ice Age, they have subsequently been altered in Arctic times when chunks of rock were dislodged from them to roll down the steep hill slopes.

BLOCKFIELDS AND FROST-RIVEN ACCUMULATIONS

The most impressive development of blockfields is found on the hills of Scaraben and Creag Scalabsdale. Here, angular debris from the intensely shattered local rock (quartzite) has accumulated to considerable depths and under the influence of solifluction has moved downhill imparting a smooth appearance to the hill form.

THE PHYSICAL BACKGROUND

Although the small terraces (terracettes) found on the highest hills of Caithness probably originated in a climate colder than the present it would appear that they are still active e.g. on the slopes of Scaraben. The herds of deer on the Langwell estate obviously use these terracettes as trackways and may in part be responsible for their continuing activity. The nearby rocky summit of Morven has weathered down into a thick spread of coarse gravel which slopes to the south. The gravel has formed into a suite of terraces, mainly turf-banked.

OLD SEA LEVELS

Skirting some parts of the coast of Caithness are marine deposits representing beaches now raised above sea level.

There are at least three localities, Achastle, Latheronwheel and Dunbeath Bays (Plate 24), where exposures of beds of well-rounded pebbles lie some 30 cm (18 in) deep on *top* of the glacial deposits. These deposits were levelled at altitudes of 29.6 m (97 ft), 26 m (85 ft) and 26.2 m (86 ft) respectively. Landscape experts find it difficult to believe that the sea stood so high on the Caithness landscape towards the end of the Ice Age and so these fragmentary deposits remain difficult to interpret, their origin and age being uncertain.

At lower altitudes are easily identifiable raised beach materials which are attributable to higher sea levels. To the north of Sarclet Haven is an interesting sequence of deposits where two beds of marine pebbles are separated by a layer of broken angular sandstone, the whole resting on a raised rock platform. Apart from the marine pebbles at Sarclet and a deposit of flat cobbles near Dunbeath Castle (both being over 6 m [20 ft] above H.W.M.) the raised shorelines of eastern Caithness are at a low altitude above the present sea level. The result of levelling raised shorelines (which often have associated rock notches and benches cut at an equivalent height above sea level) shows that their altitude declines northwards from Dunbeath and eastwards from Reay.

THE BEACHES OF CAITHNESS

As we have seen the Caithness coast is an extremely varied one from towering flag and sandstone cliffs, low rocky shores, soft cliffs of glacial debris to stretches of dune-backed strands.

These coastal sand dunes and links can be grouped into three categories, deriving their material from glacial debris, sandstone rocks and shells.

1. At Keiss and at Dunnet a long dune range running parallel to the coast is backed by a sandy machair type flat containing a number of subsidiary dunes.

2. At Freswick and Sandside Bay (Reay) the dunes are more irregularly distributed. Freswick Bay, which is fully exposed to easterly gales, is now very vulnerable to wind erosion following sand extraction. The three streams that flow into Sandside Bay carry with them a sufficient supply of material to maintain a sand-filled bay.

3. The links of John O'Groats consist of low fixed dunes of shell sand. Similar accumulations are found at the Bay of Sannick, near Duncansby, giving both areas a machair-like appearance.

PEAT

The peat cover, which still overlies approximately two-thirds of the county, was probably more extensive, some having been removed for fuel and some skinned off to release land for agriculture. Peat growth results from the continuous accumulation of partly-decomposed plant remains whose normal decay is arrested by excess moisture, preventing decomposition. Where the peat growth has been so prolific that it spreads over the contours of the land a blanket bog can develop. There are three such bogs in Caithness, at Altnabreac, Achairn and Shielton. By far the largest of these is the Altnabreac bog, whose area exceeds 8,500 Ha (c. 21,000 acres).

Peat has been used as a fuel since Stone Age times and some people still cut it by hand in the time-honoured way. However, since 1981, the Highland Peat Company from its site by the Causewaymire, has been producing peat commercially, to sell throughout Britain and, currently, to Sweden.

CHAPTER 2

THE EARLY SETTLERS

If we were to consider the whole of human history, which would take us back over two million years, then the first indications of human settlement in Caithness would be seen as a very recent event. Over this great expanse of time (the palaeolithic period) man lived as a hunter and a gatherer, exploiting what nature provided in the way of animals, fish, birds, plants, fruits and berries. There is evidence of human occupation in southern Britain, going back perhaps as far as half a million years; but for reasons explained in chapter one, Caithness, and indeed northern Britain, has been successively invaded by ice advances which would have destroyed any evidence of early human occupation, if it had ever existed.

Our story of human occupation begins in Scotland in the aftermath of the last ice retreat. People were arriving from around the 7th millennium BC, as recent work on Rhum and Jura confirms. These mesolithic folk, perhaps no more than extended family groups, relied on hunting, fishing and collecting for their subsistence. With a way of life essentially based on movement, they have left behind no permanent memorials of their existence. They are recognised by their characteristic small flints, known as microliths, and occasionally after excavation by stakeholes and hearths, all that remains of their temporary encampments. As yet, there is no unequivocal evidence for their presence in Caithness[1], although claims have been made for a possible Mesolithic date for some of the flints found in the middens and shell heaps at Freswick Sands[2].

It is in the neolithic period that we get our first firm evidence for settlement. The neolithic heralds one of the most significant advances in human history, with a change in the way of life from hunting and gathering to cereal cultivation and animal domestication. So far as Europe is concerned, the initial stage of cultivation and domestication took place in the Near East and the Balkans around 8000 BC. Thereafter, both knowledge and people spread fairly rapidly through Europe and the Mediterranean, arriving on the shores of southern Britain before 4000 BC; the earliest neolithic settlers in Caithness can now be dated to just a little after 4000 BC as a result of excavations at Camster Long (infra p38), and the period ends some two thousand years later. People were now able to settle in one place for considerable periods of time: indeed, the nurturing of both crops and animals would have required a more sedentary way of life and ultimately lead, through control of the food supply, to our civilisations, past and present.

What sort of conditions would these first settlers have found in Caithness? Recent palaeobotanical work[3] at the Loch of Winless, about 8 km (5 miles) west-north-west of Wick, seems to indicate that within this area of the Caithness plain, there has been very little in the way of natural tree cover since the end of the last glaciation. In the 8th millennium BC there may have been isolated clumps of oak, alder and elm. By the time neolithic farmers arrived, birch and pine were also present and a decline in elm may be associated with, or some time after, their arrival. Whilst it would be unwise to carry such a picture over the whole of Caithness, bearing in mind its rich diversity of habitats from coast line to plain to inland moor and hills, trees can never have been plentiful given such other factors as temperature and wind. To take the vegetation story a little further, towards the end of the neolithic the onset of wetter conditions encouraged widespread peat formation, a factor which continues to the present day.

In any area and at any particular point of time there is frequently an imbalance in the archaeological evidence for a prehistoric culture. We may have the settlement evidence preserved but not the burial, or *vice versa*.

In Caithness we have plentiful evidence for tombs but nothing substantial for settlement.

Chambered tombs are found widespread in western Europe, from south Sweden to Iberia. At present, some of the earliest seem to occur in Brittany and Portugal between 5000 and 4000 BC. It is likely that there were several independent areas where the ideas and rituals behind the building and use of such monuments developed, rather than a spread of the idea from one source. It is, for example, no longer possible to suggest that chambered tombs originated in the Aegean area, as the examples there (including such famous monuments as the Treasury of Atreus at Mycenae) are up to three millennia later in date than those in western Europe.

THE EARLY SETTLERS

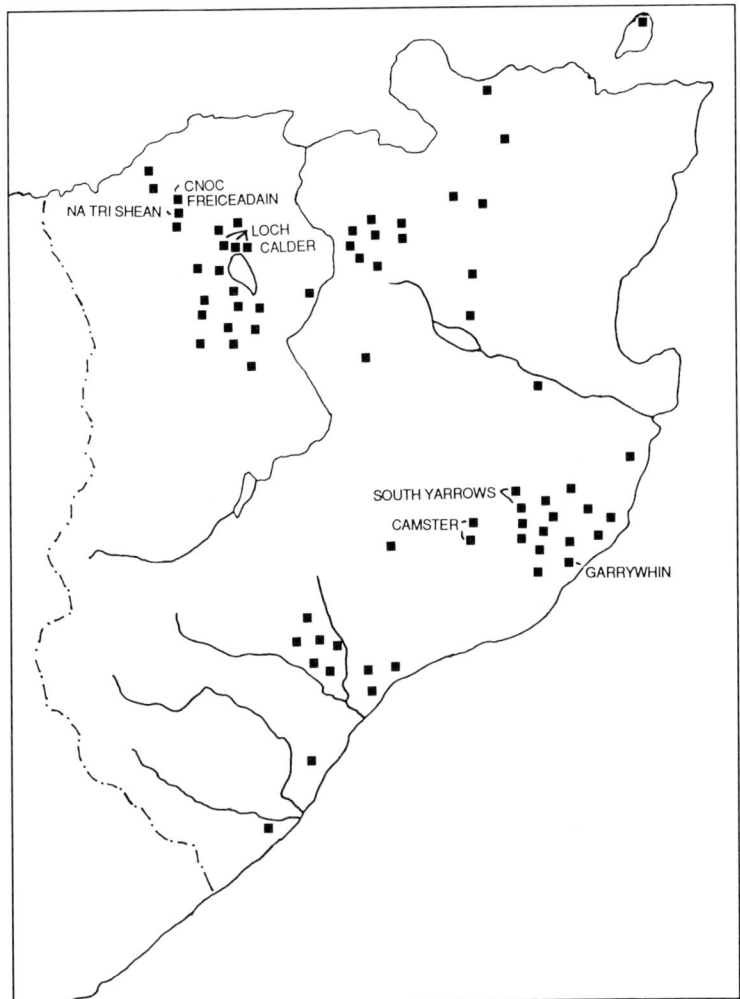

Figure 2. Distribution of Chambered Tombs in Caithness (after Henshall, with additions)

Any definition as to what a chambered tomb is, can be fraught with qualifications, not surprising in view of the facts that there are thousands of examples and they cover a period of something like three thousand years. It would be surprising if ideas were the same over such a large area, and that they remained constant for two to three thousand years. Basically, the tombs consist of a mound covering one or more chambers, which are generally accessible from the edge of the mound. The mound itself can be composed of stones, although other materials, such as turf, are sometimes used. In shape the mounds are round or long (either rectangular or trapezoidal) and they can vary in size from a few metres to enormous examples over 80 m (260 ft) in diameter or over 100 m (330 ft) in length. Although so many are now ruined, the original height of some mounds would have been in excess of 6 m (20 ft). Today, many mounds appear as just a pile of stones, but this can hide elaborate features of their external architecture. The edge of the mound may have been revetted by a stone wall; there may have been an elaborate setting of stones, known as a facade, at the wider end of a long cairn or, as we will see, at both ends in some Caithness examples.

The chambers can either open directly from the edge of the mound, or be approached by a low passage. They can be built entirely of large stones (megaliths), dry-stone walling, or a mixture of the two. Roofing of both passage and chamber was either by large slabs or by slightly overlapping successive courses of stone to produce a corbelled vault. Again there can be a mixture of the two techniques, with corbelled courses of dry-stone walling being completed by a single large capstone; this is very much a feature of the Caithness monuments. Plans of chambers can be very varied, but there are obvious limitations of size imposed by the materials and methods of construction used. Chambers can be circular, not more than 5 m (17 ft) in diameter, square or rectangular; in the latter case they can sometimes be quite long, about 27 m (88 ft) as in one example in Orkney, but they also tend to be rather narrow. Variety in chamber form is sometimes provided by internal divisions, creating a series of compartments within the main chamber (as with many Caithness examples), or by the addition to the main chamber of smaller, independent side cells which open from the main chamber. Good examples of the latter occur in Orkney, where Maes Howe is the most famous example.

So far, we have concentrated on the physical dimensions of our earliest monuments; what of their purpose? Certainly the deposition of human bones took place, including both cremations and inhumations. Sometimes large numbers of individuals, of both sexes and all ages, were buried in the same chamber. Recent excavations in Orkney, at Quanterness[4] and Isbister[5] (more popularly known as "The Tomb of the

THE EARLY SETTLERS

Eagles") have revealed the fragmented remains of over 300 people in each of the tombs. In contrast, the excavation of three chambered tombs at Loch Calder, some 8 km (5 miles) south-west of Thurso, yielded only half a dozen identifiable burials and the very fragmentary remains of four or five others[6]. Because such tombs were 'open', it is always possible that they could have been robbed of their contents, or some bones may have been removed by the community which used the tomb as part of their religious practices. The fragmentary nature of some of the burials might also be accounted for by the prior burial or exposure of the corpse elsewhere, a process known as excarnation and strongly suspected for the two Orkney tombs just mentioned. Subsequently, only parts of the skeleton were transferred to the chambered tomb. There appears to be no single answer to the burial ritual, not surprising perhaps, when we remember that the tombs were being constructed and used over a period of two thousand years, but collective burial and access over time to the chambers were clearly important factors.

Apart from human bones, excavations frequently reveal the bones of animals — cattle, sheep/goat, pigs, deer — the explanations for which are sometimes given as funeral feasts or offerings for the dead. The finds of talons and other bones of the white-tailed eagle from Isbister, and the 19th century discovery of 24 dog skulls at Cuween Hill (Orkney), might suggest another explanation: perhaps in some cases animal and bird remains could be regarded as totems of a particular family or group — Family of the Eagles, Family of the Dogs — and, again drawing evidence from Orkney tombs, Family of the Sheep at Blackhammer and Quanterness, and Family of the Deer at Knowe of Yarso. In each case there is evidence of more than 20 animals of these particular species being present, along with fewer remains of other animals, birds and fish.

The inventory of the primary chamber contents is completed by hand-made pottery, sometimes decorated, and frequently occurring only as broken pieces, and objects of stone, flint and chert, including axes, arrowheads, knives, scrapers, utilised and waste flakes.

It is always possible that tombs served functions other than containers for the dead. Many of them are conspicuous features of the landscape. In an age where there were no written records, the territorial rights for a group might have been legitimised by the presence of the tomb and its skeletal contents. If land ownership were related to family inheritance, then the ancestors bones could have provided the legal documents of the times.

To sum up, chambered tombs can be regarded as burial places, perhaps in some cases for all members of a group or family, and in others for only a select few, which are characterised by a mound covering one or more chambers accessible from the edge of the mound. With the provisos already given about generalisations, we can now examine more closely some of the Caithness examples.

There are over 70 chambered tombs in Caithness (Fig. 2), concentrated in several reasonably discrete clusters: from south to north, there are clusters in the valley of the Dunbeath Water; around the Loch of Yarrows to the south-west of Wick; and at Sordale Hill and Loch Calder, a few miles to the south-east and south-west of Thurso respectively. The tombs tend to occur on present-day marginal land, which was almost certainly more fertile and naturally better drained in the neolithic period. This may provide a clue to the location of the tomb builders habitation sites, which otherwise allude us, as their dwellings are likely to have been in reasonably close proximity to their tombs.

The history of research into the Caithness tombs is characterised by a burst of activity in the 1850s and 60s, when two eminent Caithnessians, Alexander Henry Rhind and Joseph Anderson, conducted a remarkable series of excavations. The latter in particular made many percipient comments concerning the structural history of the tombs, as revealed by his excavations at South Yarrows, Camster, Garrywhin and Ormiegill. Interest then waned and, apart from a little work by Tress Barry and Edwards earlier this century, it was not until the 1960s that interest returned. John Corcoran investigated three tombs at Loch Calder and in 1971 began the ambitious task of excavating and restoring the long cairn at Camster. His untimely death in 1975 meant that only the northern half of the cairn had been investigated, and it fell to the present writer to complete the work. The nearby Camster Round cairn was also restored in the mid 1960s, and limited excavation has recently taken place at Garrywhin.

Complementary to excavation evidence, there is that provided by field work. In Scotland, we are fortunate in having a detailed inventory of the tombs, due to the work of the indefatigable Miss Audrey Henshall[7]. New discoveries and fresh interpretations mean that we have constantly to update our information; Miss Henshall is currently working on a new edition of her work on the Caithness tombs.

We can now attempt to define the main features of the Caithness tombs. It is likely that the builders had a repertoire of ideas on which to draw, and selected from amongst these to produce the 'types' we recognise today. But we must first mention that the local Old Red Sandstone provides one of the best building materials in the whole of Britain. As it splits naturally into slabs, it is absolutely ideal for dry-stone and megalithic architecture. Much of the confident building and, indeed, of the dramatic appearance both outside and inside the tombs, is due to the ideal properties of the rock.

Caithness cairns have a range of shapes from round, through oval to

THE EARLY SETTLERS

long or amorphous, the latter probably being due to the present ruined state of the monument. The long cairns provide the greatest variety in plan, ranging in length from 24 m (80 ft) at Garrywhin, to 73 m (240 ft) at South Yarrows South. The narrower ends of these cairns are sometimes provided with projecting 'horns', creating a concave space, or forecourt, which might have served as a focus for ceremonies conducted at the tombs. The entrance to the chamber is frequently positioned in the centre of a facade, which in Caithness examples appears to have been a high dry-stone wall, two or more metres in height, between the horns. In the final stages of use, it seems to have been a common practice to block-up the forecourt areas with stones. The edges of the cairns were revetted with a dry-stone wall, sometimes with two walls, the inner being higher than the outer. The effect would have been to create a sort of bench around part or all of the cairn. The differences in length of the cairns gives rise to two types: the short horned and long horned cairns, not to be confused with breeds of cattle!

Chamber plans can be quite simple, as with the small, square chamber at Tulach an t' Sionnaich, but a very common design is one based on seven large orthostats, arranged as three pairs and a backstone. This is known as the Camster type chamber (Fig. 4) and creates a number of internal divisions within the chamber itself. There is a variant, as at Garrywhin, where the innermost pair of slabs are turned at right angles to form part of the wall (Fig. 3). The walls of the chambers are composed of dry-stone walling, which oversails to form the roof and was probably completed in the majority of cases by lintels. Unfortunately, almost all the excavated examples had suffered from roof collapse; an exception to this was the simple chamber at Camster Long as, from Anderson's description, the roof was still intact at the time of his excavation. Nevertheless, we can estimate that the height of the chamber roof would have been 2 to 3 m (6.6 to 9.8 ft) high originally. This stands in contrast to the heights of the passages, which sometimes still have their roofing intact. The passages are narrow and generally less than 1 m (3.3 ft) in height. It is rare, in Caithness at any rate, to find more than one chamber per cairn. There are some, however, and this combined with the external appearance of the cairn, suggests another possibility for the history of some cairns.

We can sometimes see what appears to be a combination of both round and long cairn at the one monument. Good examples occur at Cnoc Freiceadain (Fig. 3) and was demonstrated in the excavations at Tulach an t' Sionnaich. At the latter site, a small circular cairn covering a simple square chamber, appeared to be the first monument built. This was later enclosed within an unusual heel-shaped cairn and finally, enveloped in a long cairn (Fig. 4). This surely suggests that some cairns were composite constructions, an original structure being added to

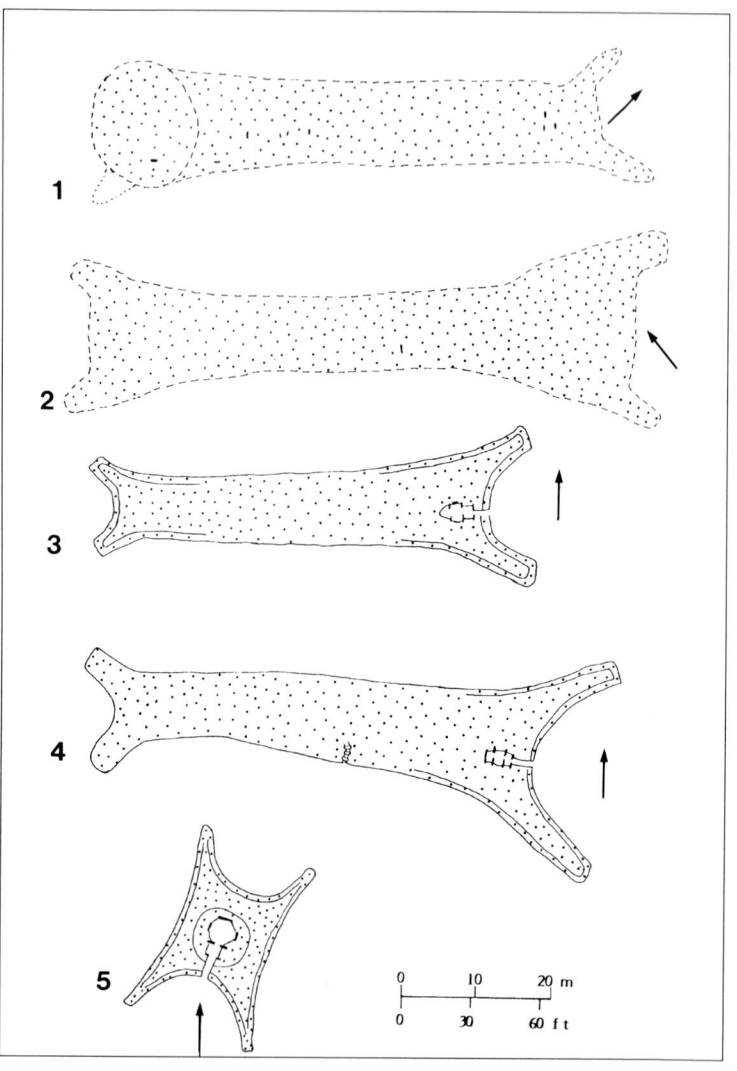

Figure 3. Plans of (1) Cnoc Freiceadain; (2) Na Tri Shean; (3) South Yarrows North; (4) South Yarrows South; (5) Garrywhin (after Henshall)

THE EARLY SETTLERS 33

through time, perhaps in response to changing rituals or a desire to create ever larger monuments. We might add here that whilst we recognise the great size of some monuments, given time, none would be beyond the capabilities of a small community (as few as 20 individuals) so far as the building was concerned. Some stones might weigh as much as a tonne, but the moving of such a mass is not a difficult task, assuming ropes (for which we have evidence from the contemporary settlement site of Skara Brae in Orkney), rollers, levers, and a knowledge of the principles of leverage were known to the builders. Suitable stone must have been available within easy reach of the chosen location for the tomb, so long distance transport would not have been a problem.

A fair proportion of the Caithness chambered tombs marked on the Ordnance survey maps are now rather ruined, and would probably only be of interest to the dedicated chambered tomb visitor. Caithness is fortunate, however, in having some very good examples which are certainly well worth a visit. What follows is something of a personal selection, but is designed to show the range of Caithness examples. Five groups have been selected and there are, generally, other prehistoric sites worth visiting in the vicinity. Three of the groups — Cnoc Freiceadain, Garrywhin and Camster — have chambered tombs in the care of Historic Buildings and Monuments (Scottish Development Department) and can be visited at all times free of charge. They are also signposted, including the paths marked by black and white poles, so they are relatively easy to visit. The other two groups — Loch Calder and South Yarrows — are on private land, but can be visited observing the usual countryside courtesies.

Cnoc Freiceadain. (Fig. 3, Plate 8). Situated on the northern flanks of the Hill of Shebster, 20 km (12 miles) west-south-west of Thurso, are two grass-covered, unexcavated long cairns. Cnoc Freiceadain (ND 013654) is the more northern of the two, and is orientated north-east/south-west with a length of 67 m (220 ft). About 122 m (400 ft) to the south lies the south-east/north-west orientated Na Tri Shean cairn (ND 012653), a little longer at 73 m (235 ft). Both cairns are prominently situated when viewed from the east and south, and the views north and west from the cairns are quite spectacular over the Pentland Firth to Orkney. Cnoc Freiceadain has a round cairn at its south-west end, almost 2.50 m (8 ft) in height. The long cairn is low and might have been robbed along the centre spine, although the presence of the tops of a number of vertical stones, set transversely to the main axis of the long cairn, could suggest another explanation. In Orkney, there are chambered tombs with plans similar to the Camster type chamber, but with the chamber elongated to take up to 14 pairs of divisional stones. They are known as stalled cairns (yet another allusion to cattle!) and the remains presently visible at Cnoc Freiceadain might represent one of these stalled cairns.

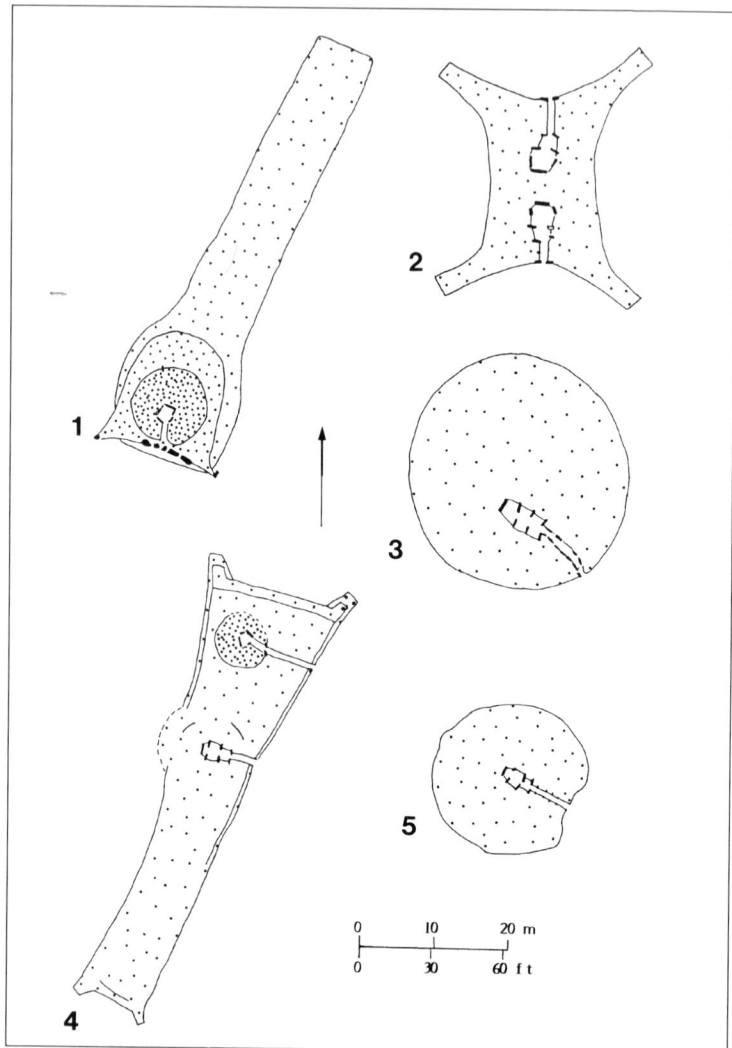

Figure 4. Plans of (1) Tulach an t-Sionnaich; (2) Tulloch of Assery A; (3) Tulloch of Assery B; (4) Camster Long; (5) Camster Round [after Corcoran (1-3); Masters (4); Henshall (5)]

THE EARLY SETTLERS

The channel along the middle would then be the result of roof collapse, but only excavation would decide if this is the correct interpretation. At the north-east end of the long cairn there are traces of horns forming a forecourt, but it is not certain if a similar feature existed at the round cairn end.

Na Tri Shean has round cairns at both ends, both being quite prominent, whilst the long cairn which joins them is again quite low. Horns are visible at both ends and the cairn does not appear to have been greatly robbed.

There are only slight indications of a chamber in any of the round cairns, but it would be a fair assumption that all three do contain chambers. Only excavation will help us to an answer here and also with the suggestion that the three round cairns were the earliest monuments, to which the long cairns were added at a later stage.

Loch Calder. (Fig. 2). On the present northern shore of Loch Calder, 8 km (5 miles) south-west of Thurso, are the remains of three chambered tombs. Destined to be submerged by the rising waters of Loch Calder, they have as yet survived such an ignominious fate and can still be seen, albeit sometimes partially submerged. They were excavated by John Corcoran[6], although at the start of his work only one site, the composite cairn of Tulach an t' Sionnaich (ND 070619) had actually been recognised. The history of this cairn has been mentioned previously (P.31) and in its final stage, the long cairn was some 58 m (190 ft) in length. The square chamber with its off-set passage, and contained with a small circular cairn, held the remains of only two individuals, a man about 30 years' old and a woman in her late teens. Farther westward along the shore are two round cairns, which had escaped recognition as chambered cairns until the start of Corcoran's excavation. In passing, it can be pointed out that it is sometimes difficult from visible evidence alone to tell a chambered cairn from a round cairn containing a cist. The latter type of monument belongs to the second millennium BC and to the next period, the Bronze Age. These two cairns are known as Tulloch of Assery A (ND 068618) and B (ND 067618). The first is a short horned cairn with an overall length of 32 m (103 ft) and, uniquely at present for Caithness, two chambers set back-to-back and entered from forecourts at the north and south ends. Both chambers are of Camster type, but with the innermost pair of divisional stones set into the wall. The southern chamber contained the remains of at least five individuals, including the tightly flexed skeleton of an adult male. The latter might represent the last burial made in the chamber. Tulloch of Assery B has one Camster type chamber, set in an oval cairn over 33 m (110 ft) on the major axis and 3.60 m (12 ft) high. Amongst the finds from the chamber were pottery sherds and flint and chert artifacts, including the tip of an arrowhead embedded in a vertebra of one unfortunate individual.

The remaining three groups of sites may all be approached from the A9 road south of Wick.

South Yarrows. (Fig. 3). There are two chambered long cairns here and both were excavated by Joseph Anderson in the 1860s. South Yarrows South (ND 304431) is the larger at 73 m (240 ft) in length, and has forecourts at both ends. The rather wider and deeper eastern forecourt has at its centre the entrance to a passage leading to a Camster type chamber, now somewhat obscured by modern building. A second chamber was located midway along the south side, although only some possible lintel stones of the passage are visible at the present day. Traces of a double revetment were found around the eastern end of the cairn.

South Yarrows North (ND 305434) lies some 300 m (1100 ft) to the north. It is now rather overgrown with heather, but the remains of a chamber can be made out at the east end of the 58 m (190 ft) long cairn. It also has forecourts and a double revetment at both ends.

There are many prehistoric monuments in the vicinity, including other chambered tombs, a broch, and one of the enigmatic stone rows.

Garrywhin. (Fig. 3). This is another area where there is a considerable concentration of prehistoric monuments, including round cairns with cists, another stone row, and a substantial stone walled fort. The chambered cairn (ND 313411) is of the short horned type, and quite small as it is only 24 m (80 ft) in overall length. It was first excavated by Anderson, who found the remains of seven or eight individuals in the outer compartment and a quantity of burnt and unburnt bone in the inner compartment, together with the usual complement of flint artifacts and pottery sherds, in the Camster type chamber. Unfortunately, much of the material from Anderson's excavations is now lost, but work in 1985 at Garrywhin succeeded in discovering a few sherds of neolithic pottery. The chambered cairn is sometimes referred to as the Cairn of Get.

Camster. (Fig. 4). Although left till last, the Grey Cairns of Camster (Plate 5) are probably the most visited of the Caithness chambered tombs, and they are certainly the most spectacular and rewarding for the visitor. There are two chambered cairns, as well as a small round cairn with exposed cist and a stone row, set in an area of flat, bleak moorland with extensive views in most directions. But all this will change as afforestation creeps round to enclose the cairns. A pity, as the restored Camster Long cairn needs the background of the sky to enhance its already dramatic appearance.

The almost completely intact Camster Round (ND 260440) cairn has a diameter of 18 m (60 ft) and a height of just under 4m (12 ft). The cairn was probably surrounded by a dry-stone wall, parts of which may be seen to either side of the passage entrance. A long, low passage leads into a magnificently lofty chamber (Plate 6) of, it need hardly be said, Camster type. Apart from a corner of the capstone, which is now missing, the chamber is intact. A rooflight has been installed in the missing space, and a little eerie light penetrates the chamber. One pair of divisional stones are particularly tall at just over 2 m (6.6 ft). Anderson found the usual repertoire of burnt and unburnt bones including, rather interestingly, two skeletons in the passage which, he suggested, had been placed sitting upright!

Camster Long (ND 260442) lies some 200 m (660 ft) to the north. It has now been completely restored, following excavation of the northern half by John Corcoran and the remainder of the cairn by the present writer[8]. The cairn measures 62 m (203 ft) in overall length, including the short, stubby horns at the north-east and south-west ends, where there are also forecourts (Plate 7). There are two burial chambers, each approached by a long, low passage but, uniquely for Caithness, they do not open from the narrow ends of the cairn, but from the long south-east side. The more northern chamber is very simple in plan, five orthostats forming a small polygonal chamber; the other chamber is the usual Camster type. Both have lost the upper courses of their roofing, which is now provided by fibreglass domes equipped with rooflights.

The external appearance of the cairn is most striking. It was surrounded for part of its perimeter by a double dry-stone revetment, the inner one being about 1 m (3.3 ft) in height and the outer about 0.35 m. On the south-east side, about two-thirds of the way along from the north-east end, we found that the inner wall ceased and that the outer had increased in height to become the only revetment in the southern half of the cairn. It should, however, be explained that the revetments had collapsed outwards and that the excavation was like a gigantic three-dimensional jig-saw puzzle to get the stones back into something like their original positions. The north-east end has a magnificent, unbroken dry-stone facade with a platform in front of it. Corcoran found that the centre of the facade had been thoroughly disturbed by Joseph Anderson, who was, no doubt, looking for the entrance to a passage in the same position as he had found at South Yarrows. Clear evidence was found for the platform which fronts the facade, but the same can not be said for the steps at the ends of the horns: They are, at best, highly speculative. This is a pity as one could well imagine a priest, or leader of the community, ascending the steps and standing on the platform in front of the dramatic backdrop provided by the facade, and addressing the audience assembled in the forecourt.

The corresponding south-west end also appeared to have a platform, but there was certainly no evidence for steps at the ends of the horns. Nor was there very much evidence for a facade, apart from some foundation courses of a dry-stone wall immediately behind the platform. The reason for the lack of a facade at this end was not far away. There used to be a sheep fank just beside the end of the cairn, and the most likely source of stone to build the fank would have been the facade itself. As it was marked on Joseph Anderson's plan, and the sheep fank was built after his work, it was decided to restore a facade at the south-west end. Incidentally, the sheep fank has now been moved to the northern end of the site.

Something of the structural history of Camster Long was revealed by Corcoran's work in the northern half of the cairn. The simple chamber was found to be enclosed in its own circular cairn, 7.50 m (25 ft) in diameter, and surrounded by a revetment 1 m (3.3 ft) high. Nothing can now be seen of the revetment of this cairn, but its position is marked to some extent by the first of the humps, which are such prominent features of the restoration and, in fact, of the cairn during Anderson's excavation, as he illustrates the site with a woodcut in his report. The same argument applies for the second hump, which covers the Camster type chamber, although the evidence here for an earlier round cairn to enclose the chamber is less certain. It had been suspected that the slight humps visible in the southern half of the cairn might conceal further burial chambers, and at one point in Corcoran's excavation it looked as if a third chamber had been found[9]. Sadly, this was not to be the case, for complete excavation by the writer of the tail of the cairn demonstrated that no further chambers had been built. The neolithic builders had simply piled stone on stone to create a massive monument. Its removal, however, provided the opportunity to investigate a piece of ground which had lain protected under the cairn. Here were found numerous sherds of pottery, flint and chert artifacts, including arrowheads and scrapers, exactly the same range of finds as are made in the chambers. There were a number of post and stakeholes, mainly on the centre line of the cairn, and these may have had something to do with laying out the axis of the cairn. Samples of organic material provided radiocarbon dates which, when calibrated, give an average age of 3800 BC. We can suggest that the cairn was built not long after that date.

The structural history of Camster Long might have involved the building of the simple chamber and its round cairn first, the Camster type chamber second, and then both chambers being enclosed within a massive long cairn. This is the sort of evidence provided by excavation which helps us to suggest interpretations for unexcavated sites like Na Tri Shean.

A visit to any of the Caithness cairns, but perhaps particularly to those at Camster, is something of an experience. To crawl, as one must, along the passages and then stand upright in the lofty chambers, gives us some idea of the awe and mystery which surely filled the minds of the tomb users. To stand outside and see Camster Long, lying like some gigantic slug on the surface of the moor, gives us some impression of the lengths to which the builders would go to perpetuate the memory of their ancestors and, incidentally, of their own presence in the Caithness landscape of 4000 and more years ago.

REFERENCES

1. Morrison, A.   Early Man in Britain and Ireland (1980) London.
2. Lacaille, A. D.   The Stone Age in Scotland (1954) London.
3. Pegler, S.   'A Radiocarbon-dated Pollen Diagram from the Loch of Winless, Caithness, North-East Scotland', New Phytologist, 82, 245-63.
4. Renfrew, A. C.   Investigations in Orkney (1979) London.
5. Hedges, J. W.   Tomb of the Eagles (1984) London.
6. Corcoran, J. X. W. P.   'The Excavation of Three Chambered Cairns at Loch Calder, Caithness', Proceedings of the Society of Antiquaries of Scotland, 98 (1964-66) 1-75.
7. Henshall, A. S.   The Chambered Tombs of Scotland, Vol 1 (1963) Edinburgh; Vol 2 (1972) Edinburgh.
8. Masters, L. J.   'The Excavation and Restoration of the Camster Long Chambered Cairn, Caithness District, 1967-80' (forthcoming).
9. Bramman, J. I.   'The Early Inhabitants' in Omand, D. (Ed) The Caithness Book (1972) Inverness.

CHAPTER 3

STONE ROWS AND STONE CIRCLES

"…..they now stand in a leaning posture, as if mourning over the departed times of a heroic age."

Worsaae.

Many centuries before the birth of Abraham, in Ur of the Chaldees, and even before the building of the pyramids of Egypt, early man in Britain was putting up standing stones. They are found throughout the length of the country standing sometimes singly, sometimes in groups, and often enclosing a circular area of ground. Erected over a period which may span some fifteen centuries, the earliest probably date from the fourth millenium BC. This was a time when the climate was drier and warmer than it is at present.

Caithness is no exception in having these hoary lichen-covered megaliths as monuments to the past. They range in height from almost 4 m (13 ft) at Borgue (ND 126266) to very small, insignificant, but nevertheless interesting stones concealed in the heather. Usually they are found on the lower ground below the 150 m (500 ft) contour. A single upright stone may be all that is left of a group and occasionally the remains of others can be found nearby. Some may have been removed for building purposes.

Although no megalithic monument as spectacular as Stonehenge is to be seen in Caithness, there are, however, examples of stone settings of a type which are unique to this part of Britain and perhaps are of equal importance. Situated as they often are in remote moorland, without the need for a barbed wire protective barrier, the visitor may walk amongst them undisturbed.

The distribution of standing stones

The distribution pattern of the standing stones (Fig. 5) is rather similar to that of the chambered cairns (Fig. 2). In each case there are concentrations around Latheron, Yarrows, to the west of Loch Calder and Reay. Although there is also a grouping of chambered cairns near

Sordale hill, there are no standing stones in this area. In the north-east of the county there are very few chambered cairns and only four isolated standing stones.

Between the above concentrations there are isolated settings which appear to link the groups together across the county. There are quite distinct patterns around Dunbeath away from the deep gorges running down to the coast. They also run from Latheron northwards along the low ground as far as Mybster, where they trend westwards towards Dorrery and then north-west to Reay. They are met at Rangag by a line coming across from Yarrows. A further line takes the low land inland from Mybster as far as Backlass. These lines may indicate the neolithic and later bronze age routeways across the county.

The absence of standing stones, and antiquities in general, in the north-eastern part of the county may perhaps be attributed to the relatively flat and poorly drained land in this area.

The single stones

There are over forty isolated standing stones which do not appear to have formed part of a group or setting but which stand alone. They are firmly set in the ground, usually with small stones around the base to help in supporting them. The height varies; some are thin slabs of local stone whilst others are quite solid boulders, as at Bilbster (ND 283538).

As in other parts of Britain folklore often attaches itself to the standing stones. Local tradition has it that a hunter broke the Sabbath by shooting deer on a Sunday. As retribution he was turned to stone and to this day can still be seen at the Borgue. A short distance to the north lies a similarly large stone, now fallen, which represents a petrified deer. Furthermore, his two dogs met the same fate and may now be seen as two small erratic boulders to the south. These small stones are still known as "the dogs". Similar mythical stories of being turned to stone are common elsewhere in Britain.

Another single stone to which there is a traditional story attached is the one situated in the parish of Bower (ND 221617) known as Stone Lud, or Liot's stone. It stands to a height of 2.5 m (8 ft 2 in) and another stone, similar in size, now lies fallen nearby. The upright stone is said to mark the burial place of one of the Orkney Earls, Liot, who died after being wounded in a battle near Spittal. In all probability, both of these stones were erected long before the Norse period. They may also have been carefully positioned because, at the time of the summer solstice, as one stands by the fallen stone, the sun would be seen to set behind the upright one, looking towards Dunnet Bay.

A single large stone, almost 3 m (9 ft 5 in) high, stands close by the side of the road at Rangag farm (ND 177449) on the road from Latheron to Georgemas. Originally it was one of a pair. The other, of similar

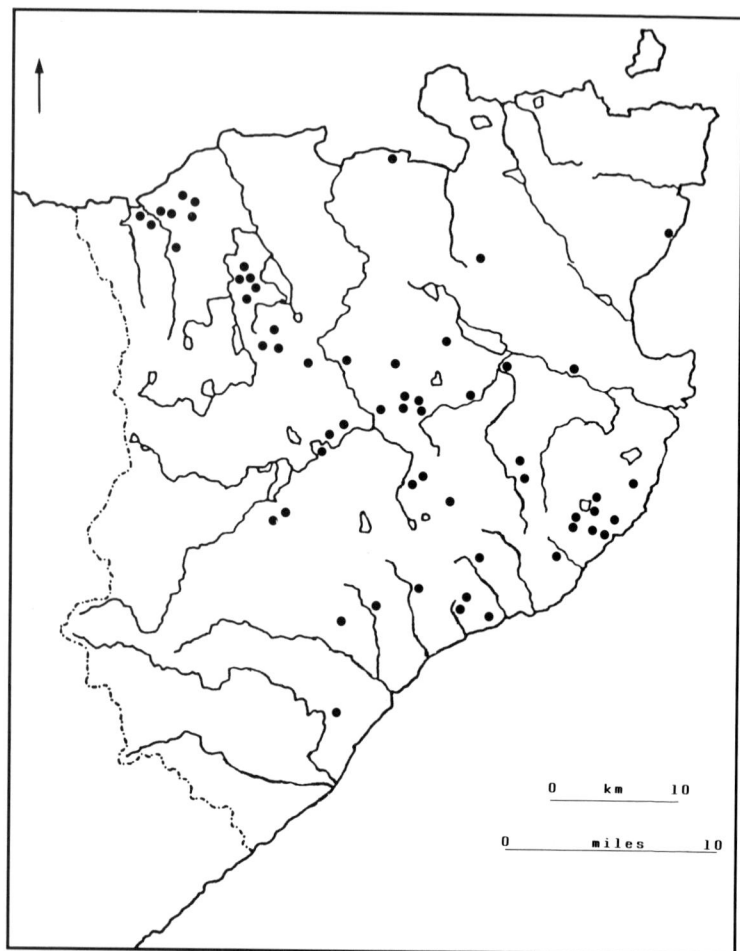

Figure 5. Distribution of Standing Stones in Caithness

STONE ROWS AND STONE CIRCLES

height, located on the other side of the road, has now been covered due to road-widening operations.

To the north of the course of Dunbeath Water is the hill of Cnoc na Maranaich on the summit of which can be seen from some distance the remains of a chambered cairn and, close by, a single standing stone (ND 132332). Attention was first drawn to the possible astronomical purpose of this stone by Professor Thom[1]. Although now leaning, it still stands to a height of 2.5 m (8 ft 2 in) and from it can be seen a well-marked dip in the horizon to the north-west formed between the distant hills. At the present day the midsummer sun sets just to the left of this notch. Around 1500 BC the last light of the sun's disc would have finally disappeared in the notch suggesting that the stone was erected for either a calendrical or midsummer ceremonial purpose.

Stone Circles

The mention of stone circles brings to mind sites such as Stonehenge on Salisbury Plain or the Ring of Brodgar in Orkney but many other settings of stones, not always so spectacular, are found throughout Britain[2].

The remains of perhaps a dozen stone circles are known in Caithness, although a number of them are now rather fragmentary. The best preserved example is that by the roadside at Achavanich (ND 188417; Plate 9), close to the southern shore of Loch Stemster (also known as Achkinloch). In plan the setting is horseshoe-shaped with its axis north and south and open at the south end. The stones are set with their main axes at right angles to the perimeter. This unusual arrangement may be a local variation as, apart from being found again at Broubster (ND 047608), it also occurs at some of the sites in Sutherland. Originally there may have been over 50 stones in this setting but there are now only about 30 still standing with the tallest about 2 m (6 ft 7 in) high. On the outer periphery, at the north-east, can be seen the remains of a burial cist, with perhaps others along the east side.

Within the vicinity of this setting are isolated standing stones to the east and a single one, now leaning, on the other side of the road. There are also the remains of a chambered cairn nearby, and at a distance of 0.5 km (500 yd) to the south-east, two hut circles: evidence of early habitation in this area.

At Aulton, Broubster, (ND 045599) is a setting of 10 stones forming part of a circle. It is interesting because at first sight there appears to be only one stone at the west standing to a height of 1 m (3 ft 3 in), but further searching reveals another fallen one nearby and a further 8 very small ones hidden in the heather. The smallest one is only 75 mm (3 in) above the surface. A further point of interest is the very large diameter of this setting which is almost 65 m (213 ft) across. Unfortunately, the setting has been damaged and some of the stones possibly removed at the north-east due to cultivation around the nearby ruined croft.

Large diameter stone settings are not unusual in Caithness. Another example with a diameter of 58 m (190 ft) is at Guidebest (ND 181351) alongside the Latheronwheel burn. There are 7 stones still standing, the tallest of which, at the west of the circle, is only 1.5 m (4 ft 11 in) high.

At Camster (ND 259458), on the east side of the road which runs from Lybster to Watten, there are 3 standing stones which may have formed part of a circle. Two are about 0.8 m (2 ft 7 in) high with the third just visible above the vegetation. They are easily seen from the road.

A single large stone stands on a heather-covered plain near Dorrery (ND 069557). It is 1.2 m (3 ft 11 in) high and is surrounded by old peat cuttings. Nearby are the stumps of two other broken-off stones which, if they formed part of a circle, would have been on a diameter of 73 m (240 ft). This is an interesting dimension because Thom has argued that a common unit of length equal to 0.829 m (2.72 ft), and which he names the Megalithic Yard, was used in setting out the stone circles. This unit would make the Dorrery diameter almost exactly equal to 88 Megalithic Yards[3].

Standing at the centre of this circle and looking south-west rises the shoulder of Ben Dorrery. About half way along this shoulder is seen on the horizon another standing stone set in a small depression. At midwinter, on the day of the winter solstice, the sun can be seen to set behind the small hump to the left of the stone on the hill and then reappear in the hollow to set again behind the stone on the horizon. If these stones were not set out carefully for astronomical purposes their positioning is a strange coincidence[4]. After all, the people who erected the standing stones were the early agriculturalists and would have required some form of indication as to the time of the year for the sowing of crops and to indicate other dates in their agricultural calendar.

The stone rows

Perhaps the most intriguing monuments of neolithic and early bronze age man in the north of Scotland are the rows of small stones set out in fan-shaped arrays. In Britain they are only known in Caithness and Sutherland, where over twenty sites have now been recorded[5]. Elsewhere, similar sites are known in Brittany but on a much larger scale and using much taller stones.

These settings of stones could perhaps be called miniliths rather than megaliths which is the term usually applied to these large blocks of stone. Often only just visible above the depth of peat which has accumulated, and sometimes completely submerged beneath the surface, they are set out with small stones usually less than 1 m (3.3 ft) in height. They appear to radiate from one or sometimes more points with the fan shape thus formed truncated at the narrow end.

The best example, and most easy of access, is that at Mid Clyth (ND 295384), known as the 'Hill O' Many Stanes'. It is signposted close by the side of a minor road off the main A9 road south of Wick. There are still some two hundred small stones set in rows radiating down the slope of a small hill. From the plan published by Thom[6] there are two separate fans. The axis of the main fan is aligned almost exactly due north and south whilst the smaller fan abuts to the west of it. The stones are set with their main axes along the rows and looking from the base of the fan, the point from which they radiate is lost over the summit of the small hill. On a clear day from the top of the rows can be seen the hills of the Banffshire coast 80 km (50 miles) away to the south-east.

It used to be a popular belief that gold would be found beneath the standing stones. That is one reason why a number of them have been removed or toppled. There were also superstitions attached to them. A farmer at Bruan is said to have removed one of the stones from Mid Clyth to use as a lintel over the fireplace of a kiln he was building. When the fire was lit the stone burst into flames but was not consumed in the process. So afraid was he that he returned the stone very quickly to the exact place in the row whence it had been removed.

In the area around Watenan are six further sites of stone rows, many of which are very ruinous, but a good example still survives at Garrywhin (ND 314413). Here, seven rows radiate from a burial cist and a total of 55 stones may be found.

Another good example occurs at Upper Dounreay (ND 12660) where the setting lies in the hollow between two small hills. The stones are very small but nevertheless are in quite distinctive rows. There remain now only about half the number of stones that were recorded when an early survey was carried out in 1871 by Sir Henry Dryden. They are situated in an area which is quite rich in prehistoric remains, including a single standing stone towards Dounreay and a number of chambered cairns.

The purpose of the standing stones

There are almost as many theories appertaining to the standing stones as there are stones themselves. Many of the ideas have no foundation other than being flights of fancy, but there are certain observations which can be made where the stones are frequently associated with other features. They may not have had a single purpose and there may well have been various reasons for their erection.

At many sites of multiple stone settings throughout Britain burials have been found and there is evidence of a possible burial at Achavanich. Moreover, the remains of a burial were located in the cist at the top of the stone rows of Garrywhin. No other stone setting has been excavated in Caithness and it is more than likely that burials exist at other similar sites.

They may have had a ceremonial purpose associated with the burial rites and there is ample evidence of this elsewhere in Britain. Perhaps they may have been communal meeting places.

The single stones may have been erected as markers. They may have been boundary or territorial indicators or erected to mark a routeway, and there is some evidence of this in Caithness.

Ever since William Stukeley published his work on Stonehenge in 1740, where he noted certain astronomical alignments, there has been an interest in the possible astronomical significance of other stone settings. It was not until the publication of the work of the late Professor Thom that the real astronomical significance of a number of the sites became appreciated. Thom carefully surveyed many sites throughout Britain where he found evidence of alignments connecting the standing stones to the rising and setting sun at certain times of the year. These alignments may have been used as a primitive calendar. Today, without a calendar it would be impossible to manage our modern society. Even so, the early farmers in neolithic and bronze age times would still have needed some form of indication of the time of the year for managing their crops. If early man recorded in stone the observations of the sun, it is just as likely that he made observations of the moon and the stars. Thom found evidence of this also, and he has suggested that the stone rows found in Caithness were used in conjunction with lunar observations. Other workers in the field have both checked the work of Thom and extended it even further. Although the findings are still somewhat controversial, there is considerable evidence to support an astronomical purpose for some of the settings of standing stones.

We can never know the true purpose or significance of the standing stones, erected by an early non-literate society. Many aspects of them must remain a mystery. Nevertheless, they form a significant part of the landscape and provide the material for an interesting study.

References
1. Thom A. and Thom A. S. Megalithic Remains in Britain and Brittany, 1978, Clarendon Press, Oxford.
2. Burl A. The Stone Circles of the British Isles, 1976, Yale University Press.
3. Thom A. Megalithic Sites in Britain, 1967, Clarendon Press, Oxford.
4. Myatt L. J. A Megalithic Winter Solstice Alignment at Dorrery, Caithness, Archaeoastronomy No 12, (Jour. Hist. of Astronomy, XIX 1988).
5. Myatt L. J. The Stone Rows of Northern Scotland, in Records in Stone, Ed C.L.N. Ruggles, Cambridge University Press, 1988.
6. Thom A. Megalithic Lunar Observatories, 1971, Clarendon Press, Oxford.

CHAPTER 4

THE BROCHS

There is little evidence of the nature of settlement in Caithness prior to the Iron Age. Monumental remains of earlier periods such as burial cairns and stone rows have survived, but there are few traces of the people themselves, including their houses, agriculture and economy. At some locations in the District there are large hilltop enclosures, such as Buaile Oscar (ND 058557) and Garrywhin (ND 312413). These have traditionally been thought of as forts, possibly belonging to the Iron Age. It now seems more likely that such enclosures may date back to the Bronze Age or to the Neolithic period and they may not in fact be settlement forms at all, but rather ritual enclosures. At other locations in the District hut circles exist, which again may date back to the Bronze Age. These tend to occur only in areas which have not undergone agricultural improvements, such as rough grazing. There is no way of knowing whether this form of Bronze Age settlement, common in the Sutherland straths, was once also common throughout the arable land of Caithness, before being removed by the dramatic land improvements which have taken place in the District in the last two hundred years.

It is only from the Iron Age that widespread archaeological traces of prehistoric settlement have survived in Caithness, with the main settlement form being brochs, which are also common in other areas of north and west Scotland. There may have been other types of Iron Age settlement within the District, such as for example, promontory forts, but there is little evidence for the dating and nature of such sites. The broch seems to have been the major, if not the exclusive, form of settlement in Iron Age Caithness.

Brochs have been an interesting topic of study for well over one hundred years, and in many ways they have come to be regarded as an enigma. They only occur in Scotland, with the vast majority to be found in the northern mainland, the northern isles and the west coast and islands. They are stone-built structures, hence perhaps their survival throughout the arable land of Caithness, whilst other less substantial settlements may have disappeared. The traditional view is that most brochs were tall stone towers with internal wooden floors, standing alone in the landscape, with the majority built between 100 BC and 200 AD. They have been regarded as the homes of local chieftains, or places where refuge could be sought in times of trouble. This image of a broch has existed for a long time, but a new understanding of the nature of brochs is now beginning to emerge as a result of modern research work largely in Orkney and Caithness.

Caithness has the largest number of brochs of any area in the north and west of Scotland, with 110 certain sites and 87 potential sites (Fig. 6). There is some dubiety about the exact identification of sites, because they frequently appear in the landscape as large grass-covered mounds showing few distinguishing features. It is possible that a grass-covered mound could contain a cairn rather than a broch, although in many cases it can be determined that the mound covers a broch from a set of regularly recurring features, such as, visible stonework, a depression in the mound top, and a surrounding ditch. One particularly distinctive feature of many broch mounds in Caithness is a stepped profile or mound-on-mound appearance. This effect is created by the underlying stone structures, and is a fairly certain indicator of the presence of a broch and its surrounding buildings.

The brochs in Caithness are spread throughout the arable land (Fig. 6). They generally do not occur within the large areas of peat which cover about two thirds of the District and it seems fairly obvious that they were related to land under cultivation during the Iron Age. The extent of cultivable land in Iron Age Caithness was less than today's arable land, as there has been considerable reclamation from peat in the last two hundred years, involving the cutting back of peat mosses and extensive drainage, sometimes of whole lochs. Brochs do not therefore occur everywhere in the arable land of Caithness, but only in those areas which were capable of cultivation in the Iron Age. Understanding the distribution of sites is however not that simple as it is possible that a number of brochs have disappeared without trace. There are historical records of the removal of whole brochs by farmers in Victorian times[1] and there may have been several unrecorded removals.

Within the cultivable land of Caithness brochs sometimes show a remarkable density of distribution. For example, in the vicinity of Keiss on the east coast of the District there are three brochs within half a kilometre of each other, two of them only 180 m (590 ft) apart on the foreshore (Harbour Mound ND 353610; Whitegate ND 354612; and Road ND 348615). There are other concentrations of sites at Westerdale in the upper reaches of the Thurso River, near Loch Watten and along the east coast of the District to the south of Wick. Some of the brochs occur so close together that it throws considerable doubt on the theory that they should be regarded as the homes or castles of individual chieftains. It seems much more likely that they were rather the farming establishments

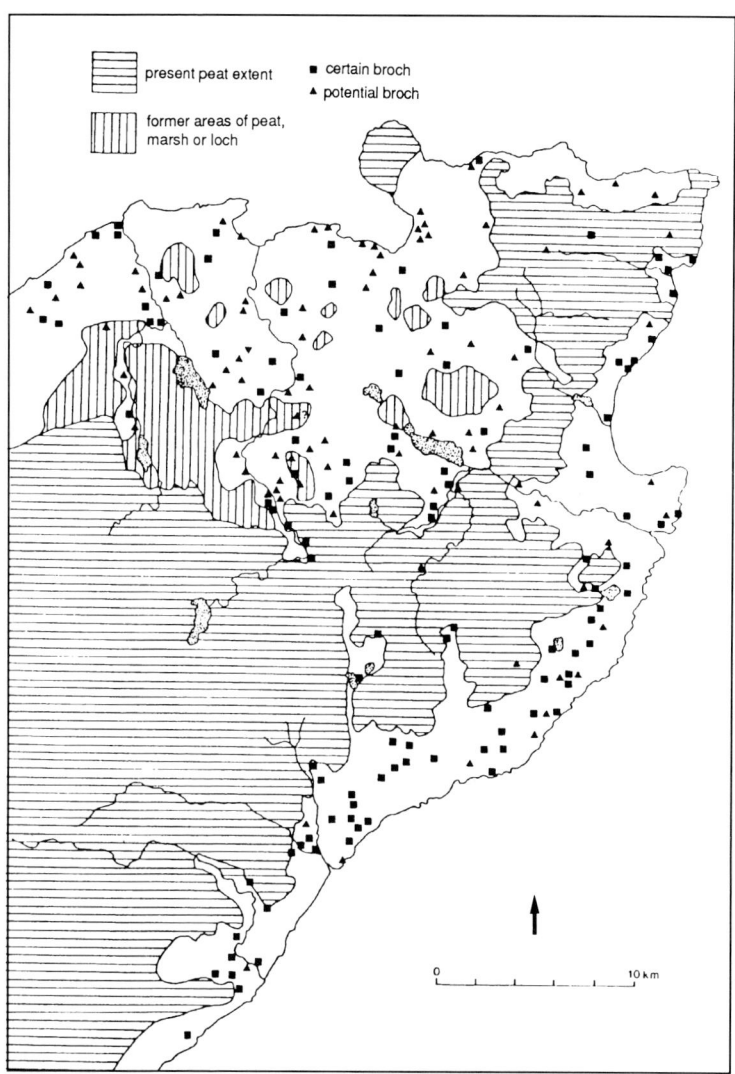

Figure 6. Distribution of Brochs in Caithness

of their time. No identifiable Iron Age field systems have survived around brochs, but this is hardly surprising in the much improved landscape of Caithness.

Knowledge of the nature of brochs in Caithness relies heavily on information obtained from old broch excavations. There has been only one modern broch excavation in Caithness, by the late Horace Fairhurst at Crosskirk (ND 025701) on the north coast of the District[2]. Prior to the Crosskirk excavation there had been only a short investigation of a broch in 1940 in advance of the construction of the spitfire aerodrome at Skitten (ND 323565)[3], and a number of antiquarian investigations in Victorian times. The first broch excavation in Caithness took place at Kettleburn (ND 349519) near Wick in 1852 prior to the removal of the remains by the local farmer[4]. Thereafter, there was a number of intermittent broch investigations until the 1890s and 1900s when a remarkable series of excavations was undertaken by Sir Francis Tress Barry and John Nicolson over a concentrated area to the north of Wick. These included the excavation of the brochs of Nybster (ND 370631) and Road near to the recently opened John Nicolson Museum at Auckengill. Unfortunately, no comprehensive record of the early excavations was kept, although there is a collection of drawings and photographs, some of which are on display in the Museum. The Tress Barry/Nicolson excavations were important because they revealed the nature of broch sites in a concentrated area of east Caithness. The features of a number of these sites are still visible today, although they are generally badly overgrown.

A substantial picture can be built of the general nature of a broch in Caithness from the sparse records of the old excavations, the details still visible at excavated sites and the record of the modern excavation at Crosskirk. A Caithness broch seems to have consisted of three main elements: the broch structure itself, surrounding buildings and an outer defensive system consisting of a rampart wall and/or a ditch surrounding the whole complex.

The broch structure is perhaps the most familiar archaeological element. There have been many articles and books written about the nature of the broch structure, describing it as a stone tower, built using a unique cavity wall construction technique. The broch of Mousa in Shetland which still stands over 12 m (40 ft) high, is frequently quoted as an example of a typical broch structure, it being assumed that all brochs resembled it. None of the excavated Caithness broch structures, however, have stood much higher than 4 m (13 ft) when dug out and there is little evidence that any had a high rising wall containing superimposed galleries within them (Plate 10). Most, however, seem to have had very thick wall bases, sometimes up to 5 m (16.5 ft) wide. It could be argued that such a wide wall base was necessary to support a considerable height

THE BROCHS

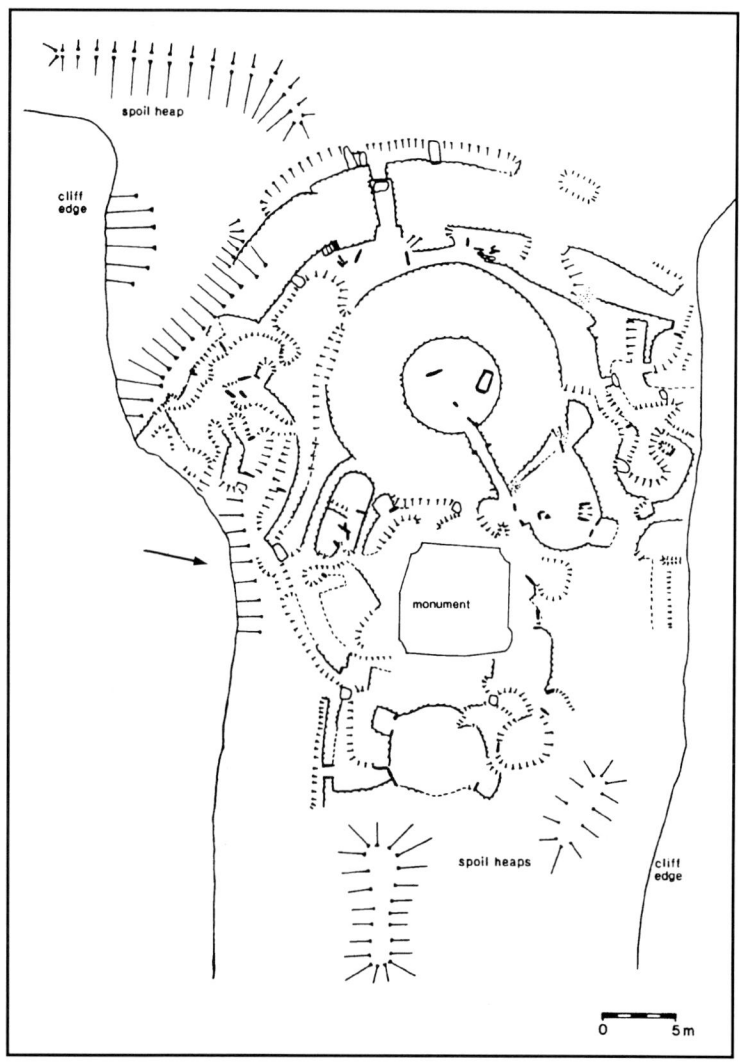

Figure 7. Nybster Broch, Caithness

of masonry, but the excavation at Crosskirk called into serious doubt the likelihood that the walls of Caithness brochs ever reached the height of the wall at Mousa in Shetland. The wall base at Crosskirk was on average about 4.3 m (14 ft) thick, but was not composed entirely of stone. It consisted rather of an earth and rubble core with an internal and external stone facing. Dr Fairhurst thought it was most unlikely that such a base, despite its thickness, could have supported a wall of any great height. In addition, the wall was considerably buttressed, presumably to support collapsing portions. Evidence of similar buttressing has been recorded at other excavated Caithness brochs, notably the Road broch, Keiss, where the original wall width would appear to have been only 3.3 m (10.8 ft) with a buttress or casing 0.9 m (3 ft) thick added at a later stage. Caithness brochs in general were probably not the towering stone built structures of the popular image, but may rather have been much squatter structures prone to collapse.

It is traditionally thought that the interiors of broch structures were furnished with wood, including a raised wooden floor supported on a ring of posts in the centre and on a scarcement at the wall. The problem with this view in a Caithness context is that modern pollen evidence has demonstrated that there was a general absence of constructional timber in the area of the Caithness plain during the period when brochs were occupied[5]. The Caithness landscape in the Iron Age seems to have had much the same treeless appearance as it has today. If timber was in use for furnishing broch structures, it would have needed to be imported, possibly from neighbouring Sutherland. There is, however, little evidence that timber was in use in Caithness broch structures, with internal furnishings being provided rather by flagstones. Evidence from brochs in Orkney suggests that flagstones could be used to create more than one floor level within broch structures[6], and a similar furnishing arrangement may have existed in Caithness. Other features of Caithness broch interiors are large underground caverns or wells and occasional hearths. The roofing of the broch structures is a particularly difficult point. It has always been assumed that brochs were roofed, but no evidence for the nature of any roofing has been produced and it remains one of the problems of understanding brochs.

The presence of buildings around broch structures in Caithness can be directly observed at 41 sites and can be inferred from surface evidence at a further 45. Given these numbers it seems reasonable to conclude that surrounding buildings are a normal feature of Caithness broch sites. The buildings are unlike the broch structure in being much less substantial. They are basically curvilinear in shape with niches and cells, the whole possibly designed to facilitate roofing with flagstones, in striking contrast to the broch structure (Fig. 7). It is possible that turves as well as stone

THE BROCHS

were employed in the construction of the surrounding buildings.

In the past it has always been assumed that the surrounding buildings were secondary to the construction of the broch structure, the latter being presumed to have originally stood entirely alone. There is now excavation evidence from Orkney, however, that a broch structure there had six contemporary houses around it[7] and it is highly possible that many broch structures in both Caithness and Orkney may have had surrounding villages from the beginning of their period of use. There is perhaps some supporting evidence for this view in the presence of two entrances to a number of broch structures in the east of Caithness, as for example at Yarrows (ND 308434), Road, Brounaban (ND 323434) and the Wag of Forse (ND 204352). At Yarrows and Road brochs it can be demonstrated that both entrances to the broch structure are primary features and it therefore remains to be asked why two entrances were necessary, if the structure stood alone, as two entrances might have been expected to increase the vulnerability of the structure. All of the brochs with two entrances, however, also have evidence of surrounding buildings and it is possible that the reason for two entrances lies in particular needs of access between the broch structure and contemporary surrounding buildings.

The possibility that brochs in Caithness may have had contemporary surrounding buildings as a general rule has considerable implications for perceptions of the function of broch sites. It strengthens the case for viewing the full broch complex as the farming establishment of its time, something akin to a small village rather than a single farmstead. It does not, however, explain the particular function of the broch structure itself. The possibility that the broch structure was intended to be a refuge for its surrounding houses is not ruled out. Alternatively, the broch structure may have been used for storage, or it may have been just another house, but clearly a rather different one from the small, cellular surrounding houses. Further evidence on the exact function of brochs will only be forthcoming from more excavation.

There seems little doubt that Caithness brochs should be seen as defended sites. Whether or not the broch structure was largely intended to be defensive, there is evidence that the whole broch village complex was surrounded by an external system of defences. A surrounding rampart or wall is visible at a number of broch sites, for example at Carn na Mairg (ND 133510) on the River Thurso. In addition a ditch surrounding the broch mound is visible, or is recorded, at 34 Caithness brochs. In some cases, such as Carn na Mairg and the Hill O'Works (ND 290625), the ditch is very deep and waterlogged. In other cases the ditch is shallow and only partially visible. It seems likely that ditches were in fact a common feature of Caithness broch sites, but they have been particularly vulnerable to destruction and infilling by ploughing and draining over the centuries. The extent and quality of the surrounding defensive system at Carn na Mairg, Hill O'Works, and other broch sites are strong indicators that defence was a very real requirement in Iron Age Caithness, although the particular threats are unknown.

The dating evidence now available for both Caithness and Orkney points to a much longer and more complex chronology for broch sites than had previously been thought to be the case. There is evidence from Orkney that brochs may date as far back as 700 BC with continual building, rebuilding, and sometimes abandonment of brochs up to at least the second century AD[8]. Thereafter, many broch sites may have been occupied into the Pictish period, although the broch structure itself may have been long since out of use. In Caithness the only available dating evidence from brochs comes from the Crosskirk excavation, where, unfortunately, the complexity of the site made it very difficult to unravel the sequence. It would appear that the broch at Crosskirk could have dated back at least to 200 BC, and may in fact be even older. It is obvious both from the record of the Crosskirk excavation and from direct observation of both excavated and unexcavated brochs, that Caithness broch mounds are very complex archaeological sites, with a deep stratigraphy spanning a much longer period than the two to three centuries over which brochs were traditionally thought to have been occupied. Caithness broch mounds may well contain evidence of several centuries of occupation from about 500 BC up to 500 AD. It is also possible that beneath the Iron Age layers at some sites evidence from even earlier periods could be preserved.

A new picture of brochs in Caithness is beginning to emerge, far removed from the traditional understanding. It will take many years of further work before brochs are fully understood throughout their area of occurrence and they will retain their enigmatic image for some time yet. In the current state of archaeological knowledge there are few certain facts. Brochs seem to have been the farming settlements of their time, housing perhaps more than one family on a permanent basis, rather than temporary refuges or the stately homes of local chieftains. They did not appear suddenly about 100 BC to disappear within a couple of centuries. Rather, they had a much longer history of use, with the idea of the broch structure probably being evolved in Orkney/Caithness where there were almost certainly already considerable skills in building with stone in an area where constructional timber was rare. Stability of settlement pattern in Orkney/Caithness seems to be indicated from about 500 BC to at least 200 AD and perhaps up to 500 AD, with a break possibly not occurring in the pattern until about the time of the Norse incursions. The link with the period before about 500 BC has yet to be established. It has long been argued that brochs represent external influences from elsewhere in

Britain, possibly as a result of population movements into northern Scotland during the Iron Age, but until more is known about the settlements which preceded brochs, there can only be speculation on this point. It is equally possible that brochs were a wholly indigenous development, arising from the particular needs of an established population which had been in residence in the north from the Neolithic period.

REFERENCES

1. Anderson, J. "Scotland in Pagan Times. The Iron Age" 1883 David Douglas, Edinburgh, p232
2. Fairhurst, H. "Excavations at Crosskirk Broch, Caithness" 1984 Society of Antiquaries of Scotland Monograph Series Number 3, Edinburgh
3. Calder, C. S. T. "Report on the Excavation of a Broch at Skitten, in the Kilmster District of Caithness" in the Proceedings of the Society of Antiquaries of Scotland 82 (1947-8), pp124-45
4. Rhind, A. H. "Notice of the Exploration of a 'Pict's-House', at Kettleburn, in the County of Caithness" 1853 in Archaeological Journal 10, pp211-23
5. Robinson, D. "Investigations into the Aukhorn Peat Mounds, Keiss, Caithness: Pollen, Plant Macrofossil and Charcoal Analysis" 1987 in New Phytologist 106
6. Hedges, J. W. "Bu, Gurness and the Brochs of Orkney, Parts I, II and III" 1987 British Archaeological Reports British Series 163 Oxford, Part III, pp12-13
7. Carter, S., Haigh, D., Neil, N. R. J. and Smith, B. "Interim Report on the Structures at Howe, Stromness, Orkney" 1984 in Glasgow Archaeological Journal 11, pp61-73
8. Hedges, J. W. (op cit), Part I, 93; Carter et al (op cit), 72

CHAPTER 5

THE PICTS

It should soon become clear that strict adherence to the chapter title would create a gap in the chronological picture of Caithness. The people known to us as the 'Picts' are justly regarded as something of a mystery, prompting F. T. Wainwright, in 1955, to entitle his collection of essays on the latest ideas on these people *The Problem of the Picts*. In the ensuing thirty-odd years the 'problem' has not gone away.

The brochs (see chapter 4) totter into disuse at an uncertain point in the first century AD, and with few exceptions, nothing is distinguishable in the archaeological record in Caithness until the late Viking remains at Freswick Bay a thousand years later. The Picts themselves first appear as a name mentioned by the Roman poet Eumenius in AD 297, where they are linked with the Irish Hiberni as enemies of the Britanni of eastern England. In AD 360, the Roman historian Ammianus Marcellinus again refers to them in the same terms, and adds that they were split into two groups known as the Verturiones and Dicalydones. Later still, other writers including Gildas and Adomnan refer to their presence and their power, until their credentials are finally established by the Venerable Bede, who, in his *Ecclesiastical History of the English People* describes them as being with the Scots, Angles and Britons, one of the four peoples of Britain, again emphasising their division into a northern and a southern group. While it is therefore clear that we are dealing with a real and powerful people, their origins are misty in the extreme, and the identifiable remains of their passing — with the notable exception of their art — almost non-existent.

The recognition of the Picts as a 'people' probably serves more to confuse than illuminate. Scholars find it difficult to agree because of the lack of corroborative evidence, but they are probably the descendants of native Bronze Age incomers — suggested by their apparently non-Indo-European language — and thus of the broch-dwellers themselves. At any rate, we do not have to see them as newcomers to Scotland, but rather a development of what has gone before. They seem not to have been a single people, but probably a confederation of tribal units whose political

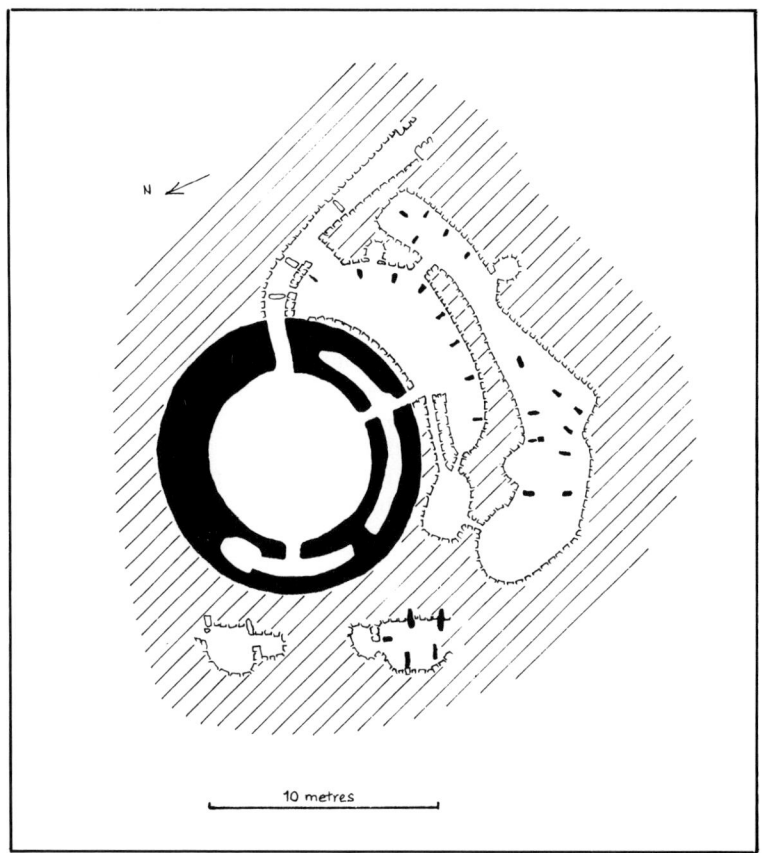

Figure 8. Broch and Aisled Dwellings or 'wags', South Yarrows, Caithness

motivations derive from a need to ally against common enemies. Their centre of power, accordingly, seems to have shifted from north to south — probably dependent on the strengths of individual leaders. Thus, under King Brude or Bridei, for example, during the 6th century, the principal court and exercise of power was based near Inverness. Earlier, and particularly during the great raid of AD 367 on the Roman frontier, it lay in southern Pictland, maybe in Fife. Perhaps, because they were not a single people, their cultural artefacts may have been insufficiently alike for us now to identify them readily.

Perhaps most obviously missing are their homes. Houses of a period which can confidently be described as Pictish are now known from Orkney, at sites such as Buckquoy and Birsay, where they precede those of early Viking date. On the mainland, however, we are presented with a virtual blank, although Caithness has its own unique contender in the form of the structures known as 'wags'. On older maps of the area, large numbers of antiquities are labelled 'Pict's Houses', but these generally apply erroneously to broch sites. However, in a number of instances, later settlements surround the brochs themselves, and amongst them are structures of a particular form which might, through modern excavation techniques, be proven to be 'Pictish' (Fig. 8). Other sites of similar type are found on their own. These are the 'wags', a type of monument found only in Sutherland and Caithness, and confined almost wholly to Latheron parish in the south-east of the county (Fig. 1). They are identified by a curious internal arrangement of pillars — either drystone or single flags — which stand around the interior, close to, but separate from the walls — thus dividing the perimeter into sections while creating an 'aisle' along the inside wall-face. Their shapes are very varied. Some are circular, others oval or kidney-shaped, while others are almost rectangular but with rounded ends. A few have secondary rooms, and could be described as 'cellular'. One of the best examples can be seen at the Wag of Forse (ND 204351; Plate 16) near Latheron, where a long, sub-rectangular building with small cells attached lies outside the ruins of what is surely a broch. Some of the stone pillars which supported the 'aisle' can be clearly seen here. Another example may be seen amongst the structures surrounding the broch at south Yarrows (ND 308434; Fig. 8) where the shape of the building has been determined by the external curvature of the broch wall. A third is to be seen at Langwell (ND 101219), where an 'aisled' structure adjoins one side of a circular building not unlike a hut circle. Elsewhere, their ruinous condition makes their plan difficult to unravel. Excavation will be needed to prove their Pictish date, but they are at present the chief contenders for the honour in Caithness. Their curious name, incidentally, appears to derive from the Gaelic 'uaimhach' or 'little cave'.

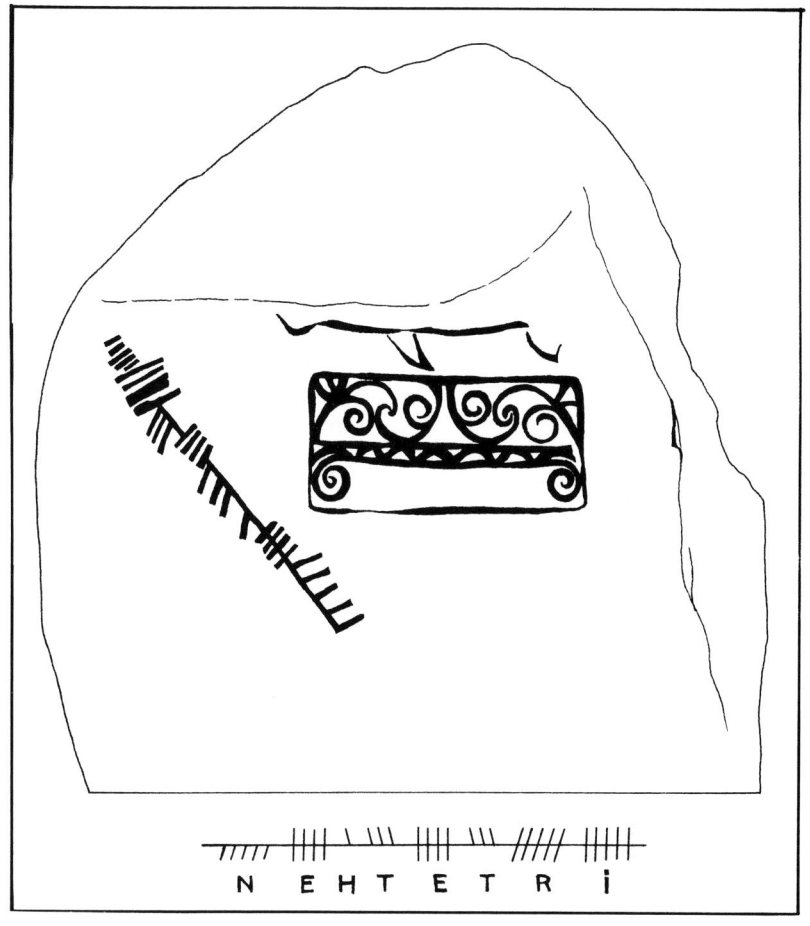

Figure 9. Class 1 Symbol Stone, with ogam inscription, from Keiss Links, Caithness

It can be assumed that unless 'Pictish' is a term which really only applies to a politically-recognised element represented by the higher social strata of tribal society during much of the first millenium AD — a position which is far from impossible, and might explain the absence of ordinary, domestic structures — they would have been farmers much as the inhabitants of Caithness had been since the Neolithic. If so, we have yet to find any traces of their agricultural landscapes — their fields, kilns, mills and so on. It is of course possible that these were the same as, or almost indistinguishable from, those of the Iron Age. Indeed, the lack of identifiably Pictish remains probably means that this was indeed the case. Elsewhere in Scotland, there are signs of the Pictish military presence in the form of fortified sites — on hillforts and duns — many apparently the re-use or refurbishment of sites first built during the Iron Age. Sites such as Craig Phadrig (NH 640452) in Inverness and Dundurn (NN 707231), near St Fillans in Perthshire have been demonstrated to have had Pictish period occupation. In Caithness, regrettably, such sites have yet to be identified. The main contenders must be the broch sites, but they are built to a different scale from the more southerly forts, and as well as being perhaps unsuitable as Pictish fortifications were probably too ruinous without undergoing considerable reconstruction. Hillforts, in the classic Iron Age tradition, do not exist in Caithness, and the author feels that those sites described as 'forts', such as Buaile Oscar (ND 059558) on Beinn Freiceadain, and Garrywhin (ND 313413) are likely to be enclosures of a different kind and of much earlier date. Perhaps as the county lies well away from the main Pictish areas of conflict, such fortifications were unnecessary. In any event, these high status sites are as elusive as the domestic ones.

Not infrequently, the religious and burial practices of past societies leave substantial remains — even when, as in the Neolithic, little else survives. In recent years, a number of burial sites have produced fragments of the characteristically 'Pictish' sculptures known as Class I *symbol stones* (see below), and are perhaps beginning to indicate a style of burial which may be 'Pictish'. Again, the best-investigated of these have been in Orkney and elsewhere outside the county. They consist of small mounds, or stone cairns, which may be both square or circular, and are often grouped together in small cemeteries. Often, the individual cairns are linked together, and may have shallow ditches surrounding them. The best examples of these can be seen at Garbeg (NH 511322), Drumnadrochit, and by Whitebridge (NH 492171), both near Inverness. Other groups show up over a wide area as cropmarks in arable fields. At Garbeg, one of the graves appears to have contained a broken fragment of a symbol stone as also did a stone cairn of similar size near Watenan (ND 312409) in Caithness. This combination of graves and broken stones is clearly significant, and may eventually shed much light on the functions

Figure 10. Cross-slab, Old Reay churchyard, Caithness

of the stones themselves. Beyond this, Pictish remains in Caithness consist wholly of their artwork in the form of these symbol stones and later cross-slabs. Let us now turn our attention to these.

It is misleading, really, to say that the stones are 'all that we have', as they are part of a rich and magnificent legacy of sculptural art which more than anything else identifies the Picts to us today. They fall into two main groups — those which carry Christian designs, and those which do not. Kenneth Jackson dislikes the use of the term 'symbol' in describing the individual design elements, and prefers to use this term for groups of designs which he suggests have symbolic meaning. Here, however, to avoid the creation of a new and confusing term, *each element* will be referred to as a symbol, as, unless Jackson's theory can be proven, that is patently what they are. The first category, therefore, consists of stones, usually undressed, which carry groups of symbols that are characteristically Pictish and non-Christian. These range from purely geometric designs such as the 'V-Rod and Crescent' and the 'Double-Disc and Z-Rod' through elegant representations of native birds and animals and the more mundane 'Mirror and Comb' to abstract creatures of perhaps mythical origin such as the so-called 'Elephant'. Incised into the surface of the stones, they are for the most part graceful and elegant designs executed with a high degree of skill. Their meaning, however, remains a mystery, and although many theories have been put forward, none is satisfactory. It is not unlikely that they represent tribal, family, or individual totems, but the reason they were carved with such care onto stone remains unclear. It has been variously suggested that they represent tribal boundary markers, tribal or marriage alliances, or memorials describing the origins and status of the individual they commemorate. However, without more direct evidence, none of these theories is provable. The instances of *broken* stones in association with graves may yet prove crucial in understanding this problem.

There are seven Class I stones noted from Caithness, of which one, from Crosskirk (ND 025701), is now missing, and three are in the Royal Museum of Scotland, Queen Street, Edinburgh. Three remain in the county — one at Sandside House, Reay (NC 952651; Plate 40) where it is built into a garden wall near the house. The second is built into a wall of the farmhouse at Latheron Mains (ND 198334). The third, which came from the stone cairn at Watenan, consists of two conjoining pieces, and is currently on display in the John Nicolson Museum, Auckengill.

The second group also carry pre-Christian symbols, but in conjunction with the Christian cross. These are carved in relief, and are usually on carefully shaped and dressed stones. The conjunction of the cross and the earlier symbols might suggest that the latter were in some way connected with Pictish religion before their conversion to Christianity by Columba around AD 560, when the saint undertook a

Figure 11. Incised crosses, Mid-Clyth graveyard (left) and Roadside, Mid-Clyth, Caithness

mission from his base in Iona to the court of King Brude — taking time out along the way to cast the Loch Ness monster back into the depths! This conversion seems only to apply to the northern Picts, as those in the south were converted by St Ninian in the 5th century, according to Bede.

Two examples can be seen in Caithness today, each with its own particular interest. The slab known as the *Ulbster Stone* — not least from the disgraceful addition of that name to the stone itself in horrendous Gothic lettering — has the distinction of carrying more symbols than any other Pictish stone (Plate 13). It can be seen in all its glory in Thurso Museum, along with the *Skinnet Stone*, recovered from the chapel at Skinnet between Thurso and Halkirk (ND 131620) in the mid 19th century. Both are fine examples of their type, and are better visited and seen than described here. A third stone, originally from Latheron and now in the Royal Scottish Museum, Edinburgh, has the added distinction of carrying an inscription in Ogam. This script was probably developed in Ireland specifically for carving on stone, as it consists of short lines in groups on either side of a median line, and without difficult curves. The groups of lines represent letters of the Latin alphabet, but transcription of the letters on the Latheron Stone produce a meaningless jumble of letters. If this is indeed Pictish, the language bears no relation to any other contemporary European tongue and is singularly unhelpful in unravelling the mystery of the stones. A second Ogam-inscribed stone, now in Edinburgh, came from Keiss Bay links (Fig. 9). It also bears the lower part of a fish, and the 'rectangle' symbol.

Besides the stones described above are a small number of other sculptured crosses which are probably contemporary, but lack the Pictish symbols. These fall into two categories — those which are on dressed slabs, and the simpler crosses carved on boulders. Built into the wall of a mausoleum in the graveyard at Old Reay (NC 969648) is a fine example of a cross-slab bearing a wheel cross whose arms and base are covered in close panels of interlace and key patterns (Fig. 10; Plate 11). A much-eroded spiral boss decorates the hub, while the upper arm of the cross shows the tool marks where a vandal of the 1980's recently obliterated the work of an earlier vandal when the stone was embellished with an unfinished memorial to one 'Robert McKay 17--' (Fig. 10).

Half-hidden under a shelter on the south side of the church at Lybster (ND 248356) is a large boulder bearing an unusual incised triple cross (Plate 15). It is thought originally to have come from near the Well of the Brethren (ND 242349) during the construction of Lybster harbour in the 1830s. At Clach na Ciplich (ND 105394), a simple, long-shafted cross is incised on a flat slab set upright on a peaty knoll. A third cross stands on the edge of the ruins of the chapel at Skinnet, whence comes the cross-slab mentioned above, with a fourth and fifth known from the graveyard at Mid Clyth (Fig. 11). Of the last two, one still stands in the

THE PICTS

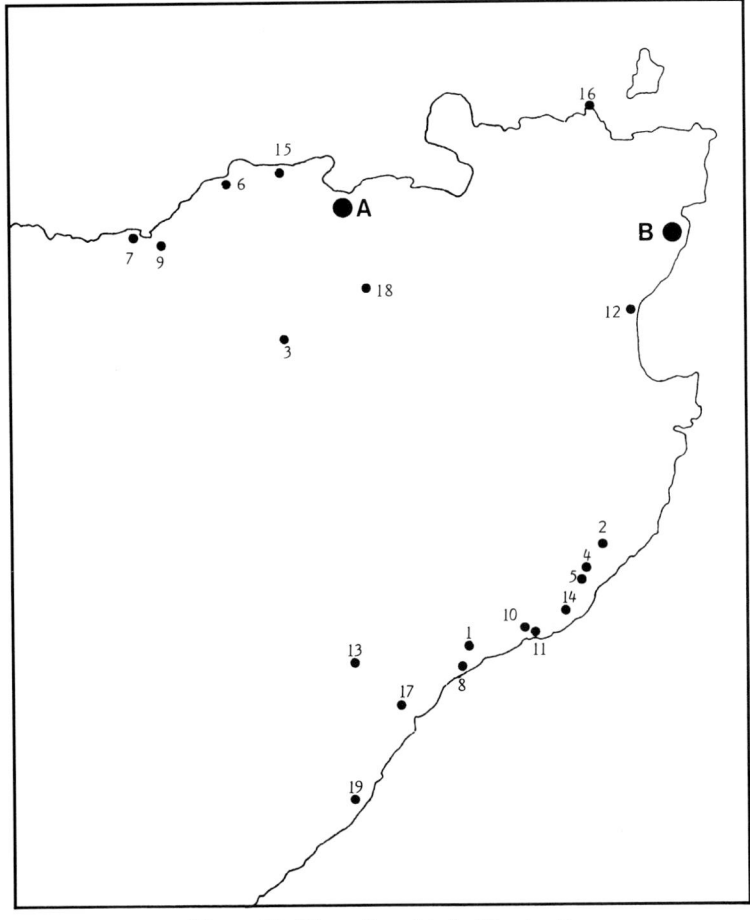

Figure 12. Sites referred to in Chapter 5

Sites Referred to in Chapter 5, Figure 12

1. Wag of Forse
2. South Yarrows
3. Buaile Oscar
4. Garrywhin
5. Watenan
6. Crosskirk
7. Sandside
8. Latheron Mains
9. Old Reay
10. Lybster Church
11. Well of the Brethren
12. Keiss Bay
13. Clach na Ciplich
14. Mid Clyth
15. Neck of Brough
16. St. John's Point
17. Ballachly
18. Skinnet
19. Langwell

A. Thurso Museum

B. John Nicolson Museum

graveyard (ND 295372), while the second is now built into the wall of a barn at Roadside Farm (ND 294373; Fig 11). Although all of these are likely to be contemporary with the Picts, they may perhaps owe their origin to the presence in the county of Irish priests, or *papar*. These eremitic monks spread out from Ireland during the early centuries of Christianity and established small cells in out-of-the-way places. Several such small monastic sites are suspected in Caithness, although none has produced direct evidence of their use. One such site stands on a small promontory at Neck of Brough (ND 061709), and another on St John's Point (ND 310751), also known as Dunmey. A third example sits above the Dunbeath Water at Ballachly (ND 157303), where a small rectangular building, thought to have been a chapel, sits atop a natural mound with a massive and most odd wall running from its foot towards the river. Much of the information about these sites relies on tradition and may not always be accurate. Only excavation will reveal the truth.

All in all, not much of the remains of the first millenium AD can be distinguished on the ground, but the county was clearly occupied, and probably thriving, during those ten centuries. Archaeologists, historians and art historians will doubtless continue to debate the issue on the basis of the available evidence, but what is most needed is *new* information in the form of identified and excavated sites, before the 'problem' can be resolved much further.

Please note that references to sites in this chapter *do not* assume there is right of access to them. Permission should always be sought from the landowner or tenant prior to a visit. Remember also to close all gates and respect crops and livestock, as without the co-operation of landowners many of these sites would be completely inaccessible.

1. Jackson, A. The Symbol Stones of Scotland. The Orkney Press, 1984
2. Jackson, K. H. The Pictish Landscape in Wainwright 129-166. Nelson, 1955
3. Wainwright, F. (Ed.) The Problem of the Picts. Edinburgh, 1955
4. Friell, J. G. P. and Watson, W. G. (Eds). Pictish Studies: Settlement, Burial and Art in Dark Age Northern Britain. British Archaeological Reports, British Series 125, 1984.

CHAPTER 6

VIKING AND LATE NORSE CAITHNESS

The image of the Vikings, taught to us as children, is one of violence, exacerbated by the picture presented through the monastic annals. Modern archaeological evidence, however, rarely supports this view of the advent of the Vikings "West over Sea" in the 9th century. If we turn to later Saga sources, although often written down in the 12th century and remote from the events described, we learn of scholars, poets and travellers. Combining this information with that recovered from archaeological investigations in the homelands of Scandinavia, we can easily see that the latter view is more readily acceptable and supportable. We cannot of course entirely dismiss the violence of some of the initial forays to the Viking colonies, but this ought not to colour our overall conception of the Viking expansions.

Our sources for the Norse arrival and colonisation of Northern Scotland clearly indicate that to the land-hungry Vikings the green sward of Orkney seemed initially to be more attractive[1]. This did not, of course, remain the situation for long, perhaps a few generations and no more, but this earlier foothold was sufficient and has had far-reaching repercussions. It is only within the last decade or so that anyone has thought to investigate in detail the Viking remains on the south shore of the Pentland Firth . . . It is highly unlikely that the lands of Caithness were ignored by the Orcadian Vikings and for most of the history of the Orkney Norse Earldom, common rulers are recorded for the two areas. The Norse heritage of Caithness is more fugitive than that of Orkney, but its presence cannot be refuted. The lack of early Viking evidence is perplexing, but there is, as compensation, more later Viking or Late Norse evidence (11th-13th centuries, as compared to the initial Viking arrivals in the 9th-10th centuries); we can examine, at least in part, the traces of Scandinavian speakers, who were perhaps the fourth and fifth generation Vikings in Caithness.

The place names (see chapter 11; Fig. 14) indicate a concentration of Scandinavian influence in the north-east of the modern county, with the indigenous population more restricted inland. The nature of this

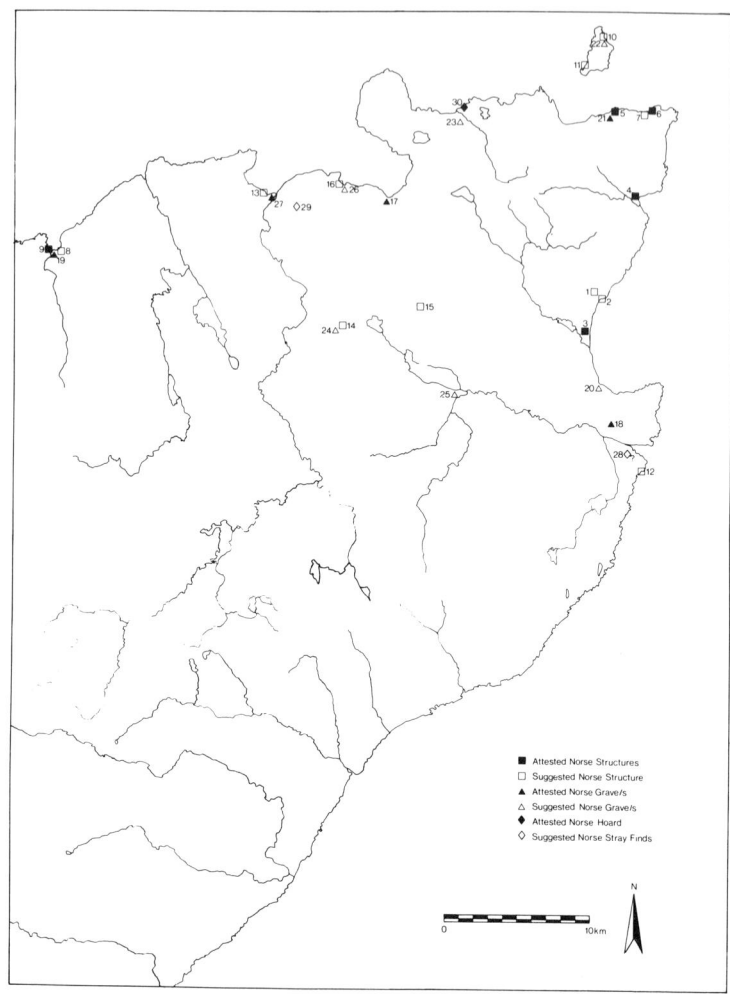

Figure 13. Viking and Late Norse Sites in Caithness
1. Keiss Broch, 2. Whitegate Broch, 3. Birkle Hills, 4. Freswick, 5. Huna, 6. Robertshaven, 7. John O'Groats, 8. Sandside Bay, Reay, 9. Cnoc Stanger, 10. Nethertown, Stroma, 11. ?Flendie Clett, 12. ?Castle of Old Wick, 13. ? Scrabster Castle, 14. ?Halkirk, 15. ?Castlehill, Bower, 16. Murkle, 17. Castletown, 18. Westerseat, 19. Reay, 20. ?Ackergill, 21. Huna, 22. Nethertown, Stroma, 23. Near Dunnet, 24. Housle Cairn, Halkirk, 25. Watten, 26. Murkle, 27. Thurso, 28. Aucorn, near Thurso, 30. Kirk O'Banks.

VIKING AND LATE NORSE CAITHNESS

apparent dominance of the local population is at present undocumented. The Norse presence in the county can be seen everywhere on the road signs — Huna, Sannick, Scrabster, Seater, Halkirk and Freswick to name but a few[2].

Finding structural traces to go with this rich Norse place name record is not, however, as simple. The 1911 Royal Commission report for Caithness[3] failed to report *any* structural remains which could be related to the Norse period of settlement in the county. Although middens and a structure were noted at Freswick on the east coast, they were not distinguished as being Viking. In our search for Norse structures the most obvious place to start is an examination of the building remains so visible around the large mounds which litter the countryside: the broch towers. There can be no doubt that they were a landmark to the Vikings a thousand years ago . . . The corpus of material derived from the study of extra-mural structures associated with brochs in the county is evergrowing. For example, at two of the brochs at Keiss, Whitegate and Keiss broch itself, there are undated structures of rectangular form in the immediate vicinity[4]. They appear to have been constructed of stone robbed from the brochs and are thus of later date. There are, however, other examples, which appear to be more convincing. A fine example occurs at Birkle Hills, Keiss, where to the north of the broch, a rectangular dry-built stone structure was excavated by Tress Barry. It was paved with slabs that included a Pictish symbol stone, which might suggest a Viking reuse[5].

Other brochs have Norse artefacts in their upper occupation layers, such as the one at Freswick Sands. This is not unexpected at this broch, given the proximity of the extensive Norse site on the Links there. The Norse occupation at Freswick has been known through earlier excavations[6] and still remains the only site of the period to be excavated in mainland Scotland. However, it is clear from re-examination of the archival data from these excavations, that the structural sequences presented in publication now need revision[7], and that the available artefactual collection has been much enlarged from material collected from the site over the years since these excavations, due to the savage erosion of the coastal margins of the site (Plates 17, 18). Detailed analysis of the midden deposits at Freswick Links has been undertaken by Durham University since 1979. The results of this work will shortly be more widely available, but already there are some exciting revelations[8]. There is evidence of extensive fishing activity at the site, mostly of substantial cod, ling and saithe (often in excess of one metre in length), which seems to be on a scale too large for home consumption. This site may even have been a commercial fish processing site for the Late Norse population of the Freswick area . . . In addition, the evidence suggests the keeping and slaughtering of cattle and sheep and the recovery of carbonised oats and barley[9] may support the suggestion of on-site cultivation indicated by plough marks under the Norse middens. Clearly the economic and environmental potential for Norse Caithness is only now being brought to the fore and in a way which even the contemporary Orcadian sites cannot at present match.

Freswick was previously the only recorded Norse settlement site in the county, although more recent fieldwork in the area is helping to broaden the picture of settlement of potentially Late Norse date. Two new settlements (Fig. 13) have been located on the north coast at Robertshaven (Ness of Duncansby) and at Huna[10]. This is an obvious location for Norse settlement, considering the close relationships there were with Orkney in the period of the Earldom.

There are possible references to the site of Huna in the *Orkneyinga Saga,* and information about graves, including a potential boat grave is available from the site. However, since 1977, sherds of grass-tempered pottery of a type and form identical to those found at Freswick have been found in the area to the east of the jetty. Recent examination has also revealed structural traces. Sand quarrying indicated that a low irregular mound at Huna was made up of a series of superimposed structures. Sherds of grass-tempered pottery were found in association with walls protruding at the upper level. Further survey work around this bay revealed two additional structures. Although conceivably representing boat nausts (even of the Norse period), the traces and possible dimensions probably indicate a more domestic use. Regrettably, the site is no longer available for archaeological examination.

A second newly recorded site on the north coast is at Robertshaven to the east of John O'Groats. Over recent years the site located in a sheltered bay, has been revealed by finds of scattered sherds of distinctive grass-tempered pottery and various artefacts, possibly of the Norse period. Approximately 200m (655ft) inland, traces of Norse midden have also been located, and in conjunction, during this work, the foundations of a substantial wall were recovered. Extensive bands of midden material, with structural features associated with the upper layer, were located in 1980. A small seasonal stream cuts through the lower midden layer which extends to the west under an overburden of approximately 3m (10ft) of sand. Both midden layers have produced grass-tempered pottery and large fish bones, as at Freswick. At the eastern end of the site, a relatively modern boat naust is built on top of stone from the underlying structure; and the whole is suffering from severe erosion.

In addition, a nearby landowner, Mr Magnus Houston of the Mill Farm, John O'Groats, has noted that further rectangular structures were located during the building of sheep pens and dips further to the west. Without excavation it is impossible to make comment on the status of this site, except to note that the Orkney historian Storer Clouston has pointed out that only two "bus" were known in Caithness, one at Freswick and the other at Duncansby.

The presence of the simple hand-made grass-tempered pottery and other artefactual evidence, in conjunction with probable building form, may suggest that there was a group of broadly contemporary sites in the north-east corner of the county. This may seem to be an obvious statement, but it is one which could not have been made even a decade ago. The grass tempering alone cannot be seen as a chronological indicator; simple forms continue throughout the assemblage and late examples have more developed forms, such as ribbed strap handles of medieval type. They are, however, more commonly found in finer fabrics farther south. These examples in Caithness would seem to be locally made copies of other vessels which had presumably been imported to the area.

Apart from these sites, there have been no other concentrations of Late Norse period settlement recorded in Caithness, although they presumably do exist elsewhere. For example, at Reay to the west of Thurso, there are fleeting references to structures in the vicinity of the graves (discussed below), although it is not always clear to which period they may be ascribed.

A further body of structural evidence, which is often ascribed to the period under consideration, is that of the castles[11]. There are some sites which, through tradition, have been attributed to this category. The site of Flendie Clett, Stroma, is one example, but without excavation this ascription can neither be confirmed or denied. Cruden, writing in 1963, suggested a Norse origin for some of the castles and Talbot continued the idea in his suggestion that the Castle of Old Wick (Plate 25) and that of Buchollie, south of Freswick, could date from the 12th century. Although there is a lack of associated structural evidence at the site, the visible remains all being of the 16th century, underlying midden deposits would seem to suggest the presence of an earlier structure. The castle at Old Wick is itself of a very simple form, being a single square tower with a series of square and retangular grass covered structures stretching along the promontory. The dating of this structure remains a mystery but must be roughly contemporary with its close parallel at Brough in Dunnet Parish. The basic argument for the 12th century dating of these structures — Kastali — is outlined by Talbot but it must be stressed that simplicity in form need not represent an early date.

Braal Castle, Halkirk (Plate 23) dated at least to the 14th century had as a possible predecessor, the episcopal manor house of Bishop Adam at Halkirk which apparently stood on the opposite bank of the river in the vicinity of the Manse, but there are now no traces remaining. Crawford has noted that the earl dwelt near the episcopal manor house, presumably

Braal[12]. This was later known as the "caput" or administrative centre of the Caithness Earldom.

Located near Scrabster, lies the site of Things'Va, lying on a gentle slope 3.2 km (2 miles) to the west of Thurso. The site is a broch (very similar to that at Tingwall, Evie Parish, Orkney) and was damaged even at the time of the writing of the Commission volume. The site of Scrabster has been examined by Talbot, and although he could not ascribe any structural remains to the 12th century, he believed that some of the pottery recovered could date to that period[13].

Another class of monument tentatively ascribed to the Norse period is the "ring work". The evidence available in the county is rather scanty and the basis for a date in the Norse period largely relies on similarities between Castlehill, Bower[14], and the earliest phase of the Norse stronghold of Cubbie Roo's Castle on Wyre. This ascription to the Norse period is of necessity somewhat tentative. Talbot, however, points out in his convincing listing of the supportive evidence, that the ring work was a distinctive feature of the Anglo-Normans in Scotland in the 12th century. The Royal Commission visit to the site of Castlehill in Bower records a substantial feature with a well-defined ditch and causeway, possible traces of walling on the counter-scarp and an entrance. It is obvious that such a site, which has a ditch around it some 10.7m (34 ft) wide, must have involved a vast amount of corporate effort and possibly some centralised form of organisation. Talbot suggests that it may have served as a campaign castle or more permanent fortification, built during the activities in Caithness of William the Lion. One feels, however, that the reservations voiced by Talbot must be repeated in the light of insufficient evidence.

Moving away from the settlement evidence, we turn to the Viking pagan graves in Caithness, which, as in Orkney, have often been recovered from mounds either man-made or natural, sand dunes and cairns. Unfortunately, there are often no precise details about the circumstances of recovery.

The grave at Castletown was located in 1786 on top of the ruins of Castlehill broch. A similar pair of oval brooches was recovered in association with a skeleton, presumably female, underlying a flat slab itself covered by a thin deposit of earth. Wilson noted that the iron corrosion products from the securing pins had preserved textile traces on the underside of the brooches. Brogger adds to these finds a jet armlet and a roughly made bone bodkin[15].

The grave at Westerseat near Wick was located near a broch, that of Kettleburn. Here a pair of dissimilar oval brooches were found in a cist of questionable dimensions. The find was made during quarrying in a gravel hillock and no other items are noted from the deposit, not even a skeleton[16].

The finest collection of graves from the Viking period, however, comes from Reay to the west of Thurso. Here, severe weathering of the dunes in Sandside Bay revealed over a number of years five pagan graves and various stray finds, representing either further graves or occupation at the site. Due to the circumstances of recovery, it is not possible to determine whether these were simply buried in the sand, or whether, as elsewhere, they were buried under man-made sand mounds, possibly even with cairns. There has been confusion concerning the finds from various grave deposits found since the beginning of the century[17].

The earliest recorded Viking grave from Reay was discovered in 1912, and comprised a skeleton found in association with a buckle from a horse bridle. There are no further details available except that the skeleton was reburied in Reay cemetery. In 1913, the action of the wind revealed a disturbed skeleton with associated artefacts which indicated a female grave. The finds comprised a pair of slightly dissimilar oval brooches, a small bronze buckle, a steatite spindle whorl and plain iron bridle bit. J. Curle ascribes to this grave a possible iron buckle and a pair of cruciform tweezers (paralleled at Birsay in Orkney). At this point there is some confusion as Greig states that the buckle and tweezers possible represent a further burial, but the problem may be resolved by the statement that these objects were found " . . . shortly after the unearthing of the skeleton . . picked up within a radius of two or three yards from the grave".

Further activity at the site in 1920 revealed a rich male grave located on the north side of the Drill Hall at Sandside Bay. An extended inhumation was located on a paved surface with the head resting on a stone. At the bottom of the grave was a deposit containing pieces of slag and burnt iron. The burial is particularly of interest for two reasons; one is that it was covered by a mound of stones, a feature common in areas of Viking activity; the other lies in the artefacts associated with the skeleton, including a ringed pin, an iron axe, shield boss, iron sickle and two pieces of flint mostly ascribable to the 10th century.

Additional grave evidence from the Viking period has been noted at Huna (see above) where Curle recorded in 1935 the recovery of a probable Viking ship burial above high water mark to the west of Huna Hotel, in an area of blown sand. He surveyed the remains in September 1936, and recorded: rivets, timber fragments, a piece of skull, a chain fragment and two possible iron rope restrainers that covered an area of approximately $2.8m^2$ $(30ft^2)$[18]. There appears to be no further information about this find and its significance lies in the fact that no other boat graves are attested even to this degree in Caithness.

We are fortunate for a variety of reasons that the runic cross (Plate 14) from St. Peter's Church in Thurso was discovered. Without this stone, there would be no attestable Viking presence in Thurso, despite numerous references in *Orkneyinga Saga*. In 1896, two graves were located near the ruins of St. Peter's Church[19]. The graves were made of rough stones set on edge and orientated east-west. It has been suggested that the present remains of the 16th century church could overlie a 12th century chapel. Some indication of this may be found in the *Orkneyinga Saga*, for Earl Rognvald was brought to Thurso on his death, which in itself might suggest the presence of a chapel site there. The Royal Commission suggests that parts of the present ruins, such as the apsidal cell which has a square exterior, may date from the 12th century.

The obvious Christian nature of the graves would strongly suggest a contemporary church in the immediate vicinity. The graves were of a child and an adult in a flexed position, with the cross slab lying on top of the adult. It is evident from the inscription that the stone was intended as a grave cover rather than an upright marker; it has been interpreted as " . . made this overlay after Ingolf his/her Father". In addition to this stone from Thurso, a second runic inscription has been noted in the wall of the tower of St. Peter's. There may well be several others to be found at this important site.

In 1985, a damaged oval brooch came to light which, it is thought, may have come from the Thurso area. It had apparently been dredged from the river and although no further details are available, it is likely to represent a further grave and is a significant addition to our knowledge of this area.

The recovery of the Norse graves at Thurso may serve to indicate the site of a possible earlier church, below or near the standing church. There seems to be no archaeological evidence of the Church for the period pre-dating the 12th century in Caithness and of that, very little is documented. There are references to a possible nunnery at Murkle, presumably linked with an organised church. The site of St. Mary's Lybster (Crosskirk) is also considered to be an early foundation.

Historical sources[20] refer to the founding of a Bishopric of Caithness prior to 1147-51 with Andrew as the first Bishop. This represented a splintering off from the Bishopric of Orkney and from that point onwards, the church was very much a tool for royal Scottish influence in Caithness. Of the pre-Bishopric structure, nothing is known. Probably the most reliable reference to the church, albeit indirect, refers to Bishop Adam being burnt at his episcopal manor house at Halkirk. This is thought to be the site of one of the most important churches (ON Ha Kirkjá) if Crawford's suggestion is to be accepted. None of this evidence however, has been archaeologically proven.

With this rather scanty evidence for the archaeological presence of Norse settlement in the county, the picture remains to be completed by a brief summary of the hoards and stray finds from the area which can be ascribed to Norse presence but which do not necessarily indicate settlement.

Perhaps the most important piece of evidence comes from Kirk O'Banks, a small chapel of unknown date located on the north coast[21]. In 1872, during excavations at the site for drainage channels behind the small church, a cist was disturbed. Initially it was thought that the piece of metal recovered was a coffin handle but when seven other similar pieces were recovered it was realised that they were bracelets or arm rings. They were lacking decoration and were all roughly the same weight and have been interpreted by Graham-Campbell as "ring money" of the type common in Scotland from the late 10th century onwards. This is, so far, the only Viking period hoard from Caithness. Its nearest parallels of form are in the Skaill hoard from Orkney. Graham-Campbell lists forty such hoards in the whole of modern Scotland, distributed mainly in the north and west, some dated by association with coins.

Stray finds of the Norse period from the Pentland Firth islands are somewhat scarce. The Pentland Skerries themselves can boast an antler comb and sherds of grass-tempered pottery both as at Freswick; and more recently Hunter has noted midden and structural traces which may conceivably be Viking[22].

The present picture of Norse settlement in Caithness, based on the surviving structural remains, is very incomplete. The apparent coastal concentration cannot be ignored, however, with Reay, Huna, Robertshaven and Freswick all located on sandy bays. These sites have been recovered because of the actions of severe erosion and are thus likely to form only a limited part of the overall picture. The distribution of stray finds may tentatively suggest a more inland spread, although the place names indicate a coastal and eastern Caithness distribution, but it is very likely that inland from the coastal margin there are other settlements awaiting examination. It is probable that these lie under the modern farms because of the success of the site chosen. It is always important to remember that the majority of sites recovered in a rural context are to a certain extent failed sites.

There is still obviously a considerable bias in the evidence for the Norse in Caithness, because most of the evidence available is in the form of graves and the associated assemblages. The graves are all, without exception, earlier than the settlement evidence we have available to us at the moment. It is hoped that the detailed study at Freswick Links will reveal traces of the earlier, Viking settlement in the county. The distribution of those graves which may be tentatively ascribed to the Christian Norse period, also seems to be largely coastal, as at Thurso or Murkle. This distribution, often in association with recorded Norse settlement evidence, is likely to reflect the actions of erosion at the coast, or in some cases the disturbance by road building or structural developments. There is no reason why Norse burial activity should have been restricted to the coastal areas of Caithness and it is sad to reflect that during the last century many inland brochs were levelled or dug into and the findings not adequately recorded. Comments by Anderson, writing in 1871, indicate that secondary occupation and interments were a common feature noted from the examination of the brochs. The evidence now, however, is tantalisingly incomplete.

The presence of Christian graves always poses problems, because they usually lack grave goods and are consequently difficult to date. The recovery of the cross-shaped runic stone from Thurso therefore assumes a disproportionate importance and, for the period in Caithness, remains unique.

One way forward, perhaps the only one, in a study of the Viking and Late Norse periods in Caithness must lie in the potential of large-scale inter-disciplinary excavations. Detailed and intensive work at sites similar to Freswick, such as Robertshaven in particular, will help to redress the presently perceived imbalance which, it is submitted, cannot have been actual, between the northern part of the Norse Earldom in Orkney and the southern part in Caithness.

FOOTNOTES

1. Taylor, A B *The Orkneyinga Saga:* a new translation with introduction and notes, 1938, Edinburgh and London.
2. Waugh D J Caithness Place-names, *Nomina* 1984, 8, 15-28. Waugh D J The Place-Names of Canisbay Parish, *Northern Scotland,* forthcoming.
3. RCAHMS *Third Report. The Inventory of Monuments and Constructions in the County of Caithness,* 1911, Edinburgh.
4. Batey C E *Caithness Coastal Survey 1980-82: Dunnet Head to Ousdale,* Occasional Paper No 3, Department of Archaeology, 1984, Durham.
5. Allen J R *The Early Christian Monuments of Scotland.* A Classified, illustrated, descriptive list of the monuments, with an analysis of their symbolism and ornamentation, 1903, Edinburgh.
6. Curle A O A Viking Settlement at Freswick, Caithness. Report on excavations carried out in 1937 and 1938. *Proceedings of the Society of Antiquaries of Scotland (PSAS)* LXXIII 1938-9, 71-110.
   Childe V G Another Late Viking House at Freswick, Caithness, *PSAS* LXXV11 1942-3, 5-17.
7. Batey C E *Freswick Links, Caithness. A Re-appraisal of the Late Norse site in its Context,* British Archaeological Reports Series (BAR) 179, 1987, Oxford (2 vols).

8. Jones A K G, Batey C E, Morris C D and Rackham D J Man and the Environment at Freswick Links, a Late Norse Site in Caithness, in Jones M K (ed) *Intergrating the Subsistence Economy,* B A R International Series 181 (= Symposia of the Association for Environmental Archaeology, 3) 1983, Oxford, 163-176 and references therein.
9. Personal communication Louisa Gidney and Jacqui Huntley, Department of Archaeology, University of Durham.
10. Batey C E *op cit* 1984, CAN 035 and 041.
11. For example: Cruden S H *The Scottish Castle,* 1963 Edinburgh and London
Talbot E Scandinavian Fortification in the British Isles, *Scottish Archaeological Forum* 6, 1974, 37-45.
12. Crawford B E The Earldom of Caithness and the Kingdom of Scotland, *Northern Scotland* 2, pt 2, 1976-7, 97-117.
13. Talbot E A Report on Excavations at Bishop's Castle, Scrabster 1973, *Northern Studies* 2, 1973, 37-9.
14. Talbot E The Ring of Castlehill, Caithness — a Viking Fortification? *PSAS* 108, 1976-7, 378-9.
15. Anderson J Notes on the Relics of the Viking Period of the Northmen in Scotland, illustrated by specimens in the Museum, *PSAS* X, 1872-4, 536-594 (pp 549-51).
Grieg S *Viking Antiquities in Scotland (= Viking Antiquities of Great Britain and Ireland Part 11, ed Shetelig H, 1940, Oslo).*
16. Anderson J 1872-4 *op cit,* 551-2
Grieg S 1940 *op cit*
17. Grieg S 1940 *op cit,* 21-4.
18. Curle A O Notebook held in the National Monuments Record for Scotland, Edinburgh. Ms 28 (SAS 461), 20-21.
19. Allen J R 1903 *op cit,* part III, 36-7
Liestol A Runes, in Fenton A and Palsson H eds *The Northern and Western Isles in the Viking World. Survival. Continuity and Change,* 1984, Edinburgh, 224-238.
20. Crawford B E *The Earls of Orkney-Caithness and their Relations with Norway and Scotland 1158-1470,* unpublished PhD Thesis, St Andrews University, 1971 (65).
21. Campbell R Notice of the Discovery of Eight Silver Rings of ancient wrist or ankle rings, in cists near Ratter, Dunnet, Caithness. *PSAS,* 1X, 1870-72, 422-7.
Graham Campbell J A The Viking-age silver and gold hoards of Scandinavian character from Scotland, *PSAS* 107, 1975-6, 114-135 (125).
22. Hunter J R The Island of Muckle Skerry, Orkney, *PSAS* 112, 1982, 518-524 (Site 4).

CHAPTER 7

THE MIDDLE AGES

Telling the story of Caithness from the Middle Ages to our own time presents problems. For the early period there is little evidence and what does exist focuses almost exclusively on the deeds of a few important individuals. The ordinary people lived and died in, for us, almost total obscurity and it is not until relatively recently that their voices begin to be heard. For the last two centuries, on the other hand, the difficulty is one of selection from the available material as we try to identify the important trends that have shaped events and our own time.

When did the Middle Ages begin? For Caithness the turn of the 12th and 13th centuries is a convenient starting point: for, in 1206, Harald Maddadarson, Earl of Orkney and Caithness, died at the age of seventy-one and his passing marked the beginning of the end of the Norse period of Caithness history.

Harald's last years, like much of the rest of his long life, were spent in holding with the sword and his wits the lands that he ruled. The threats came from both Norway and Scotland but the latter was the stronger. It was inevitable, given Caithness's mainland position, that it should succumb to southern forces long before Orkney and Shetland did. The incorporation of Caithness into Scotland, however, was not a straightforward story of continual advance; rather it took place in the form of bursts of political activity, with the initiative usually coming from the south.

The royal house of Canmore gradually extended its rule up the eastern seaboard of Scotland from the Lowlands during the 12th century. The office of 'thane', a royal official governing a province, is first mentioned during the reign of David I (1124-53), although it may have been in existence from the time of Malcolm II (1005-34). Thanages existed at Dingwall, Cawdor, Moyness, Brodie and other districts in the north-east. Likewise, sheriffdoms first appear in the reign of Alexander I (1107-24). By 1260, Cromarty, Dingwall, Inverness, Nairn, Forres, Elgin and Banff were sheriffdoms. Caithness did not become a separate sheriffdom until 1504; before then it was considered under Inverness's jurisdiction. Royal burghs which existed in the south from the same period — Forres and Elgin were declared as such in 1153, and Inverness and Nairn in 1214 — were likewise late in appearing in the north.

Secular power in Caithness in the 12th century lay in the hands of a few powerful chieftains, such as Svein Asleifarson who, though owing allegiance to the Earl of Orkney and Caithness, pursued a freedom of action that defied higher authority. Svein built and occupied at least for a time a stronghold called Lambaborg, on the site of the present ruin of Buchollie. The castle of Oldwick (Plate 25) also dates from the late Norse period and may have been the residence of the Orkney earls when they stayed at Wick. The remains of two other castles, Mestag on Stroma and Brough, are possibly of a similar age. The chronicle of Roger de Hoveden, chaplain to the English Henry II, mentions that King William of Scots (1165-1214) destroyed a castle in Thurso belonging to Earl Harald in 1196.

The Scottish king also advanced his power north under the guise of the church. Caithness was part of the see of the bishops of Orkney, aligned with Norway, but David I appointed his own Bishop of Caithness in about 1128. This man's name was Andrew, but we know little else about him and it is fairly certain that he never crossed the Ord, remaining instead in the south where his name crops up in the occasional surviving official document. According to the Chronicle of Melrose, he died in 1185 at Dunfermline. One of his acts had been to witness the grant by Earl Harald, possibly in 1181, to the see of Rome of one penny every year from every inhabited house in Caithness, a tax by which Harald hoped to ensure some well-being for his soul after his own death.

Andrew was succeeded as Bishop by John, who lived for a time at Scrabster. A letter from the Vatican in May 1198 shows that John had refused to exact the annual penny from Caithness households and asks the bishops of Orkney and Ross to compel him to cooperate. Episcopal neglect of the Earl's gift to Rome suggests that John and Harald may not have been on the best of terms and the Bishop's appointment may have been made against the Earl's wishes in the first place.

At about the same time, King William also tried to gain some control of Caithness by supporting Harald Ungi, or the Younger, in a bid for half the earldom. Harald Ungi was a grandson of Rognvald Kali Kolsson who had shared the earldom with Harold Maddadarson and who had been murdered near Forss in 1158. However, Earl Harald refused to surrender half of Caithness to Harald Ungi and crossed the Pentland Firth with a large force to meet his rival's army. In a battle traditionally said to have been fought on Clairdon hill, the old Earl was victorious and Harald Ungi himself was killed. King William, however, called on Rognvald Godrodarson, the Norse ruler of the Hebrides, for assistance. Rognvald occupied Caithness with a strong army and then withdrew, leaving three stewards, or sysselmen, in control. Earl Harald remained safely in Orkney but sent at least one man over the Firth in an unsuccessful attempt to assassinate the sysselmen.

Harald then crossed to Scrabster and violently regained control of Caithness. He mutilated Bishop John and imposed an oath of allegiance on the Caithnessmen. The sysselmen fled south. King William himself then led a large force north to a place called 'Eysteinsdal where Caithness and Sutherland meet', probably Ousdale. In the face of the superior royal might, Harald sued for peace. Part of the settlement was that the Caithnessmen should pay a quarter of their property to the King; but Harald kept the earldom.

What sort of a place was Caithness at this time? There is evidence that the climate was slightly milder than at present but still the landscape would have been broadly familiar to us — windswept and largely bare of trees, with the sea roiling against the coastal cliffs. The detail would have been very different. There were no roads: only tracks, over which the people walked or rode; and no harbours: boats were simply beached and pulled beyond the reach of the waves. Fields existed as unfenced, arable strips on the fringes of the moors, with the river valley bottoms, subject to flooding, used only as pasture or hay ground in the summer.

The first attempt to count the number of inhabitants was not done until 1755 when the result was 22,215. In 1200 A.D., it would have been much lower, in common with the rest of Scotland. In the later 14th century, Edinburgh had only about 400 houses, and throughout the Middle Ages the population of Scotland probably hovered around half a million. The population of Caithness in the 13th century was probably not more than 4,000 people. Child mortality would have been high and forty years a normal life span; only a few individuals, such as Earl Harald himself, survived into their seventies or beyond. There were no settlements of any size, Thurso, Halkirk and Wick comprising no more than a few houses and the rest of the occupied area of the county being marked by scattered farmsteads.

The excavations at Freswick, tentatively dated to the 13th century, give us an idea of the ordinary architecture of the time: long, narrow buildings with thick walls of infill between two shells of stone; in fact, not unlike the 19th century crofthouses in appearance. A long central hearth is also featured and postholes show that the roof was held up by wooden pillars. In a county largely bereft of good building timber, it is possible that some was imported from Scandinavia by Norse traders.

Analyses of the remains in the middens associated with the Freswick dwellings confirm what we could have suspected. The people raised cattle and fowl, grew oats and barley, harvested seabirds and caught white fish, using, among other things, limpets as bait. Other domestic animals and

1. Hills and coast of south-east Caithness from Hillhead, near Lybster.
(J. P. Campbell).

2. The Langwell valley, the Scarabens and Morven. (J. P. Campbell).

3. *"The Big Rock"*, *a sea stack at Shelligoe, Lybster.* (J. P. Campbell).

4. *The pyramidal stacks of Duncansby cut in the John O'Groats sandstone.*
(J. P. Campbell).

5. The round chambered cairn, with the long cairn in the background at Camster. (J. P. Campbell).

6. The interior chamber of the round cairn, Camster. (J. P. Campbell).

7. *The horned long cairn, Camster showing restored revetment walling and entrance to one of the two chambers.* (J. P. Campbell).

8. *Cnoc Freiceadain cairns, Shebster.* (J. P. Campbell).

9. Part of Achavanich stone circle. (L. Myatt).

10. The best preserved broch in Caithness, at Ousdale, showing walls rising to 3 metres in height. (J. P. Campbell).

(Photographs clockwise) (J. P. Campbell).
11. The cross-slab in the old kirkyard, Reay.
12. The commemorative stone, to the Groat family, located in Canisbay church.
13. A Pictish symbol stone, the Ulbster Stone, in Thurso Museum.
14. A Norse rune stone, found at St. Peter's Church, now in Thurso Museum.

15. *An early Christian cross carved on a rough boulder at Lybster.*
   (J. P. Campbell).

16. *Part of the Wag of Forse complex to the south of Lybster.*
   (Highland Regional Council).

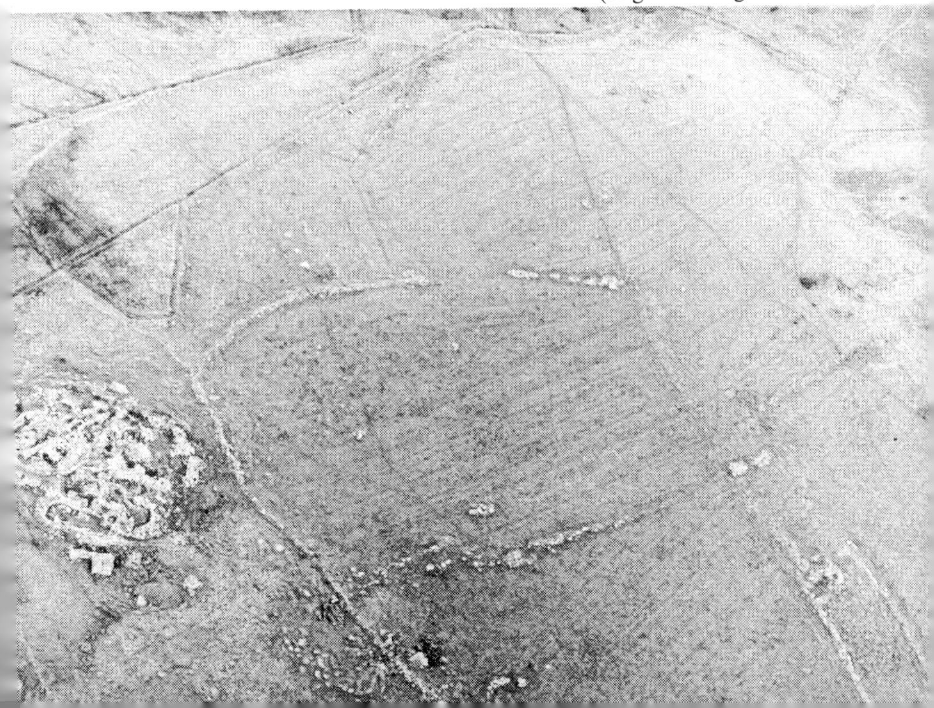

17. The dark organic layer is kitchen midden material from Norse times. Freswick Bay. (C. Batey).

18. The links at Freswick Bay. (C. Batey).

19. Dunnet Church, whose oldest parts are probably pre-Reformation. The tower dates from c. 1700. (J. P. Campbell).

20. A medieval church, St. Mary's Chapel, Crosskirk, Reay. (J. P. Campbell).

21. The 18th century church at Latheron, now the Clan Gunn centre. (J. P. Campbell).

22. Canisbay Church, whose oldest parts are pre-Reformation. (J. P. Campbell).

23. *The old castle of Braal, Halkirk.* (J. P. Campbell).

24. *Dunbeath Castle.* (J. P. Campbell).

25. *Auldwick. (Oldwick) castle, possibly the oldest in Caithness.* (J. P. Campbell).

26. Sinclair and Girnigoe castles, near Wick. (C. Cordiner 1780).

27. In the background is the old 16th century Keiss Castle. It was replaced by the 18th/19th century castle in the foreground. (J. P. Campbell).

28. *The gateway and gate lodge Thurso Castle, probably designed by Donald Leed of Thurso.* (HBD*).

29. *Watten Mains, dated 1762.* (with late 19th century canted dormers). (HBD*).

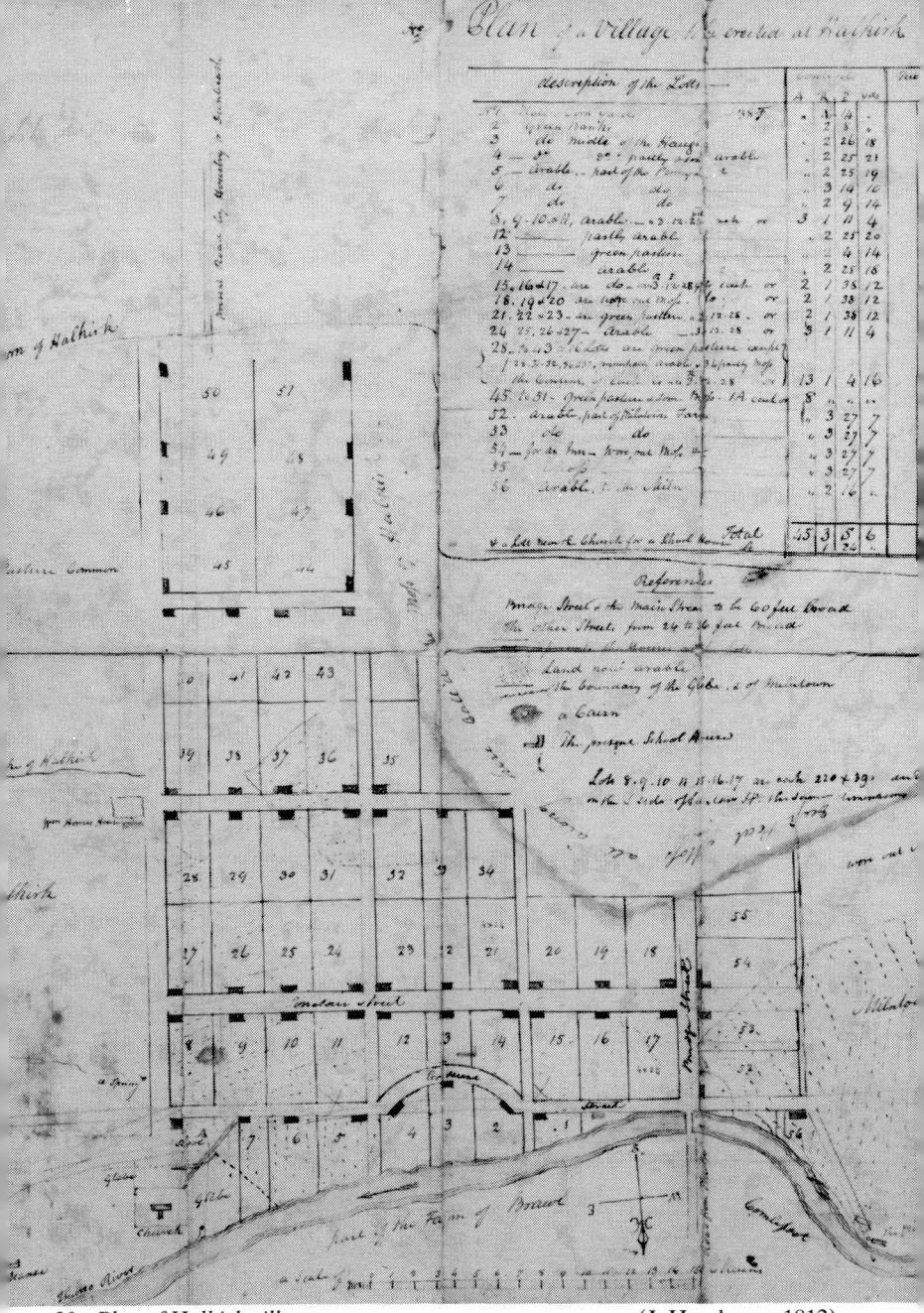

30. *Plan of Halkirk village.* (J. Henderson 1812).

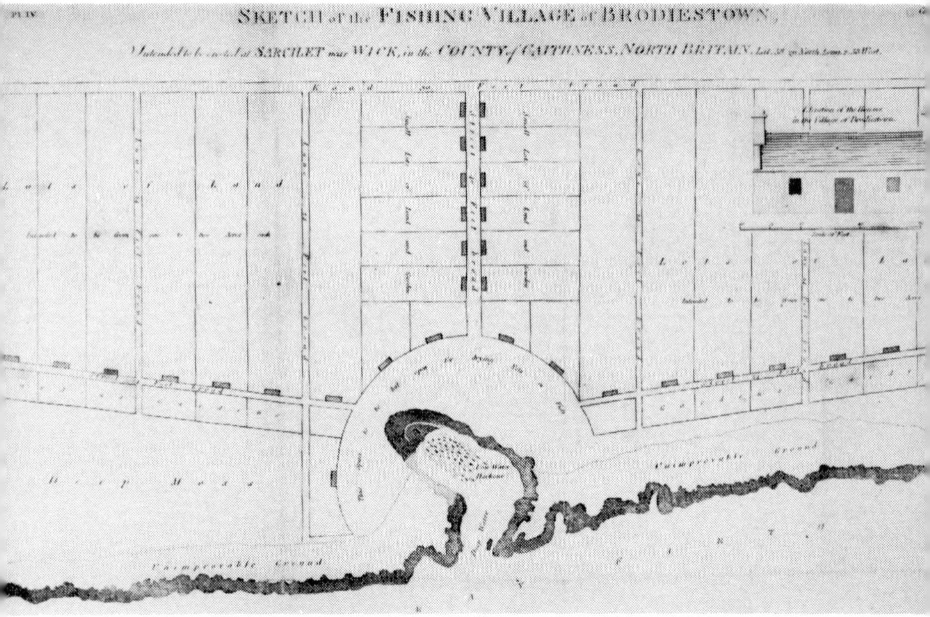

31. *Plan of Sarclet village.* (J. Henderson 1812).

32. *Plan of Old Thurso.* (J. Henderson 1812).

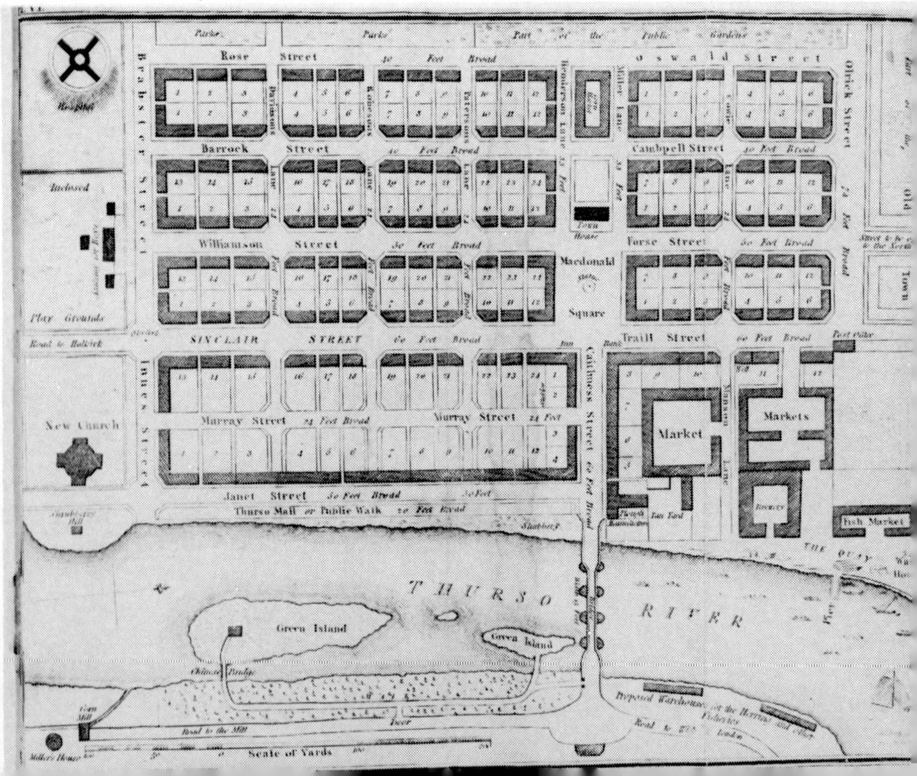

crops in use in late Norse times include horses, sheep, goats and pigs, peas, cabbage, leeks and berries and we can assume that these were current in Caithness. The diet also included butter and cheese, with ale being the main drink. Meat was preserved by pickling in brine, drying or smoking but it seems likely that for the bulk of the population a diet based on grain would have been eaten for most of the year.

In the 13th century the everyday tongue along the eastern and northern coasts was Norse. Over the succeeding two centuries it was eclipsed by Scots although many words survived in the newer dialect. Gaelic was the predominant language in the south and west. The linguistic divide was still plain in the 19th century. Throughout the Middle Ages the rubbing together of the two cultures added a special tension to feuding and reiving.

Harald Maddadarson was succeeded by his two sons, John and David. The latter died of illness in 1214, leaving John the sole Earl of Caithness and Orkney and heir to the political problems of his father. John worked on a campaign of diplomacy to establish good relations with both Norway and Scotland and appears to have been more successful in his dealings with the former than with either King William or his successor Alexander II (1214-49). He seems to have avoided involvement in the rebellions that emanated from Moray against the Scots throne. But the burning of Bishop Adam was a different matter altogether. Adam of Melrose became Bishop Adam of Caithness after the death of the John whom Harald Maddadarson had tortured. He was resident at Halkirk. How he met his death has become a part of Caithness folklore. A mob of angry farmers surrounded his home after he doubled the tithe that required payment in butter, seized him, thrust him into an outhouse and set fire to it. The Bishop probably died by suffocation, for the Chronicle of Melrose recorded that his body "although parched by the burning and, blackened by the stoning [was] nevertheless entire'. Earl John refused to respond to appeals for assistance against the mob and was later suspected of condoning the crime. Alexander II inflicted brutal punishments on those judged to have played a leading part in the atrocity. Earl John eventually fell victim to Snaekoll Gunnison, a great-grandson of Rognvald and a nephew of Harald Ungi. The dispute was once again over land and title and it came to a drunken conclusion for John in Thurso one night in 1231 when a confused quarrel burst into violence and John was stabbed to death as he hid among ale barrels in a cellar.

Gilbert de Moravia was appointed Bishop of Caithness in 1223 and during his tenure of the office, which lasted until his death in 1244, revitalised the church in the north and gave it much of its present shape. He initiated a building programme that included St. Peter's in Thurso and the cathedral at Dornoch, and divided his diocese, present-day Caithness and Sutherland, into its parishes. The boundaries of the parishes were probably set to coincide with the boundaries of existing estates. The revenues from six Caithness parishes — those of Bower, Watten, Skinnet, Olrig, Dunnet and Canisbay — were assigned, with others in Sutherland, to the upkeep of the cathedral establishment; Reay, Thurso, Wick and Latheron were reserved for the Bishop.

Gilbert chose to make Dornoch his centre of power. Politics probably played a bigger role in this than either Dornoch's milder climate or its easier communications with the south. Scots bishops were not too welcome in Scrabster or Halkirk and the Moravia or Freskyn family, Gilbert's close kin, after assisting William the Lion in dealing with Caithness in 1196, had been granted estates in Sutherland. Hugo Freskyn granted land in eastern Sutherland to Gilbert in 1211. Hugo's eldest son, William, became the first Earl of Sutherland about 1235 A.D.

The Caithness parishes are listed in the assessments of Baiamundus de Vitia, collector-general for Scotland of the papal taxes, in 1274 and 1275. Olric, Dinnosc, Cranesby, Ascend, [Skinnet], Haukyrc, Turishau, Haludal, Lagheryn and Durness, as they are spelt, contributed towards the cost of a Crusade. Chapels such as St. Mary's at Crosskirk complemented larger kirks such as St. Peter's; the present parish kirks of Dunnet, Reay and Canisbay possibly stand on the ruins of their predecessors. The various kirks must have been serviced by monks or priests with lay assistance, but no records remain of these people. The priory at Beauly was founded in 1230 and a Trinitarian order was established in Cromarty in 1271 but religious orders seem not to have penetrated Caithness to any extent, although records of hospitals, resting houses such as the one at Spittal for travellers, suggest that there was an active organisation of clerics of some kind. The Middle Ages were a time of pilgrimage, and the sites in Orkney and on the mainland associated with, for example, St. Magnus and St. Rognvald would have attracted many travellers.

The establishment of the earldom of Sutherland in the early 13th century was more or less contemporary with the emergence of the clan Mackay in Strathnaver and north-west Sutherland. Most historians of the clan put forward the view that the Mackays were descended from the earls of Moray and were exiled or forced to flee to the north to escape the power of the King of Scots, but others are sceptical of this hypothesis. Whatever the origin of the clan, the Mackays came to figure prominently in Caithness history in the later Middle Ages.

The history of the Caithness earldom immediately after the death of John Haraldsson is obscure and confused. We know that Alexander II granted the title of Earl of Caithness to Magnus, a son, grandson or possibly even a great-great-grandson of Gilbride, Earl of Angus and set in train a series of earls, known to us as the Angus Line. That the earldom should go to someone from the south is not in itself odd — Harald Maddararson was the son of the Earl of Atholl and Margaret Hakonsdottir of Orkney. Perhaps there was a link through marriage between the Haraldssons and the House of Angus.

In the middle of the 13th century, political developments in the west of Scotland led to an attempt by the Norwegian royal house to reassert its authority there. Conflicts in the Hebrides escalated into a diplomatic crisis between Hakon of Norway and Alexander II. In 1263 Hakon sailed west with a great fleet to secure his Hebridean allies. The fleet halted in Orkney in August and to protect the flank of the expedition Hakon imposed a levy and a peace settlement on Caithness. The fleet sailed west and south and the campaign ended with the Battle of Largs, a victory for the Scots, in October. Retreating to Orkney, Hakon died in Kirkwall just before Christmas. Subsequent negotiations with the Scots resulted in the Treaty of Perth in 1266 which recognised that the Hebrides and Caithness were part of Scotland.

Caithness makes another of its brief, tantalising appearances in medieval records during the Scottish succession crisis after the death of Alexander III in 1286. The name of John, one of the Angus earls of Caithness and Orkney, appears as a co-signatory on various documents — in 1289, recognising that Alexander's grand-daughter Margaret, the 'Maid of Norway' was the sole, true heir to the throne; and again in 1297, when the Earl was in Murkle, on an oath of fealty to Edward I.

Margaret died in Orkney on her way to her new realm. The records of this sad event include the itinerary and expenses of the messengers Edward I sent north to meet her. The messengers spent the night of 2nd October 1290 at Helmsdale, and that of the 3rd at 'Hospital' before riding onward to Wick on the 4th. The 'Hospital' referred to is unlikely to have been the hospice at Spittal, dedicated to St. Magnus, and it is the only clue we have to a religious foundation somewhere along the east coast, possibly at Latheron.

Caithness remained firmly on the sidelines during the Wars of Independence in the early decades of the 14th century. The nearest fighting was the capture of Skelbo Castle in 1308 by Robert Bruce's forces. Magnus, the last of the Angus earls, seems to have been content to bide at home and let events in the south run their course, only showing his hand when duty called on him to do so. Thus, in 1312, his name appears on the treaty at Inverness between Bruce and the king of Norway and in 1320 on the Declaration of Arbroath.

Crawford suggests that the Earl may have been a supporter of Bruce but was unable to act because he was surrounded by pro-English noblemen at least as powerful as he was — the earls of Sutherland and Ross and the Cheyne family.

The latter family acquired extensive lands in Caithness, including those at Oldwick and Dirlot, through marriage. Reginald de Cheyne died in about 1350 without a male heir and the estates passed through the marriages of his two daughters to the Keiths of Inverugy and the Sutherlands of Duffus.

Magnus, the last of the Angus line of earls, died in the 1320s. He may have had an heir who died in childhood, for contemporary documents refer to royal baillies or ballivi who during the heir's minority would have been administering the earldom. Interestingly, the baillie in Caithness in 1321 was Henry St. Clair, the first appearance in the county of this family. The title of earl passed to Malise, Earl of Strathearn, whose great-grandmother had been the daughter of one of the earlier Angus earls. Thus, another Lowland family followed the north road, and this time a very powerful one, Strathearn being related to the royal Stewarts. Through his second marriage to the daughter of the Earl of Ross, Malise also aligned himself with that powerful northern house.

Malise died in about 1353 without sons but with five daughters, one of whom, Isabella, his designated heiress, married William St. Clair. The earl's estates in Caithness and Orkney were divided among the five daughters. Confusion arose over who should inherit the title of Earl and it turned into a long-running series of disputes which are difficult to untangle at this distance in time. The Earl of Ross played a key role in the contest, expanding his power base northward into Orkney, an incursion of mainland Scots that drew Norway's attention to the situation. Henry St. Clair finally emerged in 1379 as the first Sinclair Earl of Orkney.

The earldom of Caithness meanwhile was divided from Orkney and passed to the Stewarts. David Stewart, a son of Robert II (1371-90), was the Earl in 1375. He died before 1389 and the title passed first to his daughter Euphemia and then to his brother Walter, who also became Earl of Atholl. Walter resigned the Caithness earldom in favour of his son, Alan, but regained it after Alan was killed in a battle at Inverlochy in 1426. Walter was tortured and executed in 1437 for his leading part in the assassination of James I, and thereafter the title to the earldom of Caithness seems to have remained vacant until, in 1452, James II bestowed it upon George Crichton, the High Admiral of Scotland, as a reward for loyal services against the Douglases.

Throughout this time when titles moved as prizes in the power games of the ruling families, the daily round of the people would have been devoted, as always, to winning a living from the land. Oats and bere were the main crops. Among the laws enacted during the reign of David II (1329-1371), one ruled that 'Ane common and equal weicht, quhilk is called the weicht of Cathnes, in buying and selling, sall be keeped and used be all men within this realme of Scotland'.

THE MIDDLE AGES

If it was intended that Caithness measures be a national standard the move failed, as Scottish weights and measures remained in confusion until the 1600s. The law has also been taken to mean that Caithness was a net exporter of grain. Again, documentary evidence for this early period does not exist but the important grain trade in later centuries could well have had its beginnings in the Norse era.

The population probably grew slowly but steadily until the middle of the 14th century. Then the Black Death spread like fire throughout Europe in the space of a few years. There are no records of the effects this plague had on Caithness. In Norway, however, between one-third and one-half of the population was wiped out and the Icelandic Annals say that Orkney was 'ravaged'. Records in Lowland Scotland agree on a third of the people succumbing. It is unlikely that Caithness escaped, although its isolation from the south may have spared its people some of the fury of the disease.

The landed families in Caithness, as in the rest of Scotland, were continually competing for influence and frequently these struggles erupted into violence, spawning bloodfeuds that could persist over generations. The landowners counted their tenants as their manpower and at the same time the tenants looked to their lords for protection from attack and help in times of distress. Clear examples of this are available for the 15th and 16th centuries when bonds sealed agreements in writing; in earlier times we can assume the existence of verbal agreements. In the Highlands the bond of loyalty between tenant and lord was strengthened by feelings of blood kinship; this was the essence of the social structure of the clan. The Sinclair earls in Caithness and the Sutherland earls obviously gained their tenantry along with their estates and claims of kinship reflect political imperatives rather than genetic realities. Unfortunately, we can only speculate how the relict Norse culture in Caithness mingled with incoming Scots influences and affected how tenants saw themselves in relation to their lairds.

The ruling families sometimes tried to settle their disputes by negotiation but these were not always successful or lasting. For example, in 1370, the Earl of Sutherland and the Chief of Mackay met at Dingwall Castle to try to end the feuding between their houses; the meeting ended in bloodshed when Sutherland's son stabbed both Mackay and his son. Written bonds, professing friendship and peace between the various ruling families, were made several times in the 15th century but again lasting peace proved elusive.

The general level of violence in northern society in the later Middle Ages was enhanced by the activities of the cattle-lifters. Raiding and plundering, a favourite pursuit of the Strathnaver Mackays, but by no means restricted to them, was carried on independently of the larger dynastic feuds.

The Gunn family emerges onto the Caithness stage in the mid-15th century when George Gunn of Halberry held the royal office of 'crowner'. Crowners, or coroners, were created in 1357 and a letter from David II in 1358 mentions an unnamed coroner of Caithness. We cannot be sure this person was a Gunn; nor can we be sure of how George Gunn came by the office, though it is probable that he inherited it.

A bitter feud between the Gunns and the Keiths persisted for several decades between the late 1300s and the late 1400s. Traditionally it is said to have begun when the beautiful Helen Gunn of Braemore was kidnapped and ravaged by Dugald Keith of Ackergill. Helen died by throwing herself from the top of Ackergill tower. A more prosaic beginning for the feud may lie with the Keiths, who, acquiring land through marriage to Mary de Cheyne, found the existing power of the Gunns a block to their own ambitions. The two families fought numerous battles, all celebrated in folklore and none more so than the last when the Keiths cheated over the arrangements made for a formal conflict by mounting two men on each of the twelve horses allowed either side. Outnumbered two to one, the Gunns were slaughtered, the dead including George the then coroner and some of his sons. The date of this conflict is uncertain but August 1478 is one possibility. One son, James, was absent from the fight; he went to live in the Strath of Kildonan and sought the protection of the Earl of Sutherland.

The Gunn family found themselves thereafter in a precarious position as hostages to the fortunes of the earls. In 1529, Sutherland of Duffus was murdered in Thurso by some Gunns, probably at the instigation of Adam Gordon. Gordon had won, by subterfuge and arms, the earldom of Sutherland; and he may well have considered Duffus, a scion of the family he had ousted, better out of the way. It has been suggested that the Gunns did dirty work for the Sinclairs as well and they also feuded with, for example, the Mackays. In 1584, the earls of Caithness and Sutherland combined forces to crush the Gunns, blaming them for all the troubles between their houses. A two-pronged attack in 1586 was finally successful; the Gunns routed the first Sinclair attack on the slopes of Ben Griam but were then pursued through the hills by the Sutherland men to be surprised and bested at Leckmelm on Loch Broom.

William Sinclair, the Earl of Orkney, was created Earl of Caithness by James III in August 1455. He lost his Orkney lands to the crown when the northern islands passed to the Scots throne as part of the marriage arrangements between James and Princess Margaret of Norway; and a few years later in 1476, he also resigned the Caithness earldom in favour of his son.

The latter, also called William, fell at Flodden in 1513 along with the Bishop of Caithness and a contingent of Caithnessmen he had brought south in answer to the king's call to arms. Before his death he had begun the building of the main Sinclair fortress at Girnigoe. When the Sinclairs became earls, they seem to have possessed less land in Caithness than the other powerful families. Girnigoe can be seen as an expression of a firm intention to rule. Other Sinclair castles were built at about the same time or later at Keiss, Mey, Brims, Dounreay and Thurso.

Sinclair power received a further boost when the family gained the hereditary office of sheriff from the crown. James IV made Caithness a sheriffdom in 1504 as part of a series of policy moves aimed to win greater control of the Highlands. The Sinclair jurisdiction included Sutherland and ran 'fra Portinculter to Pentlandfirth, and fra the eist sey to the west sey', a piece of political geography that did not sit well with the Sutherland earls in Dunrobin or with several others.

The roots of one of the most enduring pieces of Caithness folklore reach back to the late 15th century — the story of John de Groat. The oldest written record of the story appears in the *Statistical Account* of Canisbay parish, published in the 1790s; here it is stated that John and two brothers, Malcolm and Gavin, arrived in the district that now bears their name with a letter from James IV (1488-1513) recommending them 'to the countenance and protection of his loving subjects'. John's fame rests on his running of a ferry to Orkney and his ingenious solution to a quarrel over precedence among his eight sons. He built an octagonal house with eight doors so that each of his prickly offspring could have their own entrance and place at an octagonal table. A footnote to the OSA account states that the king's letter was still in the possession of a descendant around 1700. Documentary evidence for the story is now conspicuously lacking but circumstantial evidence ensures at least some truth in the legend. The Groat family (Plate 12) held land on both sides of the Pentland Firth and records of land grants to Groats date from the 1490s.

The third Sinclair earl, John, also fell in battle — in a bloody melee in Orkney in 1529. The Sinclair landholdings in Orkney and Caithness had become divided among the various branches of the family; a serious dispute arose between Lord William Sinclair and James Sinclair of Brecks over landholding rights. Temporarily bested, William crossed the Firth and sought the assistance of his kinsman, Earl John. John obtained permission from the crown to aid William and invaded Orkney at the head of five hundred men. James Sinclair of Brecks and his followers had also prepared themselves and in the struggle, now known to us as the Battle of Summerdale, the Caithnessmen were heavily defeated. Earl John fell among the dead.

The loss of over one hundred young men in Orkney coming so soon after the carnage of Flodden, when perhaps as many as three hundred Caithnessmen perished, must have rocked the county to her heels.

Historian James T. Calder (Plate 53) is probably right in recording that 'the two fatal expeditions nearly drained it of all its young and able-bodied men'.

The earldom passed to John's son, George, who ruled Caithness for over fifty years and acquired in his own time a reputation both as a brave fighter and as a cruel, astute intriguer. In his defence one could argue that, as hereditary sheriff and justiciar, he could not escape becoming embroiled in numerous feuds and disputes, both locally and nationally.

He appears to have maintained royal approval. In the summer of 1540, James V sailed north with his fleet and spent a little time in Caithness before proceeding to Scapa Flow and the west coast. The purpose of the tour was 'for the ordouring of [northern counties] in justice and gude policy'. James may have been satisfied with the way George was running things..

Several of George's neighbours sought court action against him. In 1547 Queen Mary granted him remission for the seizure of Ackergill and the imprisonment of Alexander Keith 'captain' of the castle. In July 1556, however, the Queen held a justice ayre, a circuit hearing, in Inverness, to which George was summoned 'for committing of diuerse and manifold foule and odious crimes, and accusit thairfor'. The record continues: ' because the said regent [Mary] could not get ane unsuspect assise to him, he wes put in captivite in the castell of Innerness, and thairafter transportit to Edinburgh castell, quhairin he remainit ane certaine space and thairafter wes put to friedome and libertie be ane great composition of money'.

This fine seems to have been the only instance when the Earl paid a penalty for a complaint against him. In 1549 Robert Stewart, the Bishop of Caithness, had accused him of various excesses and breaches of sanctuary, including the pillaging of altar ornaments and the chalice from the kirk of Farr. The Privy Council in May 1566 dismissed complaints that the Earl was exceeding his authority in deputising others to act for him while he was in Edinburgh on royal business. George was frequently in the capital, attending Parliament or serving other duties; for example, he was chancellor of the jury that aquitted Bothwell of Darnley's murder in 1567. In his absence it is likely that his deputies took the chance to settle a few scores of their own and, in 1569, the Oliphants, who held land and the castle at Oldwick, complained to the Privy Council about the way the Earl's men were violently enforcing their will.

The Earl's relations with the Mackays of Strathnaver and the Gordon earls of Sutherland were most crucial to the preserving of order. Over three days of what may have been tense negotiation, from the 26th to the 28th April 1549, Bishop Robert mediated at a peace settlement between George, the Earl of Sutherland and Donald Mackay of Farr.

The talks, begun at Scrabster and finished at Girnigoe pledged friendship between the protagonists 'for the public weal, for staunching of slaughter and oppression within their bounds . . . for life'.

The peace agreement was torn up in 1567. In July that year John, Earl of Sutherland, and his wife were poisoned at Helmsdale. George became guardian of John's son and heir, Alexander the Master, and married him to his daughter, Barbara, who was twice the Master's age. Sinclair's enemies suspected that he had had a hand in the murder of the Earl but there is no proof of this. The Murrays of Dornoch, 'grieved and vexed' at the influence of George over the young Alexander and at George's suspected attempt to gain the Sutherland earldom through his daughter's marriage, arranged for the youth to escape from Dunrobin to the protection of the Earl of Huntly.

George naturally sought to humble the Murrays and, in 1570, with the aid of some Mackays, the Sinclair force attacked Dornoch where their enemies had taken refuge. The town was sacked and the cathedral burned. The Bishop of Caithness, Alexander Stewart, mediated a settlement, but the Sinclairs later had three hostages killed in cold blood.

A disagreement between the Earl and his son, John, Master of Caithness, over the treatment of the hostages is claimed to have been the cause of the enmity that developed between them. John left his father's house and went to live with the Strathnaver Mackays until, yielding to repeated pleas from his father, he returned to Girnigoe where he was cruelly confined to a dungeon until he died in 1576. The traditional story is that George murdered John by having him starved and then fed salt beef until the hapless man died of thirst. In considering this crime, it should be noted that some sources, such as the Wardlaw Manuscript, indicate that George had good reason to suspect his son of conspiring against him. Nevertheless, that the Earl could allow the murder of his eldest son under his own roof is a telling display of his ruthlessness.

George died in Edinburgh in 1582 and almost immediately the Keiths and the Oliphants gathered support to petition the Privy Council not to grant to his heir, his grandson, George, the sweeping powers he had held. The petitioners argued that the old Earl had used his office to their 'greit hurt and prejudice' and that the Earl of Huntly, who was Sheriff Principal of the north, and the Earl of Sutherland had found George's powers to be 'strange and unsufferabill'. The Privy Council accepted their arguments.

A bloodfeud that lasted for four years broke out between the earls of Sutherland and Caithness in 1587. George Gordon of Marrel near Helmsdale committed 'several contempts and indignities' against the Earl of Caithness and his servants. The Sinclairs attacked Marrel in February and killed Gordon with arrows as he attempted to escape by swimming the river.

The Earl of Sutherland obtained a commission to avenge his kinsman and in the following year carried out what became known as the 'great spoil' of Latheron. A combined force of Mackays and Sutherlands cut a swathe of pillage across Caithness as far as Girnigoe. Earl George shut himself up in his castle and waited. The invaders burned and sacked the town before besieging Girnigoe unsuccessfully for a fortnight.

Sinclair took his revenge the following year, sending a force under his brother, Sinclair of Murkle, into Sutherland where they plundered Strathullie and burnt 'Ciriboll'. In 1590, three hundred Sutherlandmen again pillaged Caithness to within 9.7km (6 miles) of Girnigoe, and Sinclair retaliated with another invasion of Sutherland, leading it in person and penetrating as far as Backies, lifting a great number of cattle. An indecisive battle between the forces on the sands of Kintradwell was brought to an early end by nightfall. Sinclair had to break off the confrontation to hasten back northward when he heard that Hutchen Mackay had invaded the north-west of Caithness, plundering as far as Thurso. Mackay's force escaped before Sinclair got to the scene. Finally, in March 1591, under the arbitration of the Earl of Huntly, the Sinclairs and the Sutherlands reached a peace settlement at Strathbogie.

The 16th century drew to a close in the north with feuding that would have been familiar to Earl Harald Maddadarson. However, new ideas about government and law and order were slowly beginning to make way in the wake of the Reformation and would, in time, extinguish the outlook of the Middle Ages.

CHAPTER 8

FROM REFORMATION TO IMPROVEMENT (1560-1800)

In 1560 the Reformation made Scotland a Protestant nation. The Bishop of Caithness, Robert Stewart, was in exile at the time, banished for his involvement in the feud between his elder brother and the Earl of Arran's supporters. He returned to his native country in 1563, embraced the reformed church and retained the title of Bishop, although he was never consecrated in this role. The reformers commissioned him to plant kirks in his diocese, a task for which he was thanked by the General Assembly before his death in 1586. Most of the parishes of Caithness were in the charge of readers or exhorters — lay preachers, probably poorly educated, appointed as a stopgap measure until enough clergy could be trained. There were ministers in Reay, Thurso, Watten and Wick. Andrew Graham, the vicar of Wick, converted and held on to his benefice until 1574. This should not be put down to nifty theological footwork: the idea of reformation had been in the air for decades and Graham, like some other clerics, may have genuinely been glad of the chance to practise openly what he had long felt to be true.

We can only speculate about what ordinary folk thought of the new Protestant faith. Thurso and Bower had reformed services as early as 1561, but there is plenty of evidence to show that the old practices, sometimes debased Catholicism, sometimes faint relics of more ancient beliefs, lingered for many decades. In the 1790s, a few of these are recorded in the *Statistical Account*. Reforming zeal could stir parishioners to violence: Richard Merchiston, minister in Wick in 1633, was drowned in the Wick river after he defaced a statue of St. Fergus, the town's patron saint (see chapter 16).

The lairds, who probably saw a Reformation stemming from the lower orders of society as dangerously subversive, were at best lukewarm towards the new kirk. The Earl of Caithness is mentioned as 'an acknowledged Catholic' and the Earl of Sutherland was condemned by the General Assembly in 1587-88 for adhering to the older faith. As late as 1639, Andrew Ogston, the minister of Canisbay, complained that Sir William Sinclair of Mey was influencing his parishioners to disobey him; and in 1649 the General Assembly considered the matter of the education of the Earl of Caithness's children, their father still thought to be 'affected popishly'.

After the death of Robert Stewart, Robert Pont became the church's Commissioner for Caithness, a post similar in all except title to that of bishop. As the minister of St. Cuthbert's in Edinburgh, Pont was well placed in the new society. Two of his sons also become ministers: Zachary, who married John Knox's daughter, held the parish of Bower from 1608 to 1612, and Timothy had Dunnet from 1601 until his death sometime between 1625 and 1630. Timothy Pont is best remembered for his cartographic skills. His maps are the first attempts to represent Caithness on paper and were eventually published, with additional work by Robert Gordon of Straloch, in Blaeu's *Atlas* in 1654. Gordon is also thought to have been the author of a short description of the county in Latin, dating from the same period. Earlier mentions of Caithness are very brief and indicate that their authors had little or no personal knowledge of the place.

The last decades of the 16th century were a time of inflation, rising population and dearth, with the currency being debased and grain imported from the Baltic to fend off starvation. The amount of money in circulation in Caithness was probably small, the economy depending more on barter and exchange of services than on cash. However, a blacksmith from Banff, Arthur Smith, for some time a servant of the Earl of Caithness, was accused of forging large amounts of false coin in Thurso and flooding the north with base currency. The Earl was suspected of condoning the forgery. Smith was arrested in May 1612 by men acting on behalf of the Earl of Sutherland but the people of Thurso, angered by the Sutherland men's presence, rallied to rescue the forger; in the ensuing fight, John Sinclair of Stirkoke was killed and several others wounded.

In this uncertain religious and economic climate, witchcraft assumed an unholy importance in the public imagination and, although long tolerated, as folklore makes clear, was made a criminal offence in 1563. The first trial recorded in Caithness, of three unnamed people, followed in 1595. In 1655 there were eight trials in Wick and others in Keiss and Papigoe. Six women were tried in Thurso in 1718 and the last Caithness trial, in Canisbay, was held in 1724. A few of the accused in these trials were acquitted; the fates of most are not known. The witchcraft laws were finally repealed in 1736.

The feuding between the earls of Caithness and Sutherland and their supporters came to a formal end in March 1591, when the Earl of Huntly acted as a mediator in negotiating a peace settlement. Huntly was plain with the Privy Council about the difficulties of arbitrating between such touchy noblemen, but his efforts were successful. The resulting fragile peace survived the trouble following the arrest of Arthur Smith; and the raising of Sutherland into a separate sheriffdom in 1633, thereby making the two earls sheriffs within their own domains, removed another touchpaper from their lordships' pride. The creation of the new sheriffdom also fixed the Caithness-Sutherland border. That the resentments born of feuding could linger for a long time was amply demonstrated in 1613 when the Earl of Caithness was called upon to play a leading role in the defeat and execution of Patrick Stewart of Orkney. The Earl was supplied from Edinburgh Castle with weapons for this task of state, including 'ane grite cannon callit thrown mow', and in the ensuing attack on Kirkwall had to be restrained by the Bishop of Orkney from demolishing St. Magnus Cathedral; the Earl saw his victory as revenge for the defeat and death of his great-grandfather at Summerdale almost a century before.

Poor living conditions at home may have lain behind the recruiting in 1612 by George Sinclair of Stirkoke, a brother of the John killed in Thurso and a nephew of the Earl, of a troop of about 150 men to join the army of the Swedish king, Gustavus Adolphus. Marching through the Pass of Kringelen in the Norwegian mountains, this force was ambushed by peasants; about two-thirds were killed and the rest taken prisoner. News of this tragedy may have had a sobering effect on the Caithness people; neither the Marquis of Montrose nor the Jacobites would be able to rouse much support in Caithness, at least among the tenantry. The sons of the lairds, with more resources and chivalry to think of, continued to seek military careers abroad; several became officers in the regiment raised by the Chief of Mackay, afterwards Lord Reay, to fight in the Thirty Years War.

In 1589, only a year after the town had been sacked and burned by the Earl of Sutherland's men, Wick was made a royal burgh. James VI's charter expresses confidence that such promotion would increase the nation's foreign trade and revenues, and render the place 'more civilised', putting an end to 'thefts, rapines, murders and other oppressions committed amongst the said inhabitants'. At the time Wick was probably little more than a village, a string of dwellings roughly along the line of the present High Street. Evidence for the early history of the town is very sketchy but the discovery of coin hoards points to some mercantile activity before 1589. The royal charter did not immediately improve matters; other royal burghs seem to have resented Wick's new status. Inverness dominated trade in the north in the late 16th century and tried hard to hold its position: in 1590, a merchant called Adam Davidson of Caithness was deprived of his rights and freedoms as a burgess of Inverness for refusing to make the southern burgh his place of residence.

Was Davidson hoping to operate from Wick? We do not know.

Like Wick, Thurso had a history running back to Norse times and had been part of the bishopric before passing to the earl's estates. It, too, was a small place, clustered around St. Peter's kirk on the west bank of the river mouth, when it was created a burgh of barony in 1633 in favour of John, Master of Berriedale, the grandson of the Earl. The rights and responsibilities of the baillies of the town were first set out in 1659; this document is missing but we have its revised version, drawn up by Campbell of Glenorchy in 1680. In his survey of Scottish ports in 1656, Thomas Tucker stated that Thurso had two 30-ton sloops trading from its rivermouth whereas Wick was home port to no trading vessels. The burgh of barony also had the advantage of a thriving salmon fishery, which in the 1550s was stated as being worth £300 Scots per year. We have some information about Caithness's trade with other counties. For example, in the 1640s and probably earlier, Caithness corn was being exchanged for timber from Strathnaver; and several Wick merchants sold grain in Elgin in the 1630s.

In 1638, opposition to the efforts of Charles I to force Episcopalianism on Scotland crystallised around the National Covenant, a document at once a petition and a declaration of religious independence. John Sinclair, the grandson of the Earl, was among the first to sign it and he was soon after appointed a commissioner in charge of the collection of signatures in Caithness. The county 'for the most pairt subscrivit', and 'sindry gentlemen' tried to join the army of the Covenanters a year later but were prevented from doing so by the barrier of the Spey in spate. The Mowat laird of Buchollie stayed loyal to the king and was killed in 1645 at the battle of Alford fighting for Montrose. Conflict in England between the crown and Parliament eventually led to the Civil War and the execution of the defeated Charles I in January 1649. The Scots, albeit prepared to shed blood in defence of their faith, were appalled by the death of the monarch and declared Charles II king.

The royalist, James Graham, the Marquis of Montrose, a charismatic leader and a brilliant general, landed at Duncansby in April 1650 in a bid to put the new king safely on the throne. He had with him a small army of Danish mercenaries and Orkney levies and hoped to recruit more followers on the mainland. Caithness, however, gave him a cold reception. Many of the Duncansby tenants at first fled in alarm. When the news reached Dunbeath Castle (Plate 24) Sir John Sinclair took to his horse and rode south to alert the Convention of Estates. Montrose marched to Thurso and there issued an appeal for support. Only two lairds, Alexander Sinclair of Brims and Hugh Mackay of Dirlot, openly offered their services. Most of the county's ministers were forced to recognise on oath Montrose's authority, an act for which they later lost their charges. But, as John Henrie, a Thurso schoolmaster, told the

FROM REFORMATION TO IMPROVEMENT 95

General Assembly, they had subscribed to Montrose's 'wicked and perfidious band . . . out of carnall fear, after many temptations and threatenings'. Only one minister, William Smyth of Bower, refused the oath, an act of stubborn courage for which he was abused by some parishioners (less out of loyalty to Montrose than dislike for the minister, one wonders) and imprisoned in irons until after the Marquis's defeat. Montrose's force, augmented only slightly by his few Caithness recruits, marched south through the moors to be defeated at Carbisdale on the 27th April. On the way they captured and held for a time Dunbeath Castle.

After the defeat of Charles II's army in the autumn of 1651, Cromwell's forces occupied the whole country. A Colonel Overton marched through Caithness and crossed to Orkney in February 1652 to support an invasion of the islands by Cromwell's admiral. English soldiers were for a time billeted on the people of Canisbay. The session records of Canisbay kirk make several mentions of the occupation, which may not have been too arduous, the army's eyes being directed more at Orkney than the mainland. In 1652 the Scottish and English parliaments were united in a single Cromwellian union. John Sinclair of Tannach and George Monro of Newton represented Caithness in the discussions leading up to the union. Caithness, Orkney and Shetland, aligned for once as a single constituency, failed to provide an MP for the first parliament but were represented in the second, in 1656, by Colonel Robert Stewart. The Cromwellian parliament which was unpopular and expensive lasted until the Restoration of the monarchy in 1660. Before that, however, Caithness was the scene of more military activity.

Another royalist rebellion erupted in the north in the late winter of 1654. One of the generals, Middleton, retreated from Easter Ross into Caithness in March, pursued by Parliamentarian troops under General Monck, who wrote to Cromwell to say that he hoped to pen the rebels there 'where we hope to destroy them and that country'. By September Monck was able to record that 'Colonel Morgan hath settled Caithness in a very good posture' and had received the surrender and 'recantacion' of the royalists. Middleton escaped to fight another day; his ally, Lord Reay, surrendered on honourable terms, and Caithness was occupied for some time after. Castle Sinclair (Plate 26) was garrisoned with seventy soldiers and fifteen cavalrymen. In 1655, the session records of Canisbay complain of the presence of 'the Inglishe' causing low church attendance and of Adam Seaton 'drinking on the Sabbathe and having masking plays in his house for the Inglishe men'. Cromwell's soldiers are also credited with building the small bridge across the burn at Huna.

During the 17th century the Strathnaver Mackays were repeatedly disturbing the peace in the west of Caithness with their cattle-lifting and raiding. There were at least seven raids between 1653 and 1656 and another three in 1667. Early in 1668, the Sinclair lairds of Dunbeath and Murkle struck back at Strathnaver and came home with 900 head of cattle, many of which were probably their own lifted in previous raids. Later that year cases were brought by the Sinclairs and the Sutherlands against each other in the Court of Justiciary, a sign that the law was struggling to overcome the sword as a means of settling disputes. The Earl of Caithness was later granted remission but the lairds of Dunbeath and Murkle failed to appear in court. This gave rise to more trouble and brought Campbell of Glenorchy onto the scene.

These events and the to-ing and fro-ing across the Ord indicate that Caithness was not as isolated from the rest of the country as we might be led to believe. The bulk of the population rarely travelled more than a few miles from home — with only their feet, or possibly a horse, how could they? — but Caithness names crop up in unusual places at all times, showing that a few at least successfully sought to broaden their horizons. Between 1425 and 1494, for example, there were two students from Caithness among the 253 Scots studying at the University of Paris. A John Catnes and a Richard Catnes turn up in the Register of Burgesses of Aberdeen in 1454 and 1475. In 1671-2 William Sinclair, John Sutherland, Robert Innes and William Mowat of Buchollie are listed among the students at Aberdeen University; and two Caithnessmen, Alexander McBeth and James Sutherland, were among the crew of HMS Victory in 1805, the year of Trafalgar.

George Sinclair, the sixth of his line to be Earl of Caithness, assumed the title in 1644. During his life he incurred large debts and was being pursued by his creditors when he appealed to the Privy Council for help in dealing with his troublesome kinsmen, the lairds of Dunbeath and Murkle, both of whom had been outlawed for their non-appearance in court in connection with raids on Strathnaver. The Privy Council appointed Iain Glas Campbell, the heir to Glenorchy, to lead a troop of soldiers north in an effort to restore order. While he was in Caithness, Campbell found out about the Earl's debts. The two men reached an agreement; Campbell granted George an annual sum of £1,000 in exchange for George's title, estates and heritable jurisidictions, all to be passed over on George's death.

In 1676, George died and Campbell reaped the harvest of his deal, not only inheriting the earldom but also marrying George's widow. The people of Breadalbane, Campbell's own territory, devised a saying — 'the gold of Caithness is on the table at Balloch' — as the rents and revenues flowed south to Glenorchy's home. Campbell appointed Sir John Sinclair of Murkle as sheriff and justiciary-depute of Caithness and baillie of his Caithness lands. Although Campbell's gaining of the earldom had been ratified by Charles II, George Sinclair of Keiss disputed the southerner's right to the title. His case was considered but dismissed. Sinclair had, however, the support of most of the Caithness lairds and, it seems, of the majority of the tenants as well; Campbell was seen as a usurper who had cheated the old Earl. A campaign of harrassment began; Campbell's property and livestock were attacked, his rents were withheld, and his castle at Thurso East was pulled down.

The Privy Council gave Campbell the authority to recover his property through force of arms. In the summer of 1680, a Campbell force, under the command of Glenorchy's cousin, Robert Campbell of Glenlyon, marched north to subdue the recalcitrant Caithness people. The size of the Campbell force has been variously estimated, up to 1,100 men. Sinclair of Keiss likewise gathered men to fight, and accounts of the size of this force also vary, up to 1,500. The resulting clash between the Campbells and Sinclairs at the burn of Altimarlach (Plate 41) has been called the last clan battle fought in Scotland. Many of the legends surrounding it, for example, of how Glenorchy's men tricked the Caithnessmen into getting drunk, have to be viewed sceptically. The following description of the battle by William Dunbar, published in Macfarlane's *Geographical Collections,* rings more true than some other versions of the event.

'Upon which the Earle [Glenorchy] obtained a party of the Kings forces, and what friends he could make to assist the Sheriff of Innerness [sic] to repone him to the possesion, but he having gathered together about 300 men did enter the Countrey without the Sherif, earle George knowing of his Motion, had gathered two or three hundred Commons together, who, having gone to Week, were followed at a distance by E. John. But E. George's men, being far inferior in number and arms, resolved to return to their Houses quietly, and going without care or order, as from a fair, E. John who waited this opportunity, set upon them about a mile from Week and killed and drowned in the Water of Week above 80, beside many wounded, most part after they had thrown away their Arms and sought Quarter. for which and other crimes there is process of Treason depending against the said E. John.'

The reference to charges of treason dates this account to 1690, as in August of that year Glenorchy was implicated in the Annandale plot to restore James II to the throne.

Undaunted by his defeat, George Sinclair of Keiss continued his campaign. He besieged Castle Sinclair; some kind of artillery may have been used, which may explain why the masonry of Sinclair, built in 1606, has survived less well than the older Girnigoe. But it was not until the Duke of York, later to be James II, took an interest in the case that the title of earl was granted to Sinclair in 1681.

The Campbells remained hated intruders even after they lost the title of earl, and the harrassment that they and their servants suffered eventually persuaded Grey John's successors to sell up in 1719. The bulk of the earldom estates were purchased by the Sinclairs of Ulbster, who also acquired the sheriffship in 1735. George Sinclair of Keiss died unmarried in 1698 and his hard-won title passed to Sir John Sinclair of Murkle.

Sir John's son, Alexander, became Earl in 1705. It is interesting to note for the record that in 1707 Alexander, along with James Sinclair of Stemster and Robert Frazer, a burgess of Wick, were among those who voted against the Union of the Parliaments. James Dunbar of Hempriggs was the only Caithness member of the Scots Parliament to vote for it. After the alarms and warfare of the 17th century, Caithness settled down to a long period of relative peace, barely broken by the Jacobite rebellions. In 1700 a party of commissioners — seven ministers and one elder — appointed by the General Assembly to review 'the concerns of the Church of Christ' in Orkney, Shetland and Caithness landed at Duncansby after a rough crossing of the Pentland Firth. One of the ministers was John Brand. He found the county 'pleasant and very fertile, abounding with grass and corn, hence yearly there is a great quantity of victual exported'. He also noted that cattle and fish were cheap and said that a gentleman in Caithness could live better on 1,000 merks (about £60) than his southern peers on four times that amount. Seabirds were regularly harvested from the cliffs. The people at John O'Groats made beads from the seashells, he observed with some delight. He was less pleased with some of the religious practices that persisted in spite of the clergy's efforts to eradicate them; for example, in Canisbay, on a day about Candlemas, some were in the habit of going about a chapel on their knees and crudely baptising themselves with burnwater.

The first record of the population of the county was made sometime between 1724 and 1730 and is available in Macfarlane's *Geographical Collections*. Unfortunately, numbers are given in terms of 'catechisable souls' — generally taken to be those over ten years of age, although sometimes those over eight — and no figures are given for Dunnet or Halkirk parishes. The total for the remaining eight parishes is 11,670. In the parishes of Latheron, Watten, Halkirk, Thurso and Reay, 'at least the greater part of the common people' spoke Gaelic, 'the Irish tongue'. The accounts in Macfarlane's *Geographical Collections* existed as manuscripts in the Advocates' Library in Edinburgh where, later in the century, Sir John Sinclair came upon them and used them as a model for his *Statistical Account*..

In 1726 Wick was described as 'a small town of little trade'. Thurso, 'almost four times as populous' as her sister burgh, appears to have been enjoying at this time more of the fruits of commerce, for in 1707 she had acquired a Customs House, a recognition that irked Wick who later tried to have the House transferred there. John Brand noted that, although

FROM REFORMATION TO IMPROVEMENT 99

'ships of between 20 and 30 *last burden can come in safely' to Wick, Staxigoe was considered a more convenient anchorage in summer, especially as here the Hempriggs family kept two granaries (Plate 38). Thurso's superior reputation as a haven was however challenged in 1734 by John Stewart, an Inverness merchant, who wrote in May that year to Sinclair of Ulbster, from whom he had agreed to buy 400 bolls (26,000kg) of meal, to complain that he had been misled about the convenience of the harbour and now knew it not fit for any size of vessel.

Whatever Stewart's opinion, Thurso's trade was plenteous and varied, as this list of exports for the 1720 shows:

beef and mutton	35 last per year
tallow	near 6 lasts (each barrel weighing 2 cwt.)
feathers	17 bags
salmon	10-12 last
calfskins	near 1,000
cowhides	about 300
bere, oats and meal	15,000 bolls
codfish	about 40,000

The Thurso river had to be forded or crossed by boat but Wick at least had a bridge 'of eleven pillars built with loose stones and only timber laid over them . . . maintained by the southside of the parish for carrying them to church'. Both towns were similar in appearance, with a muddy, winding main street, lanes and a market place.

At this time, the county's agriculture was based on 'good Bear and Black Oats, the only Grain of the Countrey'. Given decent weather and freedom from warfare, the rigs usually produced more than enough to supply the people with meal and ale but famine occasionally occurred. For example, a savage one struck the county in 1634, when bad weather ruined the harvests. Tradition has it that the poor were reduced to eating dogs and seaweed and 'multitudes died in the open fields' or drowned themselves in desperation. In Elgin a collection was taken 'for the people of Cathnes quho is in distress' and raised £40.

Farming land was held in pennylands, often subdivided into halfpennylands, farthinglands and so on. The 'pennyland' was a unit of assessment of the land's agricultural value in a system that dated back to Norse times, and its size varied according to the quality of the soil, from as low as 3.2 to 7.3 hectares (8 to 18 acres) or more. A holding, whether in the possession of a single tenant or a township, was divided into infield, the arable ground, and outfield, rough pasture or moor for grazing. In

---

* (footnote) the 'last', a unit of weight, is variously defined: a last of wool was 12 sacks, of hides a gross, of fish 12 barrels, and so on. As a measure of ship's burthen, a last equalled 2 tons (2.032 tonnes).

turn the infield was divided into rigs which normally were rotated among the members of the community or township so that each household could enjoy in turn the better strips. In Caithness the system was called rig and rennal, runrig the most common term further south.

One of the earliest Caithness rentals still extant is for the estate of Brabster in Canisbay for the year 1697. The system of taxes and rents then in operation was swept away during the Age of Improvement at the end of the 18th century and at this distance in time is difficult to understand. It involved payments deriving from the Norse concept of skatt and conversions of goods into equivalents of silver. For example, William Read, who held a pennyland of land at Slickly, was noted as owing an amount of 'tallow silver . . . in payment wherof he hes delyvered to the merchand ane ox and ane cowe att 15lb 06s 8d' (in today's currency, about £1.25). Read's account also includes payments of 'multer and bannack' (fees to the laird's mill for grinding his meal), and further instalments of seed, meal, poultry and sheep. Read also kept for the factor an ox and a cow 'wanting a piece of the right luge, fyve yeirs old, come Beltaine (1st May)'.

All of Caithness's exports were raw, unprocessed goods, and the most important among these was grain, shipped in considerable amounts and enabling the families of the lairds to maintain a high standard of living. The Sinclairs of Mey, for example, indulged in books, fine wines and expensive clothes, often bought on credit on the surety of the next season's crop. Draughty, rock-head castles were abandoned in favour of more comfortable mansion houses, such as at Keiss; and other castles were modernised. Occasionally a bad harvest could bring a family to the brink of bankruptcy or beyond — in fact, Sir James Sinclair of Mey died in a debtor's prison in Kirkwall in 1732 — but generally the system seems to have worked well. Grain was carried to the ports of Staxigoe or Thurso on pack horses for transhipment to Leith, Newcastle or Bergen, among other ports. Merchants in Wick and Thurso acted as agents and importers of a wide variety of luxury goods. In this connection it is worth noting that the number of ships based in Wick or Thurso are a poor indicator of the volume of trade, as many southern vessels used both ports.

Figures for the grain trade have been put forward by several writers. John Brand in 1700 said that 16,000 bolls (approximately 864 tonnes) were exported but Aneas Bayne in 1735 gave the much lower figure of 1,600 and Pennant in 1769 the much higher one of 40,000 bolls. Some of this wide discrepancy can be explained by the annual variation in the crop and also perhaps by the gradual expansion of corn-growing land

---

(Footnote) The Caithness 'boll' was defined in 1812 as being 8.5 stone of oatmeal (about 54 kilos) or 9 stone of beremeal (about 57 kilos).

throughout the century as more fields may have been broken into cultivation. The *Statistical Account* published in 1793, states that 'in tolerable years no less than from 18,000 to 24,000 bolls (971 to 1,295 tonnes) of bear and meal' were exported.

The higher, less arable parts of Caithness depended more on black cattle than grain. By the 1790s, about 3,000 head a year, most from the parishes of Halkirk and Latheron, were being sold to drovers to be driven south to the Lowland trysts.

The even tenor of local affairs was disrupted briefly in 1746 by the Jacobites' last attempt to put Charles Edward Stuart on the throne of Britain. The Earl of Caithness and the Sheriff, George Sinclair of Ulbster, remained loyal to the Hanoverian regime but some of their kin displayed sympathy for the rebels to an extent they may have later regretted. Alexander Macbean, the minister of Inverness, noted that 'twas talked here . . that the St. Clairs would have joined the Pretender but that they durst not pass through Lord Sutherland's country'.

The muster roll of the Jacobite army identifies thirty Caithness men, although there may well have been more. Most were in the Earl of Cromartie's regiment and may have joined the rebels during the recruiting campaign led by Cromartie's son, Lord Macleod, in Thurso in February and March 1746. Cromartie's regiment seized and occupied Dunrobin Castle but was finally defeated on the day before the battle of Culloden by a force loyal to the Earl of Sutherland. George Sinclair, the laird of Geise, was among those taken at Dunrobin. The fate of all the Caithness recruits is not known but many were later sentenced to transportation as slaves in the colonies. It is also recorded that John Sutherland, the laird of Forse, raised a company from among his tenants to fight with Loudon's Highlanders on the Government side. During the military occupation that followed Culloden, anyone suspected of Jacobite sympathies was in danger of arrest. James Taylor, the Episcopalian minister in Thurso, had to flee to Orkney but he was eventually taken, imprisoned for a time and then, having proven his innocence, released. He got back home to find that his meeting house had been destroyed. It was a time when, in the name of national security, personal scores came in for a deal of settling.

In the years after Culloden a number of visitors to Caithness wrote books or letters about their travels which, with the *Statistical Account,* provide us with a comprehensive picture of the county in the last years before Improvement wrought great changes across the landscape.

Travelling was not to be undertaken lightly. The Ord had a widespread and unenviable reputation as a hazardous barrier, although when some reached it they found it less awful than they had feared. Thomas Pennant in 1769 thought the track winding up the cliffside above the sea 'infinitely more high and horrible' than the Welsh hills he knew; but Robert Forbes, a few years before, found that his 'Imagination had far outshot Reality' and said it was 'one of the finest Roads in the World, being so broad that in most places two coaches might pass one another'. He rode over it although his companions walked with their horses. It would not be until 1819 that coaches regularly undertook the route. Once into the county travelling became little easier. Roads were simply tracks and ease of passage depended on luck and the weather. Even Forbes was made to think twice when tackling the Causewaymire:

'In ane slough Mr Innes' servant, seeing the surface much broke with our crossing before him, would chuse a place for himself hard by us, and behold slumped down to ye crupper, and the horse was laid on his right leg. I cried to the other servants to get off to the poor lad's relief . . he rose unhurt, the ground being soft as a down-bed.'

There were a few carts in Caithness before the 1790s, contrary to some accounts, but they were used only for short hauls. Strings of pack horses, laden with baskets, transported bulk goods over longer distances; and on the small farms and crofts, as Pennant witnessed to his horror, women seemed to do most of the carrying of, for example, dung and peats.

The Caithness landscape in the late 1700s was open, almost treeless and bare of fences. Richard Pococke wrote to his sister in July 1760 to describe the view south-east from Stemster:

'When we came to the summit over Sir Patrick Dunbar's house [Stemster House], we had a most uncommon prospect of the broad vale in which his house stands, of another separated by low hills or eminences, with a great number of gentlemen's seats, and two churches in view, two large lakes, the fine mountains of the Paps, and that ridge which bounds the county, and the ground rising gently on all sides; but what is most singular spots of corn all over the county, contrasted with such a mixture either of heath or pasturage as rendered the face of this northern country very agreeable'.

A closer look by a modern eye would have revealed the squalor of many of the homes of the tenants: the midden at the door, the fire smoking in the centre of the main room, and the livestock housed ben under the same thatch. The two largest estates in the county now belonged to the Sinclairs of Ulbster (whose wealth had grown considerably throughout the century) and the Dunbars of Hempriggs. There were some fifty estates in all, varying widely in size and owned mostly by Sinclairs. The majority of the population were, of course, tenants.

Throughout the latter half of the 1700s the population had grown, from the 22,215 in Webster's estimation in 1755 to 23,474 recorded in the 1801 census. In around 1754, the humble tattie had put in its appearance.

Although at first regarded with suspicion, the productivity of this vegetable and the ease with which it grew soon made it the common food of the poor. From a small patch of land a cottar could provide his family with a more secure food supply than any native crop could offer. Better nutrition and health was one result; another was that the increasing numbers of cottars broke in more patches of ground on the moors to plant potatoes for their own use.

Then the practice of inoculation against smallpox was introduced. This disease was a major cause of death, particularly among children, and outbreaks occurred regularly. 'In December 1796', wrote John Williamson, a surgeon with the fencible regiments in Thurso, 'the confluent smallpox became highly epidemic and fatal . . . the epidemic was almost general and, by my calculation, one in four fell a victim.' Williamson, with the help of the clergy who preached that to fight disease was not to provoke the wrath of Providence, carried out a general scheme of inoculation, sometimes treating 120 people in a day.

A severe famine arose in 1782. Frost and snow in October devasted the crops before they could be harvested and dearth forced many to emigrate either to the Lowlands or to America. The three parishes most badly affected were Watten, Latheron and Halkirk, all of which showed a decrease in population in direct contrast to the experience of their neighbours. The parishes along the Pentland Firth, long accustomed to drawing sustenance from the sea, fared better. Landowners and elders were called upon to submit to the government the amounts of meal they thought would be sufficient to feed the poor; and cargoes of oatmeal, barley and pease were shipped from Banff for emergency relief. Thanks to these schemes the minister of Wick was able to record that 'none died of want'.

This was in sharp contrast to the effects of the great famine of 1634, and would have been seen in 1800 as evidence of the progress of society. The idea of progress was much in the air, and the old ways, some of which could trace their roots to Norse times and beyond, were falling before the onslaught of a new, rational outlook. In the 1790s the ministers of Caithness submitted to Sir John Sinclair, the laird of Ulbster and now a prominent figure in the government, their contributions to his *Statistical Account of Scotland.* Their writings are imbued with a sense of progress and they described a time of momentous change throughout the nation, in agriculture and industry. With the typical optimism of the times it was labelled the Age of Improvement.

CHAPTER 9

MODERN TIMES

In the years around 1800 sweeping changes altered the face of the Caithness countryside and set the pattern that exists to this day. The impetus for this improvement, as it was called, came from the south. The Society of Improvers in the Knowledge of Agriculture in Scotland was formed in 1723 and proved the driving force behind change in the Lowlands. The state of affairs in the north lagged behind for some time but in the wake of the famine of 1782, in a tavern in Edinburgh, Highland estate owners formed the Highland and Agricultural Society and the new ideas were taken up with great enthusiasm.

Sir John Sinclair of Ulbster (Plate 54) became an indefatigable improver. Born in Thurso in 1754 and educated at Edinburgh University, Sir John inherited debts of £18,000 and the family estate, about a quarter of the county. In 1780 he became Member of Parliament for Caithness, in time to agitate in the Commons for government relief in the famine. His optimism, interest in every subject and propensity to write about his ideas to all and sundry must have made him a source of irritation to many people; but it also led him to become the first President of the Board of Agriculture (a body set up at his own instigation) and to found the British Wool Society. His life and the story of improvement in Caithness are inseparable.

The change in agriculture began with the surveying and enclosure of fields. A new geometry of regular large parks replaced the haphazard rigs of the old system, and dry-stone walls, hedges and flagstone dykes were built to seal the land in modernity. No longer could beasts wander across the rigs tended by herd boys. Much common land was removed from public access, at least 1010 hectares (2,500 acres) by 1802 to be quickly followed by many thousands more. The formation of new farms from common land created a social upheaval, the consequences of which were not to become apparent until later. Clear at once was that the local small tenants could not afford the rents of improved ground: the new fields at Mount Pleasant, for example, formerly worth 14s (60p) an acre, were now let for £4 to £5 an acre. Southern farmers moved into Caithness and

MODERN TIMES

agriculture changed from being a way of life to a capitalised industry.

Draining wet ground and liming to counteract the acidity of the soil were also considered essential and new techniques of crop and animal husbandry were introduced. A five-year rotation of crops began and lasted as a basic pattern until well into this century. Not all of the experiments succeeded: wheat failed to flourish in Caithness's thrawn soil and cool winds and Sir John Sinclair's attempt to enliven his new plantations with nightingales ended dismally.

New steadings were built to grace the new farms. John Henderson estimated in 1812 that a farm of 60 hectares (150 arable acres) would need stabling for six horses and four garrons, byres for cattle and oxen, a loft, a threshing barn with horse-powered machinery, a kiln barn to dry grain and cart sheds. In the early days roofs were thatched but slate gradually replaced the straw or turf. Such a steading could cost £1,500, a sum beyond the dreams of the cottars and crofters who were shoved to the poorer patches of ground where a thatched cottage and dry-stone outhouses could be put up for little cash but much sweat.

Rents were converted into cash payments and by 1840 the laird of Freswick had become an exception by still collecting rents in terms of days of service. The new farmers were granted long leases, nineteen years being a common term, to encourage them to improve their properties; they also had a heavy demand for labour and many formerly 'self-employed' tenants became farm labourers.

James Traill of Castlehill, sheriff-depute and son-in-law to the Earl of Caithness, made his Olrig lands a showpiece for improvement. He also built water-powered mills for threshing and handling flax, a widespread crop in the county at the time, and planted hedges and trees in large numbers. The Reverend George Mackenzie included in his contribution to the *Statistical Account* an example of how a tenant — called Donald Coghill, but his farm is not named — could thrive when implementing Mr Traill's ideas on crop rotation. Coghill planted in 1792 1.2 hectares (3 acres) of clover and ryegrass, 0.3 hectares (0.75 acres) of turnips and 0.4 hectares (1 acre) of potatoes on his parks formerly devoted entirely to hay; 'from the advantages already reaped, he is determined to persevere in this mode of managing his farm; and others are preparing to follow his example', wrote Mackenzie.

It took several decades for improvement to spread throughout the county, from the larger farms to the smaller. In 1840, the minister of Thurso noted that a lack of capital was delaying progress. By then, almost all the common land, except for the wettest stretches of moss, such as Killimster, had been enclosed, and Watten parish alone was estimated to have 40km (25 miles) of drystone dyke.

Visitors to the county also noticed, however, that on poorer land there were the less fortunate. 'Huts and peat stacks, the one scarcely distinguishable from the other', observed one traveller of crofters' homes near Berriedale in 1829. Many of the small tenants were clinging to older techniques of husbandry; and it seems that landowners were reluctant to grant them the long leases that might have encouraged them to invest what little cash they had in improvement. In Halkirk, John Munro criticised the lairds who, instead of rewarding poor tenants for reclaiming moorland, merely increased their rents by 5s (25p) for every new acre they broke in with the spade.

Of all Sir John Sinclair's ideas, the one that had the most impact on the Highlands concerned sheep — particularly the Cheviot. High ground, unsuited to arable farming, could be used for sheep farming. It was calculated that hill ground could produce 1.4kg (3lb) of mutton for 0.45kg (1lb) of beef that the old-fashioned black cattle could manage, not to mention the valuable wool crop. Flocks of Linton, or Blackface, sheep were introduced first, but Sir John thought that Cheviots would do better. He brought a flock to Langwell where they throve and increased the value of the rental of the estate from less than £300 to over £1,600 a year.

Sir John hoped that existing small tenants in the Highlands would form co-operative sheep-farming ventures and thus remain on the land. Other landowners, burdened with debts or fired with zeal for improvement, and with southern sheepherders willing to pay large rents, were less patient. Large-scale evictions took place to allow the formation of extensive sheep runs, none more notorious than those in Sutherland. At Langwell, Sir John himself moved 80 families, many to the new village on the cliffs of Badbea. There were clearances in other parts of Caithness: tenants at Shurrery, Brubster, Shebster, Clashmore, Dounreay and other places were shifted to create vacant grazings. The minister of Reay recorded in 1840 that most of his parish, which included parts of Sutherland-shire, had been 'converted into sheep farms, and consequently, the poor people have been ejected from their houses and lands, many of them reduced to indigence and misery, and others necessitated to emigrate to a foreign land'.

The formation of new arable farms also involved evictions. Sir John recorded how he changed a tract of land along the Thurso river, occupied by 82 tenants, into 'regular' farms for 25 tenants. The evicted families formed new townships and 'cottage farms', or flitted to the towns or even furth of the county. According to the witnesses who testified to the Napier Commission in 1883, 35 crofters were evicted to make room for the farm of Rumster, 17 for Reaster and 15 for Rattar. Evictees settled in small colonies on waste ground; there were two at Reaster, called Beggars' Town and Paupers' Town.

During the period of improvement wages rose and those able to stay on the land as labourers, ploughmen or shepherds saw increases from around 25s (£1.25) per year in the 1770s to perhaps £7 by 1812. Such payment, with a house and a bit of land for potatoes, kail and a cow, offered in its day relative security. Unskilled or semi-skilled labourers earned between 6d (2.5p) and 1s (5p) a day, but women's wages could be only half as much as men's.

Hundreds of Highlanders fled from the evictions in Sutherland and Ross to seek refuge in Caithness. About 300, from Assynt and Strathnaver, moved into Dunnet before 1821 but after ten years most of them had moved again, some emigrating. Thomas Jolly wrote that they 'got into arrears with their rent . . their habits not being adapted to an industrious life'. This is a harsh judgement. The age of improvement left a trail of casualties, trapped in a pit of poverty from which escape was often via the emigrant ships.

Latheron also received immigrants, an influx that caused the parish minister, George Davidson, in 1840, to worry how they all might be catered for. He noted the demand for land, as did his colleague in Halkirk where much waste ground had begun to support 'a considerable number of dwellings'. Latheron's poor roll more than doubled between the 1790s and 1840. The other parishes fared better. The sums of money available from kirk collections and donations for distribution among the households listed on the parochial rolls were pitiably small — only 5s (25p) in most instances. Friendly societies, whose aim was to provide a simple form of insurance to their members, became common; for example there were five in Halkirk, supporting 29 widows. As elsewhere in the north, the poor were reluctant to seek charity. Finlay Cook noted in Reay that only 'sheer necessity' overcame his parishioners' antipathy to what they thought 'degrading' behaviour.

Fortunately for the people of Caithness the changes in agriculture happened at the same time as important developments in other activities, particularly fishing.

The harvesting of the sea has always played a major role in the lives of Caithnessians. John Morrison's vivid phrase for Canisbay in 1790, 'every farmer . . is a fisherman, and every fisherman is a farmer', applied equally to all the coastal parishes. Although there are records as early as 1554 of Caithness fish being sold to the Lowlands, until the end of the 18th century the focus was on fishing for subsistence rather than for export; in times of scarcity, the proximity of the shore and skill with the sellag pock or line probably saved many a household from hunger if not from starvation. The catching of lobsters for sale to merchants from London began in Mey in 1791. On the east coast from Duncansby Head to Dunbeath, a similar trade in white fish and shellfish also took place but it appears to have involved very few full-time fishermen: the minister of Wick observed that the small price paid only 'enables the fishermen, who are mostly farmers, to pay their rents much better than before' and complained about tradesmen and farm servants spending the night at the herring fishing to the detriment of their daytime work.

The catching of herring for export began in the latter decades of the century. Until the potential of this resource was realised the abundant shoals had been netted for food or for 'excellent bait to the cod-fishing'. There were stations at Dunbeath and Clyth and a larger curing establishment at Staxigoe, the enterprise of Alexander Miller who, with two partners, fitted out boats for the more lucrative Shetland fishery in the 1760s. By 1790, 32 boats fished from Wick and in the following year 44 put to sea. The herring fishery was subsidised by a government bounty but the want of a good harbour — a storm in 1791 caused 'much damage' to the boats — was clearly seen as an impediment to further development.

The British Fisheries Society, instituted in 1786, sent Thomas Telford on a tour of the north to survey the possibilities for improvement of the fisheries. Telford travelled along the Caithness coast in 1790 and found that small fisheries existed at Keiss, Staxigoe, Broadhaven, Sarclet, Whaligoe, Clyth, Forse and Dunbeath. Some of these places offered little opportunity for large development, thought Telford: Keiss was too exposed and Whaligoe he called 'a dreadful place'. Instead, he recommended that the Society concentrate its efforts on Wick, where herring landings were already quite substantial and where the bay appeared promising to his engineer's eye.

Finally, in 1803 the Society reached an agreement with Sir Benjamin Dunbar and acquired the feu of 158 hectares (390 acres) of land on the south side of the river, displacing a few tenants who then farmed the site. Telford planned the new town, naming the streets after the directors of the Society and the whole settlement Pulteneytown after its Governor. A local architect and mason, George Burn, built a new bridge across the river in 1807-08 and also began the construction of the new harbour to Telford's plan. The harbour was finished in 1811 and cost £14,000, half of which was paid by the Society and half by a government grant. A significant aspect of the proposals for the town was that no land should be allocated to the dwelling houses for any form of agriculture: Pulteneytown was to be devoted entirely to professional full-time fishing and the industry of curing.

The new town grew quickly after 1810, with houses and yards springing up and families being drawn in from the surrounding districts and further afield to win a share of the new prosperity. By 1830 the permanent population had passed the 2,000 figure. Highlanders came from the impoverished townships of the Hebrides and the west to find work. The wage for a six-week stint on a herring boat in 1840 was about £4. Travellers were struck by the dignity and quiet forebearance of these

MODERN TIMES

people who had suffered so much and commented on the stirring sight of the open-air Gaelic services on Sunday. The herring fleet at sea, the tan sails like so many birds' wings, also inspired many a pen picture. At the height of the season in August, Pulteneytown stretched to accommodate 10,000 people. The catch rose to nearly 200,000 barrels of herring and a thriving export trade carried cured fish to the markets of Europe*.

The Age of Improvement saw other new settlements grow in Caithness. Sir John Sinclair led the way with his plan for the expansion of Thurso (Plate 32), laying out a grid of streets and feuing lots for houses and gardens. In 1800 Thurso also acquired its first bridge, built by Robert Tulloch to Sir John's plan and paid for by local landowners. The village of Halkirk (Plate 30) also emerged from Sir John's desk, and to the east the long village of Castletown grew up under the direction of James Traill. Lybster began after Patrick Sinclair built a pier at the mouth of the Reisgill burn to encourage the herring fishery and was further developed by Patrick's son after the old laird's death in 1820. Major Innes of Sandside spent over £3,000 on building Reay harbour. David Brodie of Hopeville invested £61 in the creation of the landing place and steps at Whaligoe (the steps accounted for £8), laid out the village of Sarclet (Plate 31), at first called Brodiestown in his honour, and in all invested over £5,000 in improvements.

In 1825 James Traill began the shipment of flagstone paving from quarries at Castlehill. Castletown grew quickly as the quarrying industry flourished and remained a significant employer throughout the rest of the century. With the upsurge in economic activity during the Age of Improvement came a growth in transport facilities. The single most important development was the cutting of a new road over the Ord, carried out by the Commission for Highland Roads and Bridges whose chief engineer was Thomas Telford. The engineering superintendent for Caithness and Sutherland was Thomas Spence. Charles Abercrombie had surveyed the Ord route before 1802 but construction did not begin until 1809, when the new road snaked its way up the coast, leaving in its wake new bridges and embankments. Finally, in 1819 the first coach to make the complete journey from Inverness clattered into Thurso after 24 hours on the road.

Coastal shipping also increased. Murdoch Mackenzie's reliable charts of the Pentland Firth, first published in the 1740s, and the new lighthouse on the Skerries, built in 1794, encouraged more captains to brave the fogs and roosts of this shorter route from Europe to the Atlantic. Piloting became an important additional source of income for many fishermen in the area.

---

* Footnote (For a detailed account of the fishing industry see the two publications by Iain Sutherland listed in the bibliography).

Wick bubbled with activity. As well as the fishing, the town had by 1840 four rope works, a distillery, a meal mill, four saw mills, a pavement works, James Bremner's shipyard, a dozen boatyards and a foundry. A gas works was being constructed, and many new, grand public buildings graced the streets. The *John O'Groat Journal* began publication in 1836 and was joined by its rival the *Northern Ensign* in 1851. There was another side to this bright coin, however, as the minister, Charles Thomson pointed out. Especially after the fishing season the crowded, poorer streets of the town were rarely free from disease. Smallpox, typhoid fevers and skin diseases were common and the most savage epidemic, of cholera in 1832, claimed 66 lives, for a time, threatening the fishery itself, as village after village along the eastern seaboard was stricken.

The sea also took its toll of lives from among the fishermen. Drownings and accidents were frequent but individual deaths were overshadowed by the major catastrophes when, in the absence of weather forecasts and engines, sudden storms could easily overwhelm the whole fleet. The worst of these broke on the morning of the 19th August 1848 when a south-easterly caught and sank 41 boats and carried away 37 men within sight of Wick harbour. Altogether, on the Moray Firth coast, 94 men lost their lives that day. Such disasters became rarer with the installation of live-saving appliances and the stationing of lifeboats around the coast. The Royal National Lifeboat Institution gave Thurso its first lifeboat in 1860, placed others at Huna and Ackergill in 1878 and, in 1895, took over the running of Wick's lifeboat, previously supported by the Harbour Trustees.

Between 1811 and 1841 the population of Caithness grew by over 54 per cent; thereafter the rate of increase slowed but the peak of 41,111 was not reached until 1861.

During this same period there was also a revival in religion. To keep pace with the rising population, the government funded Thomas Telford to build new kirks, for example, at Berriedale, Keiss and Lybster; and new quod sacra parishes were created around these. An evangelical spirit seized many in the rural areas; some individuals, who practised, argued and preached an uncompromising brand of Calvinism and frequently fell out with the ministers to lead small breakaway sects of their own, became collectively known as 'The Men'. The extent to which this spiritual zeal was fed by the social upheaval of the Clearances is open to debate but at the time the revival was sincere and far-reaching and led to the Disruption.

The Church of Scotland fell into two camps, the Evangelicals and the Moderates, during the early 1800s. The main issue was patronage — who should decide on the minister, the congregation or the landowner? The

MODERN TIMES

debate was loud and long, and involved the House of Lords, and finally split the Church. At the General Assembly in 1843, four hundred ministers and elders walked out to form the new Free Church. By this act of courageous rebellion in defence of the principle that a minister was answerable to his parishioners and not his patron, the ministers angered many landowners and lost their manses and kirks. But their congregations stuck with them. The Free Kirk was a truly popular institution and later, in the 1880s, its ministers were to play an important role in the crofters' campaign for land reform. For some time after the Disruption, until new kirks could be built, services were held in the fields or any convenient place; at Keiss the herring store was used, but at Dunbeath the landowner would not allow even the erection of a turf bothy for shelter.

A struggle for religious freedom was one way in which the tenantry could cock a snook at their landowners. Increasing destitution gave rise only fitfully to more overt political protest; and Caithness was cushioned by the herring against much of the unemployment, poverty and emigration that scarred the Highlands in the 1820s and 1830s. In 1846, however, disease hit the potato crop. Famine stared the poorer tenants in the face. The patience of the people of Caithness, like that of many of their neighbours throughout the country, was finally tried by 1847.

The *"Groat"* reported on the 5th February the 'turbulent spirit' of the people of Wick who, led by a piper and a drummer, had taken to marching through the streets to protest against the shipments of grain from the harbour. The authorities, finding that the reading of the Riot Act and the drafting of special constables failed to quell the anger, called in the army. Two companies of the 76th Regiment, later augmented by men from the 27th Foot (the Inniskillens), were shipped from Fort George. The sense of outrage at the exporting of food while people starved was countrywide: Ackergill fishermen refused to help the soldiers disembark; in Thurso the river was blocked by small boats, guns were mounted on the braehead by the townsfolk, and pilots refused to bring in grain ships; in Castlehill harbour people invaded a Leith grainboat; marchers demonstrated on Dunnet sands. The soldiers were assaulted as they guarded the quays and dispersed the people with bayonets. On the evening of the 24th February, a party of the 76th fired on the crowd when they were ambushed with a hail of stones under the Academy brae in Wick, William Hougston, a cooper who was passing at the time, was shot in the wrist, and a girl called Macgregor was wounded in the arm. Finally, order was restored: the grain shipments went ahead, the carts rolling down to the quays in Wick and Thurso under armed guard.

By the middle of the century the county had assumed much of the pattern of life that persisted for the next hundred years. The census returns for 1851, ten years before the population was to peak, give us glimpses of every household. For gentlemen such as Henderson of Stemster, an army captain on half pay, a Justice of Peace and the farmer of 445 hectacres (1,100 acres), life was comfortable: he employed 38 permanent and 60 occasional labourers on the farm as well as a groom, cook, laundress and housemaid. At the other end of the scale circumstances must have been far less satisfactory for Margaret Keith who worked a 0.8 hectares (2 acre) croft at Faulds and shared her cottage with her daughter and grand-daughter. Almost all the neighbours of the Keiths and Hendersons in the parish of Bower drew their living from the land, as crofters, farm servants or labourers. The smaller holdings were concentrated on the poorer stretches of ground, for example on the fringes of Stemster, Bowertower and the Hill of Brabster. The few tradesmen and craftsmen, whether shoemaker, gardener, blacksmith, carpenter, tailor or mason, frequently had a bit of land for a cow or potatoes. Bower was also home to a couple of handloom weavers, old men, their craft now made obsolete by the easy importation of factory-made cloth. Several old women and men described themselves as retired farm labourers and paupers. The census also records the presence on some farms of herd boys, fourteen or fifteen years old, tending the cattle as their first step on a long, steep ladder of agricultural servitude. Unmarried workers lived as lodgers with their masters or on the larger farms in bothies: seven men — three ploughmen, a shepherd, a cattle tender, a groom and a 'scholar' — shared the male bothy at Stemster, while its female counterpart housed the dairymaid and her assistant, two outdoor workers and a 'farm servant'. Both men and women, eight all told, shared the bothy at Tister, and it may have been such co-existence of young people that excited the ministers to see bothies as dens of iniquity.

In 1851 the number of herring boats at Wick topped the 1,000 mark; for over ten years it remained at this level, reaching a peak in 1862 with 1,120 boats. Then important changes overtook the industry: boats grew larger, often too large for the smaller havens around the coast, who began to lose their fleets to Wick where they could be accommodated by continuing expansion of the harbour. The larger boats, decked and shooting new cotton nets, could catch more fish than their predecessors. Although the number of boats operating from Wick fell, the amount of herring caught per boat rose from about 100 crans in 1846 to over 250 crans in 1895. The total catch fluctuated from season to season, usually falling between 70,000 and 110,000 crans.

In July 1874 the railway line connecting Thurso and Wick to Inverness was finally completed, eclipsing the old coach service. The new line supplemented by the coastal steamers and the telegraph, extended to the county in 1868, effectively drew Caithness into the mainstream of British life. Newspapers and, after 1872, compulsory primary education

MODERN TIMES

also wrought their own revolution; folk no longer had to rely on the pulpit and the packman for news of the outside world. Wick, Thurso, the larger villages and rural areas alike enjoyed the new growth of shops and services; and new schools and kirks sprang up throughout the 1870s. Tourism grew on a modest scale as visitors saw and wrote about the hectic activity during the fishing season.

Agriculture continued to progress on the larger farms: in 1876, for example, reaping machines were tested at Westerseat. The harvest that year was, however, a poor one and the persistence of bad weather in the following spring — snow fell in April and May — threatened the livelihoods of many crofters. Depression began to creep over the industry. The all-important tattie crop, the food of the poor, yielded less than was hoped for; and at the feeing markets, where farm servants sought employment with the larger farmers, wages on offer began to drop.

In the early 1880s agitation for land reform swept the north of Scotland. On Skye rent strikes brought in police, five of them sent from Caithness, and troops to restore order among the crofters; in Caithness, farmers organised meetings and called for rent reductions, and the laird of Clyth encountered 'strong language' when he refused a general revaluation of rents to his tenants. Tenants in Latheron produced a petition, described as 6.4m (21 ft) long with a double column of signatures, for the House of Commons in March 1883, and a Crofters' Alliance met in Bower in the following month. Letters appeared in the papers describing evictions and other oppressive acts by landlords.

The government responded by setting up the Napier Commission to investigate the conditions of the crofter in the Highlands. In October 1883 the Commission heard testimony in Caithness and the published evidence gives us a detailed picture of crofting at the time. The Commission counted 1,387 crofts in the county, defining the occupiers as small tenants without leases who depended on the land for a 'material portion of (their) occupation, earnings and sustenance' and paid an annual rent of not more than £30. The size of Caithness holdings ranged from about 0.8 to over 12 hectacres (2 to over 30 acres), on average being larger than those in the Highlands. The crofters had horses, sometimes shared between crofts, a few cattle and sheep and, another respect in which Caithness differed from her Highland neighbours, large numbers of pigs were kept.

James McCulloch, the Free Kirk minister of Latheron, described his parishioners' grievances to the Commission; in summary, they stand to represent the feelings of all crofters and protested the loss of access to hill pasture, no compensation for improvements to land and buildings, insecurity of tenure, excessive rents, damage to crops by game animals and shortage of land. The outcome of the Napier enquiry was the passing in 1886 of the first Crofting Act, ensuring small tenants security of tenure, fair rents and the right to claim compensation for improvements to their holdings.

The land reform movement also wrought changes in the political representation of Caithness in Parliament. At the beginning of the 19th century, the county's MP was, who else, Sir John Sinclair of Ulbster. He lost the seat for six months over 1806-07 but was able in 1811 to see his son, George, take his place. George Sinclair was finally defeated in 1841 by George Traill of Rattar, who represented the Liberal Party and remained MP until 1869 when Sir Tollemache Sinclair was elected. Until the Reform Act of 1832, electors numbered only a handful (only those holding land with a rental value of £400 could vote) and seats were bought and sold with large sums of money. The Reform Act enlarged the electorate (and got rid of the absurdity whereby Caithness was paired with Bute as a single constituency) but in 1882, at the height of the land agitation, the voters' roll for the county numbered only 1,223. The passing of the Franchise Bill in 1885 increased the roll to about 4,000 and in December 1885 Dr Gavin B. Clark of the Crofters' Party won the seat from the Liberals. Dr Clark was a Scot working in London, noted for his writings on land reform and socialist issues; his reputation won him Caithness, for he did virtually no canvassing before the election. Clark's reputation proved his downfall in 1900 when his supposed sympathies for the Boers in South Africa turned Caithness against him; on his election campaign he was called a traitor in Wick and forced in Halkirk to seek refuge in the Ulbster Arms from his angry constituents. He was defeated by Sir Robert L. Harmsworth of the Liberal Party. Throughout the century Wick was part of another constituency, the Northern Burghs, with its own MP. The present constituency of Caithness and Sutherland did not come into existence until 1915.

In the 1880s attention was focused on the crofters. Meanwhile the larger farms were beginning to concentrate on stock rearing. By the turn of the century, the Board of Agriculture's statistics showed that of the quarter of the county's area suitable for farming only about one-third was devoted to grain crops, the rest being for grassland, hay or turnips. This basic pattern has persisted to the present day and the county has developed an enviable reputation for its cattle and sheep.

The First World War forced a violent break with the past for many people. Men and women from Caithness served in all theatres, with the bulk of recruits joining the Seaforth Highlanders. Unlike the Victorian wars, the fighting in Europe had a widespread and immediate impact at home. The casualty lists in the papers appeared with dismaying regularity and by the time of the Armistice in 1918 almost every family had been touched by tragedy. *The Sword of the North,* published in 1923, gives many details of the War and records the names of 922 Caithnessians who lost their lives.

MODERN TIMES

After the War the flagstone industry at Castletown began to decline, as the costs of quarrying and transport rose and as the new, cheaper concrete became available for paving stones. The period of the War had, however, given the herring stocks around the Scottish coast a chance to recover from the heavy fishing they had endured for over a century and in 1919 Wick's catch was 99,845 crans. In 1921, however, the catch dropped to almost one-half of this; and stayed at the same level in 1922. The peak of the 1920s was reached in 1926 with 136,956 crans; in that year the fleet fishing from the harbour at the height of the season passed 300 boats. Thereafter, with some fluctuation from year to year the catch declined. In 1930 it was disastrous and 1931 saw Wick's worst season to that date — only 30,497 crans. Catches rose in 1932 but the costs of the fishing were now putting fishermen in an acutely distressful financial situation. Wick's staple industry had failed. The rise of the seine-net fishing offered some hope for the future. Some villages, such as Keiss, which had begun to concentrate on crab-fishing at the turn of the century, sought other kinds of fishing.

The number of registered unemployed in Wick grew from 547 in January 1929 to over 1,000 and soup kitchens were run in the winter months for poor children in Wick, Thurso and some of the villages. In 1931 the dole amounted to 12s 6d (62½p) a week for a single man, 10s 6d (52½p) for a single woman and £1 for a married man. In July 1937, a determination to look on the bright side led Wick to crown her first Herring Queen, Reta Shearer.

Farm servants were also having difficulty finding work; the papers commented on the large numbers of flittings at term day, and many chose emigration, fuelling a trend that had been evident for many decades. The population of Caithness in 1931 numbered 25,656, almost half of the peak figure reached in 1861. All parishes showed a decline, the largest in Latheron (more than 60 per cent), the least in Thurso and Wick. Agriculture, however, remained the largest single occupation, employing over one-third of the county's workforce.

The Second World War brought an end to the depression of the 1930s. Caithnessians fought in all the armed services but, more than its predecessor, this was a 'people's war'. The front line could prove to be one's own doorstep. Wick was bombed on several occasions; prisoners of war were billeted in the county; the RAF operated from new airfields at Wick, Thurdistoft and Skitten; the Home Guard drilled and exercised.

In the late 1940s and early '50s Caithness struggled through the years of post-War austerity. The 1951 census revealed the population, at 22,710, to be at the level last existing in 1801; and for many young people emigration was still the route to a better livelihood. Then rumours began to circulate that the government planned to build an atomic power station in the county. The first inklings reached the pages of the *John O'Groat Journal* in September 1953 and, after much speculation and to-ing and fro-ing, were confirmed on 1st March 1954 when it was announced that the decision had been taken to site Britian's first fast breeder reactor at Dounreay.

Councillor J. Abrach Mackay of Castletown spoke for all his colleagues when he called this development 'a most welcome event of unprecedented importance to the county'. So it turned out. A major house-building programme trebled the size of Thurso; a new high school, a technical college and new roads were constructed. The spherical steel housing of the first Dounreay reactor, familiarly the 'dome', became an unofficial symbol of Caithness's place in the modern world, almost as the sails of the vast herring fleet had been in 1860s. Dounreay also brought a large number of immigrants to the county, from England and other parts of Scotland, and Thurso's streets echoed happily with a novel mixture of accents. The incomers were affectionately nicknamed 'atomics'. Just as the construction of Dounreay (Plates 58,59) was going ahead in 1957, the herring meal and oil plant at Shaltigoe, a last effort by the Herring Industry Board to revive the fortunes of the fishery, closed its doors. The Dounreay development came at the right moment; and it reversed population decline and created new opportunities. In the 1981 census Caithness had 27,380 people and, in a sample analysed for occupation, only 8.3 per cent were farmers or farm workers. With its workforce of over 2,000 people, Dounreay has remained the single largest employer in the county to this day.

The dangers of such overdependence have not been ignored. There have been many schemes and attempts to introduce more diversity into the local economy. Some new industries have flourished while others have only managed to stay viable for a short time in the face of the disadvantages imposed by Caithness's geography, particularly the distance from the large southern markets. The North Sea oil industry has not so far had a great impact on Caithness. A pipe assembly plant at Wester has provided employment only intermittently and, although Wick has a role as a support base for the rigs, many Caithnessians have had to move to Orkney or Easter Ross to participate in the oil bonanza. Oil from Beatrice Field, discovered in 1976 only a few miles off the south-east Caithness coast, is piped ashore in Easter Ross. In March 1986 the government granted licences to prospect onshore along the Pentland Firth and elsewhere in the county.

What of the fishing? For a few years in the early 1980s there was a complete ban on the catching of herring in the North Sea, the stocks of this resource being so depleted. The white-fishing fleet has also shrunk: Wick still sees landings of fish but now the focus of the industry has shifted to west coast ports, closer to the lucrative Atlantic shoals. Inshore fishing still provides a living for some families in the coastal villages.

In 1762, a visitor to Caithness was advised to take 'some good bread with me. . . Caithness, being so poor and despicable. . . I could have no good thing to eat in it'. The same traveller found when he arrived 'one of the most plentiful and hospitable countries in the whole world'. The tourism industry now makes a valuable contribution to the county's economy.

In the past few years land use issues have centred on the conflict between conservation lobbies and forestry. Caithness has never been greatly endowed with trees, at least not since the last Ice Age that ended some 10,000 years ago. The Forestry Commission created extensive plantings at a few sites such as Rumster and Dunnet but it was not until private forestry acquired large tracts of land on the Caithness-Sutherland border that conflict arose. Tax-incentive schemes encouraged wealthy investors to put money into forestry. Conservation bodies argued that the 'flow' system of lochans and peat deposits in the heart of Caithness, internationally recognised as a unique wildlife habitat, was being needlessly destroyed. In March 1988 the government withdrew the notorious tax breaks that were seen by many to encourage blanket afforestation.

Most of the protagonists in the debate agree that balanced land use, with farming, forestry and conservation needs all taken into consideration, is the way forward. Schemes to promote small-scale forestry by local crofters and farmers have yet to make such headway but the diversification of agriculture looks like becoming a new topic of importance as overproduction within the European Community is leading to the imposition of quotas and other restrictive measures.

Unemployment is high in Caithness (at the time of writing it is around 14 per cent of the workforce) and the county is currently experiencing a small rate of emigration. Against this background a stormy battle over the future of Dounreay occupied the headlines throughout 1987.

When Dounreay was being built in the late 1950s, some concern was expressed over working on the Sabbath and the high wages at the new plant that local employers could not match — the nuclear industry itself aroused no widespread fears. By 1987, however, a number of Caithnessians had doubts about the safety of further expansion at Dounreay and especially about the wisdom of opening there a plant to reprocess nuclear waste. A public enquiry, fired with much debate, was held but the outcome is not yet clear.

The prospect of life without Dounreay is shadowing the future of Caithness, and this short history has to end on a note of uncertainty. But there is a dogged, quiet determination in the Caithness spirit, more Norse than Celtic, that has in the past and can again turn adversity into opportunity.

SECTION TWO

CHAPTER 10

SETTLEMENTS

INTRODUCTION

The establishment and growth of many villages and towns in the north of Scotland was intimately linked with the mass movement of people, often involuntarily, from the countryside. This dislocation, in Caithness, was in the main due to landlords finding it more profitable to lease their land in some other way. This 18th and 19th century monetarism often had drastic social consequences, with entire valleys being cleared of people. For example, in the south-east of Caithness, the straths of Ousdale, Berriedale and Langwell were virtually emptied. Many of the evicted from Langwell, some 28 families in all, formed a crofting village on a barren, grudging shoulder of peaty land perched above the perilous cliffs at Badbea, just after the turn of the 19th century. The sad little settlement has long since died; a monument, erected in 1912 to the memory of those who had lived there, is an added pathos to the scene.

Another derelict settlement, founded by evicted families in the 1830s is Broubster, which was established in the form of a square. To its cruck-timbered cottages came families who had been removed from the adjacent lands of Shurrery, Shebster and Broubster.

However, the purpose of this chapter is to discuss communities that are still very much alive, making a traverse along the coast from Berriedale to Reay before moving inland to the villages of Halkirk, Spittal and Watten (Fig. 1).

BERRIEDALE

Snuggling between the steep inclines of its notorious Braes lies a pleasant wooded dell, Berriedale (Plate 64) with a nucleus of houses including the heavily-antlered smithy by the old roadway and a further cluster on the raised beach at the conjoined outlet of the Berriedale and Langwell Rivers. On a steep face by the rivermouth lie the fragmentary ruins of Berriedale Castle, a site which might be Beruvik of the *Orkneyinga Saga*. Perched high on the slope above the castle are the two towers (used in the days of the herring fishery) known as "The Duke's Candlesticks."

DUNBEATH

Like the Langwell valley, the lovely Dunbeath Strath was emptied of its people in the 1840s, when 80 families were forced to move elsewhere to make a living. Many of them became involved in the herring fishery which had begun at the rivermouth about the year 1790. So prolific were the catches that by 1838, 76 boats were fishing from the tiny harbour. Small settlements arose to the north (Portormin) and south (Balcladich) of the rivermouth. Others developed near the Telford bridge and at Inver, which had the markethill nearby.

The lovely Dunbeath Strath has come to be associated with writer Neil Gunn who was born in the house adjacent to the village shop. As a boy Neil explored the river in detail getting acquainted with the antiquities, particularly the broch not far from his home. On the opposite bank of the river to the broch was Milton Inn, athwart the pre-Telford road, where Glenorchy's troops sheltered prior to the battle of Altimarlach near Wick in 1680.

A visit to Laid Hay Croft Museum gives an insight into the basic but cosy dwellings and outhouses the crofters lived in during the 19th and early 20th centuries. Laid Hay provides a stark contrast to the castle of Dunbeath (Plate 24) which may date as far back as the 13th and 14th centuries. The castle looks north towards the harbour to some of the restored buildings of the Dunbeath Preservation Trust, whose unique heritage project work can be seen in the strath and at its headquarters in the old village school.

LATHERONWHEEL

Latheronwheel Hotel, reputedly the first building constructed in the planned settlement of 1835, has a commemorative plaque set in its gable end. To this day the hotel is known as "The Blends," so named after a proprietor who blended his own whisky in the 1890s.

It was the wish of the landowner Captain Dunbar, that the new village should be named Janetstown, after his wife. However, the suggestion fell on stony ground and the village remains named Latheronwheel. Each incoming tenant was allocated a 0.8 ha (2 acre) feu with the right to fish from the small but busy harbour, which at this time had a fleet of over 50 vessels. Now, only a handful of boats use the small haven.

The houses of the feuars were built on the north side of

Latheronwheel burn, extending in a U shape down towards the old coast road which crossed the Burn by the ancient bridge that, wrongfully, has been associated with General Wade. There does not seem to have been a shortage of incoming tenants due to the many people who moved into Latheronwheel Strath following the Clearances.

LATHERON

The small hamlet of Latheron grew at the junction of the A9 and the A895, better known as the "Cassie Mire" road, which was constructed, towards the end of the last century under the direction of the indefatigable Sir John Sinclair.

The significance of the herring fishery to the local community was all too clearly spelt out by the writer of the *New Statistical Account* who predicted that "upon its permanency or failure . . . depends the future continued increase, or rapid decrease of population."

Prominent on a knoll beyond the prehistoric standing stones at Latheron is the old bell tower which may date to the later 17th century. It is believed that this detached tower was constructed because the configuration of the land prevented the sound of the local church bell carrying any distance. The old church, built in 1734, on the site of an earlier church (part of which survives) has now been tastefully converted into the Clan Gunn Centre. Such was the influence of the many people who settled in the area following the Kildonan clearances that Gaelic services were held in the church until the 1830s.

According to tradition a monastery was sited near the present church and dressed stones recovered from the field have been referred to locally as "The Chapel Stones." Other archaeological finds from the area include Pictish symbol stones. All that survives of Latheron castle is a fragment of wall by the side of the burn.

LYBSTER

The place name Lybster, like so many in the settled parts of lowland Caithness is of Norse origin.

Clearly, people were living in the area long before covetous Norse feet pounded along the shingle of nearby Shelligoe beach: witness the diverse monuments of ancient times, including the spectacular stone age burial tombs at Camster.

It seems likely that the mouth of the Reisgill (Old Norse hris — brushwood, and gil — ravine) Burn was an attractive area for early settlement as, on the north brae above the harbour, on a stone, was found carved a cross and a shallow depression (Plate 15). This stone was removed to the old church of St. Mary's (built in 1836) and subsequently located beside the central parish kirk at the north end of the village.

Further evidence of an early ecclesiastical interest in the area is provided by the old name of Lybster Bay, Haligoe, the holy goe, and the Brethren Well to the west of the burn mouth. Moreover, during the early 19th century, excavation of the land by the river to provide a harbour led to the discovery of a substantial burial ground. Such place name evidence, along with the carved cross and cemetery, might suggest an early monastic settlement at the head of the bay.

We could speculate, then, that on their arrival in this area, possibly in the late 8th or early 9th century AD, the Norse came upon a peasant society of Picts already christianised through the zealous missionary activity of the Celtic church. The bay was christened by the Norse "Haligoe" and their early settlement to the east of the inlet perhaps focussed on their hall, the "skali," now commemorated in the name Skaill at the south end of the village. There was of course no "village" in those times. Indeed, there was no village in the whole of Latheron parish even as recently as the 1790s!

The 19th century had dawned before the first planned settlement in the parish became a reality; its originator was the local laird, Patrick Sinclair, a character of considerable energy, who had a capacity for losing money.

Patrick Sinclair was a cousin of Sir John Sinclair of Ulbster, that distinguished son of the county better known as Agricultural Sir John. Patrick joined the Black Watch and while in Canada served under General Amherst. After a varied career he returned to Lybster in 1784 to his home at the Hall or Ha', now usually referred to as Lybster Mains (Plate 47).

In his fifties he married and decided to extend his house, whose oldest parts may date back to the 17th century. A library and a reception room were built, with fine plaster ceilings and decorative cornices.

Around the turn of the century Patrick Sinclair planted 40 ha (100 acres) of his estate with birch, alder, elm and ash. The old trees are now dying off but have been replaced with young conifers.

Agricultural Sir John's land innovations no doubt influenced his cousin at the Ha' as reclamation and drainage schemes were initiated and he even experimented with growing wheat in various parts of his estate, which stretched from Swiney in the south to Clyth burn in the north.

In the year 1810 Patrick Sinclair decided that he could best encourage the growth of the fishing industry by constructing a wooden pier at the mouth of the Reisgill Burn. There were already a few boats engaged in lobster fishing, which was rapidly expanding along the Moray Firth. Having built the new pier he decided to rename the sea inlet Amherst Bay, in memory of his commanding officer in Canada. That same year, at the age of 74, he received his last promotion to Lt. General.

As an increasing number turned to the summer herring fishing many people (including those dispossessed of land in parts of Sutherland) were attracted to the vicinity of Lybster village, which Patrick Sinclair first planned in 1802. Soon, the small village had an influx of people who had a variety of trades such as coopers, fishcurers, boatbuilders, ships' chandlers and shopkeepers.

So rapid was the growth of activity at the harbour that in 1817 the Fishery Board for Scotland officially recognised Lybster as a fishing station. To mark the success of Lybster as a fishing port, the General fixed a miniature herring barrel to the south-east gable of the Ha', where it can still be seen.

The early development of the village coincided with the important new lines of communication in Caithness being laid out under the supervision of the eminent Scottish civil engineer, Thomas Telford. In fact, the line of Telford's new road (now the A9) ran across the north end of the main street of the village which was named Quatre Bras, commemorating the battle in which General Sinclair's two sons had taken part. Here, too, the Free Church was built in 1848.

In 1820 Lt. General Sinclair died at the age of 83, the oldest general in the British army. His grave lies in what was once his own land at the Ha.'

His son Temple Frederick Sinclair succeeded to the estate and he continued the development of the linear village by laying out a square off the lengthy main street. Temple, like his father, was a staunch Whig and so he named the four sides of the square after politicians of the Reform Ministry of the 1830s: Grey's Place, Russel Street, Jeffrey Street and Althorpe Street.

The junction of the old coast road and the southern end of the planned square became known as The Cross. Two houses in the village with dates of 1802 and 1833 above their porches are reminders of the foundation of the settlement and its first phase of expansion.

A feu disposition, dated 1833, from Temple Sinclair to James Sutherland, fishcurer, 5 Grey's Place, Lybster, gives an interesting insight into how carefully the village layout was planned. Sutherland was obliged to "build and erect a substantial stone house and to cover the same with blue slates."

The street in front was "to be 50 feet in width, whereof 24 feet are to be laid with the common materials of the high road and six feet reserved on each side for a foot pathway . . . to be flagged with stone."

The road and pathway were to be made "at the sole expense of the feuars," proportional costing depending on the length of the house frontage. To ensure that the paths and streets were kept in good repair, the sum of 3/- (15p) had to be paid annually by each feuar to the proprietor, who had decreed that no outstairs, outshots, dunghills or

SETTLEMENTS

other nuisances were to encroach on the street!

By the late 1830s the parish had developed the classic coastal highland economic way of life of dual dependence on land and sea.

In 1838 the *New Statistical Account* reported that 2592 people in the parish were employed in fishing for herring with 325 boats in Latheron parish: 71 at Clyth; 101 at Lybster; 10 at Swiney; 32 at Forse; 32 at Latheron and 76 at Dunbeath. By this time Lybster, with a population of around 400, had become the third greatest herring station in Scotland after Wick and Fraserburgh.

Some harbour improvements were made in 1832 when a stone pier was erected along the west bank of Reisgill Burn where it entered the sea. In the 1850s much of the main quay was built. The west wall of the harbour basin was constructed to a length of 91 m (300 ft) and a weir was made near the outlet of the Burn spanned by a fine 18.6 m (61 ft) high bridge. The substantially improved developing harbour led to an import trade of coal, timber and salt.

The peak of the herring fishery was reached in the 1870s, but within a decade the dark clouds of recession had gathered. Despite the gloom harbour improvements continued and the lighthouse was built in 1884.

By the beginning of the First World War the industry had all but collapsed and local folk would never again witness dozens of tiny boats sailing heavily to port with the silver darlings. Nor would they wonder at the throng of fishery workers from the west filling the night air with the haunting music of the Gael.

By the 1930s the harbour was a desolate area, but an energetic harbour committee soon restored its picturesque appeal as well as increased its safety as a haven. The evocative era of the silver darlings has long gone but the basin is still a lively focus of the village where men feel the call of the lonely sea and sky.

Although railheads had been established in the county in the 1870s it was 1903 before the Lybster branch line from Wick was laid with stops at Thrumster, Ulbster, Clyth and Occumster, the train taking ¾-hour for the 13-mile journey. The line was a boon to folk along the coast, particularly the many pupils who went to Wick High School after an early apprenticeship in the village school. Towards the end of the second World War its future looked bleak and the line was closed in 1944.

Like all village communities Lybster had its fairs; one of them lasted for three consecutive days; up until 1910 it was held in the main street but was subsequently transferred to the black park which became the site of the golf course some 60 years ago.

Such fairs provided moments of light relief in the annual cycle of toil. Yet, the villagers found time for the occasional game of knotty which was a kind of shinty played with a cork from one of the herring nets. W. G. Mowat records that huge numbers played on either side in the local cow's park, the goals being a ditch at one end and the former coach road at the other.

Three licensed premises remain in the village from the former proliferation of inns. The Commercial Hotel, previously called Bruce's Hotel, dates from the first half of the century. The Union Inn, later the Bayview Hotel, is known to have held a licence as far back as 1881. The Portland Arms Hotel is perhaps of early 19th century date, but an inn site there dates back to the previous century. This was obviously a prime site with the opening of Telford's road and the inauguration of a horse-drawn coach service from Inverness to Caithness in 1819. . . . The era of relative isolation from the rest of the country was over.

SARCLET

Having made a tour of Caithness in 1790, Thomas Telford, the distinguished Scottish civil engineer, submitted a report to his political masters, suggesting port developments in Caithness including one at Sarclet. In the year 1800 the haven was developed by Captain Brodie, tenant of Sir John Sinclair, and within two years there were 21 thatched houses (Plate 31). Sarclet shared in the early 19th century prosperity from the herring fishery, but as the size of vessels grew, its role declined and the settlement deteriorated into a depressing straggle of houses. In recent times modern houses have replaced the dilapidated single storey structures in the planned village.

WICK

Like many another town the history of Wick is obscure, but it is highly possible that the oldest nucleus of a settlement lay close to the mouth of the river where the small haven provided shelter. There are early references to Wick in a Norse saga when Earl Ronald came to Caithness and was entertained at "Vik," (Plate 25) perhaps at Auldwick Castle, an early stronghold, to the south of Wick. And in the Bodleian Library, Oxford, an old map dated to c. 1250 has Wick as the only settlement noted in Caithness.

In the year 1503 Wick was made the seat of the sheriff court; in 1589 it was raised to the status of royal burgh by King James VI. The town must have looked a sorry sight when the accolade of royal burgh (giving it important trading rights) was bestowed upon it, as, it had been burned and looted the previous year by the Earl of Sutherland as part of a feud with the Earl of Caithness, who virtually owned the town and the lands around it. Wick in the late 16th and 17th centuries was apparently still a very small town, as judging from a map of 1608 by Timothy Pont (see Chapter 15) it was divided into four straggling groups of buildings scarcely 1.6 km (1 mile) in length.

SETTLEMENTS

A clearer picture of the royal burgh emerges in 1660 when documentation indicates a settlement of 500 people, with ten merchants, six tailors, five weavers, four smiths, five shoemakers, four coopers and four glovers. Although Wick itself had no vessels (Thurso had two sloops) trade was taking place including items such as: timber, tallow, hides, wool, millstones, beef, mutton, port, butter, cheese and whisky.

In the early 18th century Wick was still a "small town of little trade"; in 1760 it was described as "pleasantly situated in a little bay which has no harbour." Relative to Thurso the town's population growth was slow, as a writer of 1735 observed that the population of Thurso was approaching 3000 people, about three times the figure for Wick. In the 1790s, the population was at a similar level when the contributor to the *Statistical Account* was bemoaning the fact that the town had no harbour.

The great spur to the town's development was the phenomenal growth of the herring fishery, primed by the construction of Telford's harbour (begun in 1803 and completed in 1810) on the south side of Wick River. By the year 1816 the new planned settlement of Telford's "Pulteneytown," was well established. It took its name from a one-time director, who eventually became Governor, of the British Fisheries Society, Sir William Pulteney. Other streets in the new town have the names of directors and officials of the Society, such as: Argyle Square, Vansittart Street, Kinnaird Street, Huddart Street, Breadalbane Terrace and Smith Terrace.

With the accelerating success of the fishing (particularly the summer herring catch) an increasing number of families left the land to try their luck at sea. The new harbour with all its attendant facilities meant that fishing could now become a full-time occupation, a radical change from the traditional role of crofter-fisherman. The neatly laid out new town of Pulteney, with its focus on Argyle Square and its central green, was soon teeming with people from all parts of Caithness. (For further details of buildings, see chapter 13). Eye witnesses have also recorded the crowds of incoming highlanders who filled the harbour quays eagerly seeking work.

By 1835 there were 830 boats fishing from Wick and by 1862 the figure had exceeded 1100, crews coming from all over Britain to fish for the 'silver darlings'. In those hectic days of the zenith of the herring fishing, the population of Wick could swell from 7,000 to 18,000 people.

Such a thronging populace was good for business as the thriving markets on the North Head (in July) and the High Street (in November) could testify. At the latter the curers settled with the fishermen for past fishing and engaged them for the coming season at a fixed price. A feel for the days when Wick was the herring capital of the world can still be gained from a visit to its excellent Heritage Centre.

Wick and herring may no longer be linked synonomously in the public mind, but a new product has substituted the herring in that respect, Caithness Glass (Plate 61), which opened its factory in Wick in the early 1960s and has had considerable commercial success, with subsidiary units in Oban and Perth.

To the rapidly expanding new town was added a distillery, in 1826. Most of its product is used for blending but some is bottled as a distinctive malt whisky known as "Old Pulteney". Perhaps over-indulgence of the product prompted the comment in the *New Statistical Account* that, "at all seasons of the year whisky is drunk in considerable quantities, but during the fishing season enormous potations are indulged in". The writer was inspired to further comment about the inhabitants of Wick parish: "Maniacs are very rare. Idiots.......are remarkably common"!

In the early 19th century "greater Wick" consisted of four settlements: Broadhaven and Louisburgh (both of which were established by Sir Benjamin Dunbar of Hempriggs), Wick and Pulteney. For many years Wick and Pulteney had their separate town councils until the two settlements amalgamated into one burgh in 1902. The considerable expansion of Wick in the late 18th and early 19th centuries largely destroyed traces of the older burgh, with the 16th century church of St. Fergus and part of Parliament Square being among the few survivors.

The long sinuous High Street, a continuation of the main road from John O'Groats is the spine of old Wick, with a number of lanes and closes off-shooting from both sides. One of these, Tolbooth Lane, commemorates the former Tolbooth, long since gone, whose successor was the town hall, with fine cupola, built in Bridge Street in 1828. The focal point of the old town would have been the market place and the site of the former market cross is indicated by stones set into the road.

There is a tradition that the original parish church of Wick stood near the eastern extremity of the High Street at Mount Hooly, a name that suggests early ecclesiastical associations. The church was then transferred to the western end of the High Street. Perhaps a number of buildings stood on the western site before Wick Old Parish Church was dedicated in 1830. It is reputed to have one of the widest unsupported span in Scotland at that time, its rafters resting on the side walls without any other interior support. In 1843 the minister the Rev. Charles Tomson "came out" in the Disruption and took most of the congregation with him to form the Free Church (now Bridge Street Church).

Close by the Old Parish church is the interesting fragment of a much older church, dedicated to St. Fergus but usually called Sinclair's aisle as it was supposedly built by George Sinclair, 4th Earl of Caithness, in the 16th century.

SETTLEMENTS

STAXIGOE

Kelp burning for the production of alkali, was well developed on the north coast of Caithness in the first half of the 18th century. From Gills, for example, the burned kelp was taken by small boats to both Thurso and Staxigoe for shipment south. At this time Staxigoe was the only port to the north of Cromarty and had a flourishing grain export to various ports in Scotland and Europe such as Bergen, Hamburg and Gothenberg. The volume of trade in cereals, especially oats, was so considerable that girnels (grain stores) were built at Staxigoe by the Earl of Caithness in the late 16th or early 17th centuries (Plate 38).

Obviously some fishing was taking place in the 18th century as Thomas Pennant on his tour in the far north in 1769 commented, "near Staxigoe creek is a small herring fishery, the only one on the coast; cod and other white fish abound there; but the want of ports on the stormy coast is an obstacle to the establishment of fisheries on this side of the country".

The earliest commercial development of the herring fishery in Caithness was from Staxigoe (see Chapter 9) which became such a flourishing community that letters to the future county town were addressed, "Wick, by Staxigoe". In 1830 quays were built and within 20 years there were 31 boats manned by 125 fishermen working from the small port. With its fishing activity and trade Staxigoe developed into an attractive village whose red tiled roofs gave a Low Countries aspect to the small settlement.

KEISS

Settlement along this coast goes far back into antiquity and the cluster of brochs suggests a well-populated area in the Iron Age.

A fortified dwelling of more recent date appeared with the Z-plan structure of Keiss castle, built about the end of the 16th century. The first meeting of the Baptist church in Scotland was held here in the middle of the 18th century. The service was conducted by the owner of the castle, Sir William Sinclair, who became the church's first pastor.

The new castle of Keiss, built in 1760, had major additions to its structure in the 19th century (Plate 27).

The present village, whose layout can be dated to the early 19th century, attracted more people to the area with the completion of James Bremner's harbour in the 1820s (Plate 39). Some of the houses fronting the picturesque harbour have been tastefully renovated and the fine Telford manse of 1827 gives an impressive entrance to the village.

DUNNET

Referring to Dunnet, the *New Statistical Account* (1841) claimed that "there is nothing that can be called a village in the parish". The present village developed around the church as people dispossessed of land in the districts of Assynt and Strathnaver came into the area in the 1820s and 1830s.

Dunnet Church (Plate 19) bears a strong resemblance to the old kirk of Canisbay and undoubtedly dates from pre-Reformation times, with architectural features suggesting a 16th century or even earlier date. One of the most distinguished ministers at Dunnet was the mapmaker Timothy Pont (see chapter 15).

The communities of Brough and Scarfskerry, like Dunnet, evolved with the relocation of people compulsorily removed from their small tenant holdings. Many of the men of these settlements joined the merchant navy, a tradition that still exists.

CASTLETOWN

The place name Castletown derives from the earlier form, Castlehill. However, there is no documentary or archaeological evidence to suggest that there ever was a castle here, but it is possible that the Shelly Hillock, an ancient kitchen midden, could have been mistaken for the ruins of an old stronghold. Another plausible explanation is that the broch site lying to the west of the quarries was interpreted as a "castle". On top of the grassy knoll that enveloped this old broch was discovered a skeleton which was buried with two superbly executed "tortoise" brooches characteristic of the Norse period.

Although the Norse and earlier peoples farmed the area it was probably the late 18th century before improvement of the land had taken place in Olrig parish, placing it ahead in agricultural developments of many other parts of the county. For example, the *Statistical Account* commented on the high grade oats of the parish which were in much demand elsewhere in Caithness. In addition to the typical crops of bere, oats and potatoes, quantities of flax were grown, the processing of this crop being carried out in the landlord's mill. The landlord (see chapter 15) was the renowned James Traill (1758-1843), son of Dr. Traill, parish minister of Dunnet, a man of dashing energy and a zealot in agricultural improvements. To the flax mill he added a grain mill (Plate 51) and introduced the first threshing machine to the county. He was well aware of the bareness of the landscape and planted trees around his policies where the rotation of crops had already been introduced and "draining, ditching and enclosing are carried on with spirit". One of the major drainage schemes was the Loch of Durran which yielded considerable quantities of marl to sweeten the adjacent soils.

Traill, who became Sheriff-depute of Caithness in 1788, was a contemporary of Agricultural Sir John Sinclair of Ulbster. He married Lady Janet Sinclair, daughter of the Earl of Caithness and soon became proprietor of the fine mansion of Castlehill House, which, unfortunately, was burnt down in the 1970s. From Castlehill he directed his major agricultural reforms and industrial initiatives. It was inland from his house that the extensive plantation of trees (ash, plane, elm, oak and larch) was established. He also laid out a number of roads in the parish and built the harbours of Castlehill (Plate 35) and Ham, to the east of Dunnet Head.

Close to Castlehill house and near the surface of the ground were good quality, finely-bedded fissile flagstones, ideal for paving slabs, walling and roofing. The rapid growth of population in the county (as elsewhere), the expansion of villages and the construction of harbours provided a great fillip for quarrying operations.

TABLE 2

STATISTICS OF EMPLOYMENT AND PRODUCTION OF FLAGSTONE AT CASTLEHILL, CAITHNESS

	Tons	Value	Persons Employed
1856	7,000		
1858	16,600		
1895	15,545	£18,206	
1896	24,257	31,906	
1887	21,633	28,131	403
1889	17,818	22,484	404
1899	23,029	21,934	478
1900	18,794	17,378	454
1901	20,951	20,241	500
1902	34,804	23,239	414
1903	15,907	20,252	301
1904	18,187	20,404	402
1905	17,528	12,998	324
1906	15,534	10,109	205
1907	15,306	5,770	142
1908	9,880	6,409	191
1909	9,914	7,936	201
1910	7,400	5,605	154
1911	6,036	4,153	145

Although exploitation of this quarry at Castlehill began in the 1790s, the splitting of local stone into flags did not achieve the status of an industry until 1825. The work force at the site built up rapidly and soon over 100 men were employed in the quarry which was connected to the harbour of Castlehill by a bogie track. Many of the work force were part-time but it is nevertheless astonishing to find that by the turn of the 20th century there were 500 men on the Castlehill payroll and an estimated 900 similarly employed throughout the county.

A map of 1822 shows that Castletown was then a tiny hamlet, but it soon expanded as quarry workers took advantage of Traill's offer of free flag trimmings (with one clean face) for house building. And so by the late 1830s the village had expanded into a neat linear settlement consisting mainly of single storey cottages, some of which have been tastefully preserved. By 1840 the population had reached 320, the latest estimate being around 1000 people.

The flagstone was split from almost horizontal beds by means of wedges and levers, the normal practice being to remove as thick a slab as possible, subsequently splitting it into more manageable sizes. The stones were then "dressed", i.e. cut into squares or rectangles at the cutting beds.

The quarries were wet and uncomfortable places in which to labour and so little work was done in winter. Work in the industry was hard and the wages usually poor. For example, the *Caithness Courier* of 5th May 1866 reported that the workers held a meeting to discuss rates of pay as they had not had an increase for 30 years! In March 1872 the workers went on strike claiming that their wages were inadequate to support themselves and their families. The management conceded the first instalment of a half day on Saturday, the *Courier* hoping that "none will abuse the new privilege by spending it in a public house!".

Like Halkirk, Castletown can boast of a very attractive village hall, gifted by Miss Margaret Traill, daughter of the Sheriff. This handsome building (in need of restoration) with its beautiful oriel window was opened with suitable ceremony on New Year's Day 1867.

Road communications to Castletown had improved significantly before the full impact of quarrying was felt in the area. One route, the Castletown-Dunnet road, sometimes posed a problem as dunes became ruptured in strong winds and sand piled high along the road. In fact it was the 1950s before adequate stabilisation of the dunes was achieved by the Forestry Commission.

Submissions to the Napier Commission Report showed that many of the tenant crofters on Traill's estate were also employed as labourers in the quarry. The tenants bitterly resented their rack-renting and

SETTLEMENTS

complained of the iniquitous practice whereby they were obliged to buy their provisions from the laird's store. They were even compelled to purchase their coal from the estate at whatever price the owner cared to charge. Making official complaint about this despicable truck system was made particularly difficult for the tenants as the procurator-fiscal was the factor of Traill's property!

The optimism of a visitor writing in 1893 to the local press that it was "gratifying to observe the commercial prosperity of Castletown" was shortlived. Within two years the flagstone workers were on a two day week as were the workers in the other major quarries of the county. Trade slumped alarmingly after 1902 and the subsequent closure of the works at Castletown proved disastrous to the community. A relief fund for the unemployed was set up and disillusioned men left the area to seek work elsewhere, many going overseas.

By the 1920s most of the Caithness quarries had closed with severe competition from synthetic stone. It seemed sad that a worthy product which had been used in most of the large towns of Britain and exported to Ireland, Germany, India, Australia, New Zealand and South America should meet such a catastrophic slump in trade. Indeed its virtues were extolled so frequently in letters to their offices that the Caithness Flagstone Company decided to publish a list of testimonials which typically contained remarks such as, "they are superior to any other flags".

The flagstone trade has long gone, but another stunning commercial success has been developed in Castletown, with the establishment of the deep-freeze factory, Norfrost (Plate 60). The factory employs more than 200 people producing 6000 freezers a week, over half of them for export. Norfrost has its own research and development section making special purpose machines, including robots, for the factory.

THURSO

Thurso is located at the south-east corner of a pronounced bay in a pleasant aspect with fine coastal views to the promontory of Dunnet Head and the high cliffs of Hoy.

Although Thurso is mentioned in the Norse sagas, very little is known about its history until the Middle Ages. Even then its trade might have been significant because in 1330 King David II had Thurso's unit of weight adopted throughout Scotland.

One of the early castles in Caithness, almost certainly of Norse origin, is believed to have been located in the area now occupied by St. Andrew's manse. From this old castle the neighbourhood takes the name Castlegreen. The castle was destroyed by the troops of King William the Lion who stormed into Caithness to avenge atrocities inflicted on Bishop

John by the Norse Earl Harold Maddason. The site of the bishop's castle was probably the "borg at Skaraboldstad" at Burnside, which was partially excavated in the early 1970s to reveal an oblong structure with kitchen range.

Because the fertile lowlands of Caithness were so heavily settled by the Norse, it seems certain that a local law-court or "ting" must have existed. Donald Grant in *Old Thurso* suggests that such a site might have been at Thing's Va or Scrabster Hill. Not far away, the gallows stood on Gallahill, where according to tradition, they had been used since at least Norse times.

When Christianity came to Thurso is not known but the earliest ecclesiastical site is ruinous St. Peter's Church, standing in what is one of the oldest parts of the town. It may well have been founded in the early 13th century by the renowned Gilbert, Bishop of Caithness from 1222-1245 AD. Most of the existing structure of St. Peter's appears to date from the 16th or 17th centuries, including the beautifully traceried window in the south transept. Within the churchyard, which has some fine old tomb stones, was found a small stone with runic inscriptions (Plate 14). The old church was used for religious services until December 1832 when it was replaced by the new and imposing St. Peter's Church in Sir John Square (Plate 54).

To the north-east of the later Thurso castle, built to the east of the river, sits Harald's Tower, where Harald the Younger of Caithness fought, and was killed by, Earl Harald of Orkney in 1196, at the battle of Clairdon. For a period the tower, built by Agricultural Sir John on an old chapel site, was used as a mausoleum for the Sinclairs of Ulbster.

Thurso castle, close to the river mouth, was built in 1660 by George, the 6th Earl of Caithness. After the castle came into the hands of the Sinclairs of Ulbster, a wing was added in the 1830s. Some forty years later Sir Tollemache Sinclair, a considerable benefactor to the town, virtually rebuilt the whole edifice. Unfortunately, in 1952, structural defects made it necessary to abandon the castle.

Prior to the building of the castle, Thurso was made a free burgh of barony by King Charles I in 1633, conferring on the town a number of commercial privileges more limited in scope that those of the royal burgh of Wick. The Barony Charter also conferred the right to hold four fairs, only two of which, Petermas and Marymas, survived any length of time. These fairs were held in what is now the town square, where the bustling fishwives also sold their wares by the Auld Fish Stone.

Throughout the middle ages Thurso had an important trade with the continent and for nearly two centuries it was the principal seat of the Sheriff Court. By the mid 17th century Thurso, according to Custom House records, was exporting from its rivermouth considerable quantities of meal, fish, meat, oil and skins and importing salt, wine, timber and iron. Its significant trade with the Netherlands is commemorated in the name of Rotterdam Street. An earlier and much less salubrious name for this thoroughfare was the Black Gutter.

In 1735 Aeneas Bayne, whose manuscript *Survey of Caithness* reposes in Inverness library, wrote of Thurso, "It is a neat little fashionable town......with one principall street, severall wynds and sufficient buildings in it". Around the rivermouth huddled the oldest part of the town, the "Fisherbiggins"; in the area of what is now Durness Street was "Booragtoon", where the small dwellings thatched with straw held down by simmons had their "boorags" or mossy peats stacked alongside. At this time the town's water supply was furnished by three wells, one of which, the Meadow Well, survives in Manson's Lane.

At the turn of the 19th century Thurso was still a small town with one main thoroughfare which ran from the bridge (first constructed in 1800 but substantially rebuilt in 1877) via Traill Street, commemorating Sir James Traill who established the flagstone industry, Rotterdam Street, High Street and Shore Street down towards the sea. The houses in Shore Street, part of the Fisherbiggins area, have been tastefully restored, including the circular Turnpike, dated 1686.

Of the three tolls that formerly existed in Thurso, one survives, at the junction of the A836 and A882. The others were located by the Station Hotel in Princes Street and at the junction of Olrig and Durness Street. The coming of the stage coach in 1819 was a catalyst to improving the town's roads; the next major breakthrough in communications was the year 1874 when the railhead reached its northern limit in Thurso.

The first planned phase in Thurso's development resulted from the late 18th century proposals of Sir John Sinclair for a New Town (Plate 32), a rectilinear layout of spacious streets focusing on Macdonald Square, later named Sir John Square, in the developer's honour. The principal architectural interest of his development, which lasted throughout much of the 19th century, lies in the elegant houses of Janet Street (Plate 45), named after Sir John's mother. From the square, which has a statue of Sir John, ran Sinclair Street, commemorating the family name. Facing it now is the imposing facade of the library, formerly established as a school for boys, the Miller Academy, in 1862 (Plate 48). Parallel to Sinclair Street is Princes Street, so named to honour a visit in 1876 by the Prince and Princess of Wales.

Another fine building of the period is the elegant Town Hall, completed in 1871. Next door is the town's museum with its superbly comprehensive herbarium of naturalist Robert Dick, whose house still survives in Wilson's Lane (Plate 55). Just over a decade later in 1882, another important amenity was added to the town, with the construction of the Esplanade, from which runs the coastal Victoria walk past the

Murray mausoleum, formerly a chapel site on Pennyland Farm. In nearby Pennyland House was born William Smith the founder of the Boys' Brigade. (For details of other buildings, see chapter 13).

The third phase of the town's growth followed the First War and continues to the present day. It includes the local authority developments on either side of the river as well as the Atomic Energy Authority's estates at Ormlie and Mount Vernon.

SCRABSTER

It is a bracing walk along the Thurso esplanade, towards the haven of Scrabster ("Skarabolstathr" of the Norse sagas) which has been an important local harbourage at least since the days of the Vikings.

The village (Plate 63) lies cosily in the lee of the corrugated cliffs cut in the glacial till. Its deep water harbourage, once a hive of activity during the heady days of the herring boom, fell on poor times in the inter-war years but has since been rejuvenated. Apart from fishing boats there are many pleasure craft and Scrabster has had a regular ferry service to Stromness since 1856.

In 1862 the lighthouse at Holborn Head was completed. The coastline west of the lighthouse is of enormous interest with its great slabs of rock, heavily jointed and exploited by the sea to produce geos, caves, arches, blow-holes and the dramatic sea stack known as The Clett.

REAY

The hard, dark diorite rock of north-west Caithness produces a lumpy landscape peculiar to this part of the county. Between this rugged terrain and the U-shaped Sandside Bay, framed between two headlands, lies Reay village.

An abundant supply of sediment is brought down to Sandside bay by the vigorous streams, aiding the build up of dunes and the evolution of links, now partly occupied by a fine 18-hole golf course.

Apart from Cnoc Stanger there are signs of prehistoric settlement in the area, with chambered cairns, standing stones, stone rows, hut circles and brochs. Viking evidence also came to light with the discovery of skeletons near the site of the village hall.

The area's ecclesiastical history is splendidly represented by the old church (perhaps of 12th century date) at Crosskirk (Plate 20) and reconstructed remains of part of the old church of Reay which lies in the north-east corner of the kirkyard. On the walls are some ancient panels and shields as well as a sculptured stone, its face intricately carved (Plate 11).

In the churchyard are a number of old tombstones with interesting heraldic devices, inscriptions and customary symbols of mortality such as the skull and crossbones. The present parish church is a splendid building dating from 1739, its "jougs" set into the south wall. The manse was added in 1788.

Further interesting inscribed stones are located at Sandside House: one is a small rectangular block of sandstone incised with two circles, the smaller containing an equal-armed cross. The other is set upside down, against a wall close by the house. It is an oblong sandstone block some 1.4 m (4 ft 7 in) long and 0.6 m (2 ft) wide with engraved Pictish symbols of a triple oval, below which is a mirror case and underneath that a mirror and comb (Plate 40).

In the village is a market cross (with missing upper limb) said to have been removed from Old Reay which was situated nearer the sea. In height, it stands 1.3 m (4 ft 3 in) above the ground and in width across the arms measure some 0.6 m (2 ft). Reay market was held on what is now Ben Ratha Court. It took place on the first Monday in September, the last occasion being the year 1913.

Old Reay could claim to be the oldest village in Caithness and clearly in late medieval times it was a settlement of some importance. Its charter of 1516 is an indication of its early significance. The 18th century writer Aeneas Bayne had this to say.... "The town of Reay close by the seaside seems to be a place of considerable antiquity and in which there are vestiges thereof yet to be seen, but is now almost covered with sand. The privileges of this town tho' ancient, are very few, having only two mercats in the year: one in the latter end of August called Marymes, and the other about the middle of December called Kenlamas fare."

In 1751, according to the *New Statistical Account*, there was a tremendous waterspout which cut a new channel between Reay village and the shore to reveal the ends of seven houses and the ruinous remains of several others. Presumably, this exhumed settlement was the old medieval village, where, perhaps the market cross once stood.

The present twin settlements of Reay are clearly of more recent date, the older nucleus settling around the parish church and the old inn (Plate 62) which may date from the early 19th century, as mention is made of it in the year 1822. Between the old inn and Borlum House was the birthplace of the 'Apostle of the North' (see chapter 15). Travel to and from Reay must have been difficult as there was no road to the west of the village until the 1820s.

The growth of Reay was associated with the movement of people from the land during the evictions of the 19th century. The tenant of much of the land to the south of Reay at this time was reputedly John Paterson of Borlum who leased land from Captain Macdonald who resided at Sandside House, a fine mansion, mentioned by Bayne (1735) along with other dwellings in the area such as Borlum and Isauld.

It was Paterson who carried out the evictions from Shurrery, Broubster and Shebster, many of the dispossessed heading north towards the coast. According to local writer Donald Mackay (Jenny Horne) there were over 100 families removed in the great clearance of 1838. Although this appears to have been the most drastic of the clearances in the Reay area, the earliest removal of folk was from Helshetter (to the south of the village on Sandside Burn) in the 1770s, the emigrants leaving Scrabster only to have their vessel wrecked in Shetland.

A fascinating insight into rural life in the Reay area during the early part of last century was provided by John Couper who penned his childhood recollections around 1860. (They were republished in the *Caithness Couriers* of July 1975).

In his early life Gaelic was still widely spoken in the district. Agriculture was primitive, the old rigs curving their way across the landscape. Rotation was unknown and only the larger farms had turnips.

The predominant crop was oats which fed people and animals, the straw being "woven" and put to many uses: partitions within the house, curtains for beds, window screens, carpets for the flag floors and the making of general purpose baskets called "cassies".

It was customary in those days to bleed the cattle in summer and boil the blood to make "Bleedy Stugs", a delicacy for hungry folk!

Cow's milk was an important source of nourishment, whether drunk or converted into butter or cheese. There are two fine surviving examples of old stone cheese-presses set into the wall of a house in the west end of the village with another at Sandside House.

Nourishment was also taken from the sea, with herring sought from Forss and Sandside Bay, just below Fresgoe, where there are a few stones left of the old harbour, reputedly built to engage destitute men. Not far away is the location of a snuff mill; another survives at Crosskirk Bay.

Despite privation for many, the contributor to the *New Statistical Account* for Reay could record "some years ago the best of dress of the women was a blue duffle coat; now they appear on Sabbath days in silk and muslin gowns, shawls and straw bonnets".

A bed of limestone to the west of Sandside House was exploited as early as 1802; another was opened up inland at Ary-Leive and was worked on a large scale in the 1840s (surviving until 1890) as the rapidly-growing population broke out more hill-land, sweetened it with lime and fertilised it with seaweed. Shell marl, from the beds of the former lochans was dug up from a variety of pits in Upper and Lower Dounreay.

A small vein of lead was discovered near Reay, but much greater interest was aroused by the iron-rich nodules (haematite) which were exploited between 1870 and 1873 by digging three shallow pits. The vein was not as rich as initially expected and only one boat load of some 150 tons was shipped from Sandside harbour which had been built by the famous engineer James Bremner.

From Sandside harbour there is a fine view of the Atomic Energy Authority's establishment at Dounreay (Plates 58, 59) a site begun in the mid 1950s which has subsequently developed into a symbol of advanced British technology.

HALKIRK

The derivation of the place name Halkirk appears to be from the old Norse Ha-kirk-ja, meaning "High church".

There is dispute among scholars as to whether the Picts living in the far north of Scotland were brought in to the fold of Christianity by missionaries of Columba in the 6th century or by those of Ninian of Galloway long before Columba was born. What is beyond any dispute is the large number of chapels in the parish dedicated to saints, e.g. to Columba at Dirlot and to St. Trostan, who has five dedications in Caithness, two of them in Halkirk parish, viz., at Westfield and Westerdale. The old parish kirk on the outskirts of the village stands on or close to a site known as Tor Harlogan, signifying an early dedication to this missionary who crossed the Moray Firth from Buchan.

At the nearby chapel of St. Thomas, Skinnet, stood a beautifully carved Class II Pictish symbol stone, one of the two outstanding examples (the other being the Ulbster stone) found in Caithness. Both stones are now housed in Thurso Museum. Unfortunately the Skinnet Stone, probably dating to the 7th-9th century AD, has been broken into a number of pieces, a sorry fate for this beautiful piece of relief monumental sculpture.

Perhaps the original focus of settlement in the area where Halkirk village now stands was the old castle at Braal, now a roofless rectangular keep pleasantly situated among woodlands on the west bank of Thurso River. An 18th century traveller, Cordiner, commented on the "aged trees spreading near the castle" and the river which "yields plenty of salmon". He wrote favourably of the large garden by the castle with its "rows of fruit trees, bearing plenty of apples, pears and cherries".

Braal Castle (Plate 23) was at one time the principal seat of the Earls of Caithness. As far back as 1375 King Robert II granted Brathwell (Braal) Castle to his son. (The adjacent new castle of Braal, of late 19th century date, has been converted into flats). In 1222, there occurred a dark deed that put the name of Braal on the pages of Scottish history. The incident was caused through the insistence of Bishop Adam to double the butter tax that he received as tithes from his flock. Greatly resisting this imposition, an angry crowd made for Braal Castle, residence of the Earl of Caithness, who was asked to protect the people from the prelate's exactions. One legend had it that the Earl refused to intervene in the dispute; another, that he advised the mob to burn the bishop in his butter. Whatever the advice, the unfortunate prelate was seized and put to death. So incensed was the Scottish King Alexander II by the crime that he came north with soldiers and avenged the bishop's death by causing much bloodshed in the area. Adam was succeeded by the distinguished Bishop Gilbert Moray. Following the barbarous crime at Braal, Gilbert decided to move the bishopric to Dornoch, where the cathedral church of the see now stands.

Halkirk parish continued to be the stage where many bloody skirmishes and clan feuds were enacted (such as the desperate battle at Harpsdale between the Keiths and Gunns) but more settled times had arrived before John Sinclair of Ulbster, grandfather of Agricultural Sir John died, leaving a sum of money for the construction of a stone bridge over the Thurso River, opposite the lands of Comlifoot (Plate 49).

However, as twelve years elapsed before the work was begun, the story soon gained credence that the delay was due to the influence of the devil. When the structure was finally completed it was believed that the devil made a rendezvous there every night. Little wonder few folk would cross the bridge after sunset!

It was almost another 60 years before the indefatigable Sir John Sinclair reputedly mustered his tenants and pushed a road through from Latheron to Georgemas, and ultimately to the bridging point of the river at Comlifoot, Halkirk.

The 19th century had turned before Sir John Sinclair drew up his plans for a settlement at his grandfather's bridge, using land that was not suitable for the plough: the moss of Halkirk.

The plan for a new village (Plate 30) was drawn up in 1803 and, in the fashion of the time, was laid out on a grid iron basis with each of the 22.3 x 0.4 ha (55 x 1 acre) holdings delineated and numbered.

The principal thoroughfare at Bridge Street was to be 18.3 m (60 ft) broad and the lesser streets to measure 7.3 to 7.9 m (24 to 26 ft) in width. Dotted along the streets were communal wells, two of which survive on Bridge Street.

Family names are commemorated in Sinclair Street, Lane and Square as well as in George and Camilla Street. An inn site was allocated on Bridge Street (opposite the end of Sinclair Street) with space for shops to the south of it. It was envisaged that Halkirk would grow into a thriving market centre, but the nearness of Thurso ensured that this would not be so. Only now is the original grid plan being filled in.

The handsome village hall known as the Ross Institute is so named after John Ross, who was born at Gerston in 1834 and emigrated to Otago, New Zealand, in 1861. The business which he developed soon

SETTLEMENTS

expanded until it had branches in all the main towns of New Zealand. In 1911 the Ross Institute was opened, the electric clock (the first in a public building in Scotland) in its tower being a donation of another son of Halkirk, David Murray.

Many people in the area were saved from destitution by receiving contributions from the fund of the Halkirk Village Society, whose accounts in the early part of the last century showed a figure of £300, an enormous sum for those times. Further provision was made for the needy with the construction of the Poor House (now converted into flats) at Halkirk in 1856. It served the west end of the county, the east having a poorhouse, now virtually ruinous, at Ben-a-chielt, by the Causewaymire road.

Distillation of the "barley bree" has had a long association with Halkirk. For nigh on 100 years the spirit was distilled at Gerston. The earliest distillery foundation, which goes as far back as 1825, survived some 50 years producing whisky of considerable merit, which was a favourite of Prime Minister Sir Robert Peel. There is now little trace of the original distillery, but not long after its demise another distillery, the Ben Morven, was established close by in 1886. The Still House is all that remains of this once large complex. Ben Morven never acquired the distinction of its predecessor and after a period of financial difficulty, it closed in 1911.

SPITTAL

The settlement of Spittal, takes its name from the hospice dedicated to St. Magnus of Orkney. The earliest reference to this hospice is in a charter dated 1476. Close to the hospice site is a chapel, dedicated to St. Magnus, part of whose gable still survives.

There used to be an annual market on Spittal Hill but from c. 1827 it was held on Sordale Hill on St. George's Day, thus giving the recent derivation of the place name Georgemas. In nearby Halkirk there was an annual St. Magnus market which was held on the Tuesday prior to the 26th December.

During the later 19th and early 20th centuries the Spittal quarries had a prolific output of flagstone and the quarry is one of two (the other at Calder) still operating in Caithness.

WATTEN

The *Statistical Account* (1790's) claimed that there were many private stills in Caithness, particularly in the Watten area! At the time of its publication there was no village, just a few houses collectively called

Achingale. Even at the time of the *New Statistical Account* (1841) there was no village, so its evolution at the road junction and bridging point of the Acharole Burn is very recent. The bridge, dating from the first quarter of the 19th century had a toll house (still in existence) for collecting dues. Across the road from the old toll is the community centre housing the clock made in 1845 by the famous inventor, Alexander Bain, who was born at Leanmore in 1810. A statue commemorating him stands outside the community centre.

CHAPTER 11

PLACE-NAMES

The 20th century visitor to Caithness, equipped with Ordnance Survey map, or the local who is already familiar with the names, will be instantly aware of the blend of languages which occurs in Caithness place-names. Scandinavian, Gaelic and Scots place-names are clearly evident and the presence of the three languages makes Caithness a particularly interesting area to study. There is an unfortunate lack of place-name information prior to the arrival of the Scandinavians (c. 800 AD) but the Norse inhabitants of Orkney during the 9th century were certainly aware of the existence of Picts to the south, as the name *Péttlandsfjörthr* 'Pictland Firth' clearly indicates when it is used in *Orkneyinga Saga*. The name *Caithness* itself which also occurs in *Orkneyinga Saga* as *Katanes* 'headland of the Cats' specifies that these Picts belonged to the tribe known as *Cats,* a name which is still preserved in the modern Gaelic name for Sutherland, *Cataibh* 'among the Cats'.

Other place-names which appear to be Celtic in origin but which substantially predate the main movement of Gaelic-speaking people into Caithness were probably in use prior to 800 AD but lack of documentary evidence makes it impossible to be certain of the origin of these place-names. *Dunnet* (ND204768) is one such example. It has been equated with the **tarvedu(nu)m* 'bull fort' which appears on Ptolemy's map of the north of Scotland. The element *dunum* seems to have developed in sense from 'hill' to 'fort', either of which could be aptly applied to such a prominent headland which would have been an obvious situation for fortifications.

Many people have speculated on the absence of pre-Norse place-names from Caithness and, no doubt, many more will do so in future. Archaeological evidence may produce some of the answers but, in the present state of knowledge, no clear solution can be provided. Perhaps, when the Scandinavians arrived, the land was sparsely populated and a disproportion between numbers of Scandinavians and indigenous inhabitants led to a swamping of earlier place-names.

The Scandinavians who arrived near the beginning of the 9th century probably came either direct from the west coast of Norway or via neighbouring Orkney. Norse settlement in Caithness is predominantly coastal and the location of place-names displays an obvious awareness of the benefits of being situated within reach of a major inland waterway such as the Wick and Thurso Rivers or within reach of the sea, both of which would have provided food and transport to link the Caithness Norse with their neighbours in the Northern Isles. There is every reason to suppose that contact between Caithness and Orkney was close and frequent and a similarity in the place-names used suggests that there were many parallels in the development of settlement in the two areas.

It is most probable that the earliest Scandinavian place-names in Caithness were names which referred to topographical features. In a landscape empty of one's compatriots there is no need to define the position or function of a farm in relation to a neighbouring habitation and, therefore, place-names such as *Murkle* (ND166696) were coined in the form recorded in *Orkneyinga Saga* — *Myrkhol* 'dark hill'. A glance towards Murkle from *Sibmister* (ND165662) will confirm the accuracy of this description even at the present day. Another example of a topographical term being used as a habitative name is, of course, *Wick* (ND360510) from Old Norse *vík* 'a harbour'. This place-name is also recorded in *Orkneyinga Saga* which is an excellent source but, regrettably, it mentions few place-names[1].

Previous writers, notably Hugh Marwick in his excellent book *Orkney Farm Names*[2] and W.F.H. Nicolaisen in his equally admirable *Scottish Place-Names*[3], have identified the various terms used to indicate farms in the Scandinavian community in the north of Scotland: terms such as *stathir, setr/sætr, bólstathr, garthr* and *kví*. It has been previously assumed that there were no place-names containing *stathir* in Caithness which, if it were true, might suggest a significant difference between Caithness and its northern neighbours but, in fact, it is very probable that both *Drumhollistan* (NC926640) and *Gerston* (ND123594) contain the element *stathir* which has developed into final -*stan*/-*ston* as in Orkney place-names such as *Knarston, Hourston* and *Tenston*. *Drum*- is, of course, Gaelic *druim* 'a ridge of a hill' and it has been attached to an earlier Scandinavian -*Hollistan* 'farm/homestead of a man named Holi'. In *Gerston* likewise, the first element is probably a personal name, *Geirr*.

Caithness is different from Orkney and Shetland in that the tendency to abbreviate earlier Scandinavian names is much more pronounced in Caithness than in the Northern Isles and although this can be most clearly seen in place-names containing *bólstathr,* it is a general tendency and presents innumerable problems to the unfortunate person who is attempting to unravel the etymology of the names. Severe truncation of a name may suggest a failure to understand its component parts and the earlier arrival of Scottish English or Scots as a force to be reckoned with in

PLACE-NAMES

REAY
Achunabust	ND994645
Broubster	ND028612
Loanscorribest	NC984640
Lybster	ND025685
Shebster	ND017640
Stemster	ND041658

THURSO
Aimster	ND117633
Scrabster	ND102704

OLRIG
Sibmister	ND165662

DUNNET
Wester	ND231727

CANISBAY
(Brabstermire)	ND324695
(Brabster)	ND323678
Stemster	ND367721
Stroupster	ND333663

WICK
Bilbster	ND280531
(Lower) Camster	ND253456
Haster	ND327505
Hunster	ND351486
Ingimster	ND296535
Killimster	ND313566
Nybster	ND363633
Sibster	ND324530
Stemster	ND337506
Thrumster	ND336453
Ulbster	ND325410
Wester	ND327593

HALKIRK
Achkeepster	ND168516
Achlibster	ND116523
Achscrabster	ND088632
Mybster	ND164526
Sibster	ND152593

BOWER
(Brabster)	ND215611
(Brabsterdorran)	ND224603
Camster	ND209608
Nipster	ND217587
Stemster	ND178619
Tister	ND192615

WATTEN
(Achlipster)	ND244486
(Badlibster)	ND247493
Bylbster	ND260540

LATHERON
Camster	ND261417
Guidebest	ND182353
Leodebest	ND184346
Loedebest	ND138322
Lybster	ND248355
Occumster	ND267355
Rumster	ND215374
Stemster	ND188446

N.B. Bracketed names have only been recorded once because they are obviously derivatives of a single Scandinavian original.

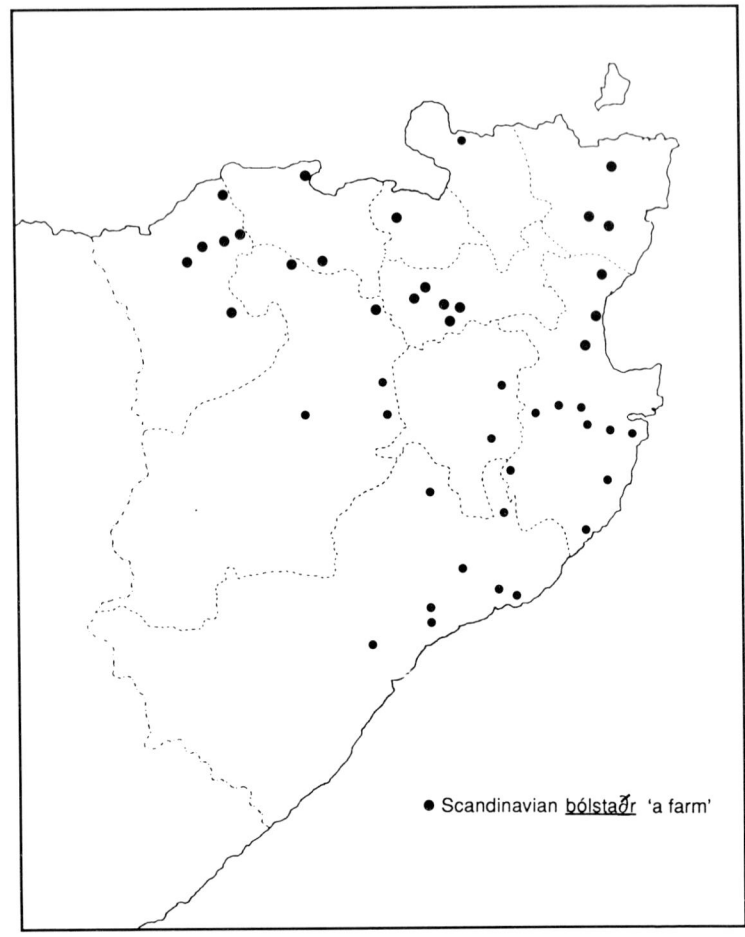

Figure 14. Place-names containing bólstathr — a farm. The distribution of the place-names is a clear indicator of the extent of Scandinavian settlement in Caithness

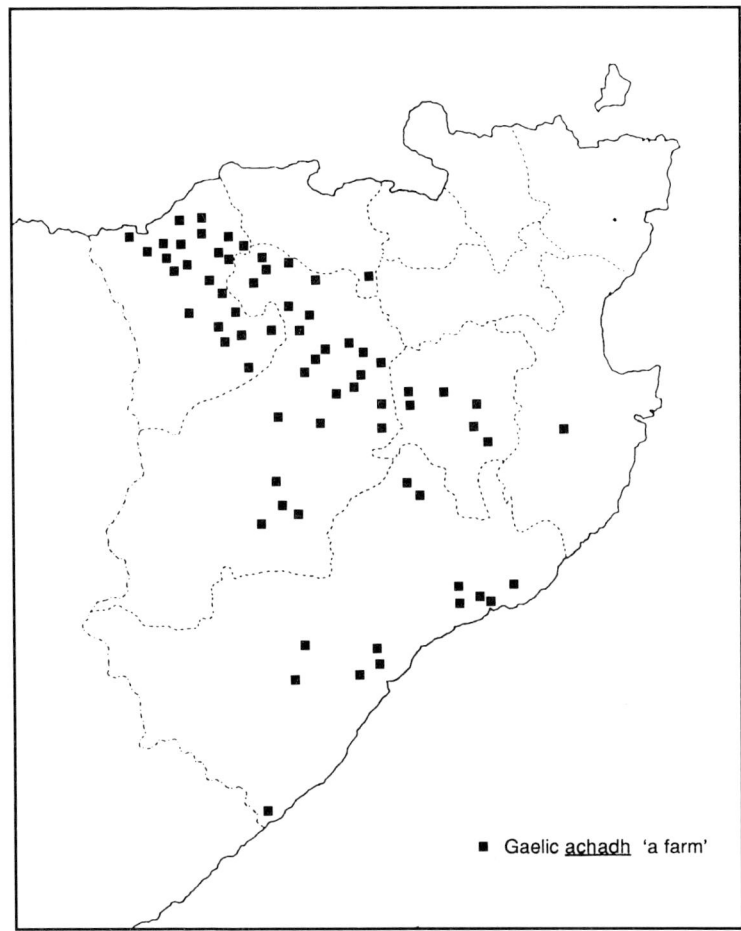

Figure 15. Place-Names containing Gaelic achadh — a farm. The distribution of these place-names is a clear indicator of the extent of settlement by Gaelic-speaking people in Caithness

REAY

Achadh na Gaodha	NC940646
Achalone	ND038631
Achanon	ND067582
Achaveilan	ND005623
Achbuiligan	NC991657
Achforsiescye	ND023596
Achiebegg	ND023624
Achiebraeskiall	ND017652
Achiegullan	NC988647
Achieviegle	ND043642
Achimenach	ND022639
Achimore	ND023644
Achins	NC958641
Achnabeinn	ND044572
Achnacarich	ND019586
Achnacly	ND039598
Achrasker	NC992636
Achreamie	ND014671
Achreregan	ND027622
Achsteenclate	ND037546
Achunabust	NC995645
Achvarasdal	NC995621

HALKIRK

Achadh Beathaig	ND047420
Achadh a' Chracairnie	ND073513
Achadh Chairnleith	ND053451
Achadh Mor	ND093431
Achaeter	ND052618
Achagie	ND096575
Achalone	ND152566
Achanarras	ND153552
Achardale	ND119563
Acharynie	ND112481
Achavarn	ND085597

HALKIRK (cont'd)

Achavrole	ND102592
Achcomhairle	ND160559
Ach Hacon	ND057641
Achies	ND134552
Achgremach	ND048634
Achingoul	ND103546
Achkeepster	ND168516
Achlachan	ND144532
Achlibster	ND116523
Achnacoile	ND080537
Achnavast	ND079640
Achscoriclate	ND082442
Achscrabster	ND088632
Achvidigo	ND152493

WATTEN

Achalipster	ND244486
Acharole	ND218515
Achingale	ND245535
Achnamoine	ND178537
Achoy	ND226533
Achverga	ND174536

LATHERON

Acharaskill	ND157432
Achastle	ND233345
Achavanich	ND179428
Achavar	ND260373
Achavrole	ND166313
Achinavish	ND090304
Achnaclyth	ND099337
Achnacraig	ND075192
	ND239344
Achnagoul	ND166325
Achorn	ND137303
Achow	ND230366
Achsinegar	ND226355

WICK

Achairn	ND303502

THURSO

Achingills	ND152631

Caithness may account for this difference between Caithness, Orkney and Shetland. There is also the fact that Gaelic was spoken in the west and south of Caithness, which could have affected the pronunciation of Scandinavian place-names. Some examples of place-names containing *bólstathr* which have undergone abbreviation are: *Brabster* (ND324695) — *breithr* + *bólstathr* 'broad farm'; *Camster* (ND261417) — *kambr* + *bólstathr* 'farm on the ridge'; *Killimster* (ND313566) — possibly *kylna* + *bólstathr* 'farm with a corn-drying kiln'. Place-names containing *bólstathr* are common in Caithness and are spread throughout the county [Fig. 14].

The abbreviation of *bólstathr* in turn makes the identification of place-names containing *setr/sætr* problematical, except when the element occurs on its own as in *Seater* (ND355726) near Canisbay (ND344725). The use of *setr* without a defining element or specific to locate it more precisely in relation to neighbouring farms indicates that the farm was occupied at an early point in the Scandinavian settlement of Caithness and there are other place-name indicators of early settlement in the area behind *Duncansby Head* (ND406732) to support this contention. The names *Canisbay* and *Duncansby* are unusual in that they are the only two examples in Caithness of place-names containing Old West Scandinavian *bǽr* which, in Norway, seems to have been generally used of an isolated farmhouse and perhaps also, originally, of cultivated land. The latter comment is particularly interesting because it is likely that the first element in both of these place-names is a Celtic personal name and the land may well have been cultivated by these Celts or their ancestors when the Scandinavians arrived to intermingle with them.

In the case of *Canisbay* the personal name is debatable but it may be *Cano*, a rare name and probably of Pictish origin. Canisbay Church was dedicated to the Celtic Saint *Drostán* whose name is associated with the founding of the monastery at Deer in Aberdeenshire and, in the Gaelic notes in *The Book of Deer*, mention is made of a Clann Chanann who held lands locally.[4] Perhaps the Norse knew the occupant of the farm as a member of the Clann Chanann and added their own genitival *-s* to this form. *Duncansby* is more straightforward in that it occurs in *Orkneyinga Saga* as *Dungalsbær*, the first element of which is the Celtic personal name *Dungal*. *Duncan* first appears in writing as an alternative to *Dungal* in the mid 17th century but the pronunciation of some local informants still preserves a strong hint of the earlier *Dungal*.

This is an appropriate point at which to pause and pay tribute to the local informant whose contribution to place-name studies is so vital. Local pronunciation frequently assists in the interpretation of an obscure place-name and local knowledge of the situation of a name is likewise invaluable. Folk etymologies have to be treated with caution in that many different stories may be given in explanation of a single place-name, but it is well worth the effort of sifting through the many colourful tales to find the elusive kernel of truth.

Let us now return to those place-names in which *setr* occurs in conjunction with a defining element or specific. As stated earlier, they are difficult to identify because of the shortening of names containing *bólstathr* but, even assuming that there are some *setr* names which have not been identified as such and which would swell numbers slightly, this place-name element does not enjoy the same ubiquity in Caithness as it does in the Northern Isles, particularly in Shetland. Perhaps the general flatness of the land and the tendency for settlement to concentrate on the coast did not, on the whole, encourage the establishment of farms of the *setr* type, i.e. hill farms rather than farms situated on flat, fertile soil.

Examples of place-names which probably contain *setr,* or the related *sætr* are: *Helshetter* (NC963628) in which the specific is possibly Old Norse *hella* 'a flat stretch of rock', and note that *setr* has become *-shetter* due to Gaelic influence (cf. Gaelic *siadair* 'a shieling'); *Hunster* (*ND243641) in which the specific is probably *Hundi,* a Scandinavian personal name or, alternatively, *hundr* 'a dog'; *Roster* (ND260401) in which the specific is most probably *hross* 'a horse'.

Place-names containing *garthr* 'a farm with yard enclosure' are also comparatively infrequent in Caithness and the same comment can be made with reference to the *stathir* names mentioned earlier. In fact, the picture emerging is of an area in which, for some reason, it was unnecessary to distinguish minutely between farms by making extensive use of terms which more closely define the nature or function of a farm. There could be at least two interpretations of this phenomenon — either Caithness was less densely populated than the Northern Isles during the period when Scandinavian place-names were being coined or a large number of names have been subsequently lost due to the early arrival of other name-forming linguistic groups in the area.

Some Scandinavian place-name elements were taken into the Caithness dialect of Scots, just as numerous Scandinavian lexical items occur in the dialects of Orkney, Shetland and Caithness, and the fact that these elements were regularly used in the post-Scandinavian period makes it very difficult to date such place-names and also explains why, in some cases, they are so much more numerous than place-names which were coined at an earlier date. For instance, Old Norse *kví* was adopted as *quoy* and, in this form, it described a marginal farm on the outskirts of an already existing farming community. The numerous place-names containing this element might lead the unwary to assume a much greater farming expansion during the latter part of the Scandinavian period than probably took place. In some instances a place-name is obviously Scots because *quoy* is combined with a Scots specific, such as Heathery Quoy, but it is not always so clear cut because many Scandinavian descriptive terms were also borrowed and were used in subsequent centuries, often in a form indistinguishable from a Scots equivalent, such as Sandy Quoy.

Borrowing from one language into another generally involved borrowing from Old Norse into either Gaelic or Scots, or both, but there are a few instances of Scandinavian borrowings from the Gaels whom they encountered on their sorties to and domicile in the islands of the western seaboard. A notable example is Old Norse *ærgi* 'a shieling,' borrowed from Gaelic *airigh*. Both of these terms occur quite frequently in Caithness place-names. The Scandinavian version *ærgi* is particularly intriguing in that, like *stathir,* it tends to be combined with a personal name which implies secondary rather than primary settlement and perhaps also that such farms were seen as having a very specific function, possibly in terms of the actual farm buildings or of the farming activities associated with the farms. Examples of place-names containing *ærgi* are: *Skirza* (ND387684) — recorded in 1635 as *Skersarie,* in which the personal name could be *Skerrir* or possibly *Skári; Blingery* (ND307492) — in which the personal name is most likely *Blæingr.*

Mention of contact between Gael and Scandinavian leads to commentary on the Gaelic place-names which are so plentiful in the west and south of the county. It is likely that Gaelic-speaking people began their slow penetration of previously Scandinavian-occupied territory in the 13th century, although it is most probable that some Gaelic-speaking people were on and within the borders of Caithness in the 12th century. There is little evidence to suggest lengthy intimate contact and mutual exchange of farms between Gael and Scandinavian. Place-name evidence points to gradual infiltration, perhaps as farms were vacated by the Norse, some of whom may have withdrawn to the greater security of Orkney.

The Gaels certainly knew the Scandinavian place-names well enough for them to have acquired permanent existence as names, whether or not the Gaels understood them, and the Norse farm names were largely retained with occasional Gaelic additions and alterations. The term *achadh* 'a field, farm' (Fig. 15) is sometimes prefixed to earlier Scandinavian place-names. *Achadh* is a very general term for a small farm, used throughout Gaelic-speaking areas of Scotland, and like *bólstathr* it seems to have been used to imply the natural progression from cultivation of fields to the establishment of associated farm buildings. Examples of place-names containing *achadh* in Caithness are: *Achunabust* (NC995645) — *achadh* + *Unabust* 'the farm of a man called Uni (genitive *Una*)'; *Achlibster* (ND116523) — *achadh* + *Lybister* (as recorded in 1612) 'farm on the slope'; and, finally, the intriguing

Achnagoul (ND 166325) — 'field of the foreigner'. Could the 'foreigner' have been a stray Scandinavian in territory regarded as Gaelic-speaking? The majority of *achadh* place-names, however, are purely Gaelic in origin, which is not surprising given that the element had a long and productive life throughout the period when Gaelic was spoken in Caithness.

Another Gaelic naming element which has had a long and productive life is *baile* 'a farm, homestead, village'. Unlike *achadh*, however,*baile* is never combined with a former Scandinavian place-name in Caithness which is, perhaps, what one would expect given that it contains no suggestion of development in meaning from 'field' to 'farm' and, therefore, no implication of Gaels initially cultivating fields close to Scandinavian farms, the names of which were eventually subsumed in Gaelic place-names, using the generic *achadh*. Examples of names containing *baile* are: *Balnahard* (*ND117554) — 'farm on the high ground'; *Balbeg* (ND161533) — 'small farm'; *Balnabruich* (ND155295) — 'farm on the bank, border or brim'; *Ballone* (*ND162319) — 'farm on the meadow, marshy ground'. The *baile* names in general have the appearance of being more recent in form.

A very few Scandinavian place-names slipped readily into Gaelic because of an apparent similarity to a Gaelic word. Forms of the place-name *Reay* (NC967647) recorded in the 13th century indicate derivation from Old Norse *rá* which can mean either 'a corner, nook' or 'a long stretched-out elevation', both of which would be appropriate to the situation of the place. The long vowel of the Old Norse *rá* has led Gaelic-speakers to equate it with *ràth* 'a fort', in which the final *-th* is silent in pronunciation, and from this equation has developed the more recent place-name *Beinn Ràtha* (NC954613).

Some Scandinavian words have been borrowed into Gaelic and are regularly used in place-names. The most common of these is Gaelic *geòdha* from the Old Norse *gjá* 'a steep-sided inlet of the sea'. The word was also borrowed into the Caithness dialect of Scots as *geo* and, in that form, it occurs around the coastline of the county and is regularly used in everyday speech. Examples of place-names containing Gaelic *geòdha* and Scots *geo* are: *Geòdh' Sheumais* (*NC949661) — *Seumais* = James; *Limpet Geo* (*ND134699) — the shellfish were probably used for bait in in-shore fishing; *Standstone Geo* (*ND188692) — the reference is probably to an unusually prominent stone in the water; *Marry Geo* (*ND 227742) — Scots *mar* 'clay, mud, mire; specifically a fine bluish or whitish clay'; *Thristle Geo* (*ND379648) — Scots *thristle* 'the prickly thistle'; *Fullie Geo* (*ND357616) — Old Norse *fugl* 'a fowl, bird'; *Ceann Hilligoe* (ND264351) — a tautologous name in which Gaelic *ceann* 'head, height' duplicates an earlier Old Norse *hóll* 'a hill' which, in turn, has been anglicised to *hill.* Perhaps the most interesting of all the *geo* place-names is *Gie-Uisg-Geo* (ND009694) — the most probable explanation of this strange place-name is that *Gie* represents Gaelic *geòdha* and Scots *geo* was added at a subsequent date once the meaning of the original name became obscure to Scots speakers. The central element is Gaelic *uisge* 'fresh water', possibly with reference to a stream draining into the *geo*.

Another Scandinavian loanword used in Gaelic place-names likewise refers to a coastal feature reflecting the Scandinavian preoccupation with the sea and the parallel willingness of the more land-orientated Gaels to utilise Norse coastal nomenclature. The term in Gaelic is *sgeir,* from Old Norse *sker* 'an isolated rock in the sea'. *Sker* was also borrowed into the Caithness, Orkney and Shetland dialects in the form *skerry* and it is a very popular naming element. The island of Stroma in the Pentland Firth has two topographical names containing Gaelic *sgeir,* which is exceptional since the vast majority of place-names on Stroma are of Scandinavian or Scots origin. The two names, *Sgeir Bhan* (*ND364777) and *Sgeir Gut* (*ND361782) were probably named by Gaelic-speaking fishermen for whom the rocks served as landmarks or 'meiths' to use the equivalent Caithness dialect term. *Sgeir Bhan* is 'white Skerry' but the descriptive element in *Sgeir Gut* is impossible to decipher, as frequently happens to place-name elements which are not couched in the language which is in regular local use.

In those parts of Caithness in which Gaelic was spoken in the 20th century, however, Gaelic place-names, particularly topographical names, can usually be understood by a native Gaelic-speaker. Several older Caithness people, although not Gaelic-speakers themselves, can offer a translation of many of the Gaelic place-names on the 6" Ordnance Survey map but, regrettably, a large number of these place-names are no longer used. They have fallen into disuse partly because Gaelic is no longer spoken but also, and more significantly, because they refer to features of the landscape which no longer play an active part in the 20th century lifestyle. Fewer people are directly dependent upon the land in the 20th century, particularly upon the moorland areas which form a large part of the flat Caithness landscape and, therefore, moorland place-names are especially subject to gradual loss. There are many evocative Gaelic place-names whose atrophy is to be regretted: *Cnoc Alltan Caoruinn* (*NC997498) — a musical name which means 'hill of the stream of the rowan tree'; *Cnoc na h-Imriche (*NC988542)* — 'hill of the flitting' — probably with reference to the summer flitting to the shielings; *Tota an Dranndain* (*ND038579) — 'the ruin through which the wind whistles'. The latter name refers to a broch in an advanced state of dilapidation and the Gaelic word used for the ruin, *tobhta,* is a loanword from Old Norse *toft, topt* 'a green, grassy place; a homestead; an enclosure'.

Another aspect of name loss is that people living close to the land make many distinctions between variant examples of the same landscape feature which are, in the course of time, replaced by a blanket term in another language. The numerous Gaelic words for water courses, for instance, have often been replaced by the much more general Scots term 'burn' which can apply to a variety of stream types. Gaelic words for streams include the following: *allt, abhainn* — general terms for stream; *meur* — literally 'a finger', but used to describe a small, narrow stream; *féith* — rents in moor or bog-land made by water; *clais* — a very small stream, ditch; *ùidh* —slow-running water between two lochs.

The transition from Gaelic to Scots in the west and south of Caithness is sufficiently recent to allow us to examine many of the features of transition from one language to another in a place-name context. There are several examples of place-names which have been either wholly or partly translated into Scots and which continue in use in the new language: *Druim na Ceud* (*ND003662) — 'ridge of the hundred' has become *Field o' e' Hunner* and the tradition relating to the place says that one hundred men were buried on this ridge after the fierce battle between the Mackays of Sutherland and the Caithness men in 1437. The battle is known as *Ruaig Shannsaid* 'Pursuit of Sandside'; *Glupein na Drochaide* (*ND003688) — has become *'e Green Brig* which is an adaptation of the original 'Gulping of the Bridge' — no doubt an onomatopoeic reference to the sound of the sea under a natural arch of rock.

Many Gaelic terms which are commonly used in place-names are borrowed into the Caithness dialect of Scots by the simple device of using the term, or an anglicised variant of it, in conjunction with the English definite article. For example: *The Achins* — a corrupt form of Gaelic *achadh; The Tulloch* — from Gaelic *tulach* 'a hillock, mound'. This particular usage does seem to suggest that the Caithness Scots speakers understood these Gaelic forms and could use them as nominal constructions in their own language.

It is probable that speakers of Scottish English or Scots arrived in Caithness c. 1400, moving up the coast to Wick and then round to Thurso. As has already been mentioned, the numerous Scandinavian lexical items which now occur in the Caithness dialect of Scots argue forcibly in favour of the likelihood of prolonged contact between and intermingling of Scandinavians and Scots in Caithness. Like the Scandinavians, the Scots seem to have favoured coastal sites with ready access to that vital communication route, the sea. Place-names in Scots are now scattered throughout the county and have the effect of unifying the areas in which Gaelic and Scandinavian place-names separately predominate.

PLACE-NAMES 153

The widespread influence of Scots can be most clearly seen in the use of place-name elements which indicate the progressive subdivision and organisation of the landscape into economically viable agricultural units. The home farm of an estate, situated on the best land available, is usually referred to as '*X*' *Mains* or, alternatively, as *Mains of* '*X*'. There are numerous examples of Mains farms and the following are a selection: *Borrowston Mains* (ND017691); *Mains of Brims* (*ND043711); *Mains of Olrig* (ND183666); *Greenland Mains* (ND246676); *Philip's Mains* (ND299729); *Ackergill Mains* (*ND354541); *Lybster Mains* (ND253363); *Calder Mains* (ND094597); *Thura Mains* (ND256621); *Mains of Watten* (ND253563). It is noticeable that a very large number of these Mains farms occur on former Scandinavian farm sites or, at least, so close to the Scandinavian farm site that it is the Old Norse farm name which survives as specific. Obviously the Scandinavians and Scots combined their desire to be near the sea with sound judgement of the potential for agriculture of the land they chose to farm or, possibly, the argument should be the obverse — that they chose the site near the sea because the quality of the land was good in such sites.

The smaller land unit known as a *croft,* or *croit* in Gaelic-influenced parts of the county, is very common in Caithness, although the terms *croft* and *croit* are not themselves frequently used as naming elements. It is much more common for such a small farm to bear a topographical name which identifies it in relation to the surrounding landscape rather than a name containing the generic *croft* which would specify the nature of the farming unit more precisely. This is hardly surprising in a county where crofts are so numerous as to render superfluous the repeated use of the generic in place-names. Examples of names which do actually contain *croft* are: *Croft of Sibster* (*ND312538); *Croft of Northfield* (*ND348482); *Crofts of Achimore* (ND023644). The latter place-name suggests several small landholdings occurring in a limited area, which goes a long way towards explaining why crofting was a subsistence occupation, providing a meagre living which could be eked out by fishing if the croft was appropriately situated. Explicit names such as *Boggy Park Croft* (*ND138672) lead to an understanding of the hardship of the crofter's life.

Two further terms which are commonly applied to small farms can be seen in *Croft of Northfield* and *Boggy Park Croft. Field* and *park* are obviously similar in development to Gaelic *achadh* which was discussed earlier. *Mayfield* (ND151662), a place-name which occurs throughout Britain, is also present in Caithness and the reference is probably to the hawthorn or "may" tree, although the name can refer to May festivities. *Heathfield* (ND106668) is another commonly occurring place-name in which the reference is to the quality of the soil and the vegetation. Similarly, there are at least two examples of *Blackpark* as a place-name in

Caithness (ND287642) (*ND070302) in which the colour *black* is probably likewise being used with reference to vegetation, i.e. heather as opposed to grass. A place-name which actually combines all three elements — croft, park and field — is listed in the Sinclair of Dunbeath estate papers for the year 1718 as *Park of Crackersfield Croft*, very clearly illustrating the process of progressive subdivision of the land. *Meadow* occurs very infrequently as an element in Caithness place-names but the example which invariably springs to mind is the intriguing *Aquavitae Meadow* (*ND352508). (One wonders what colourful tale lies behind this reference and suggestions would be gratefully received!).

Old Scots *rigge* 'a strip of arable land' appears very seldom in Caithness place-names, although *rig* is still in regular use as a lexical item in the Caithness dialect. In fact, the only two place-names which, to the writer's knowledge, contain the element, actually share the same specific although the generic is singular in one name and plural in the other. The names are *Hemp Rigg* (*ND378677) and *Hempriggs* (ND352474) and the reference is obviously to the regular sowing of hemp as a crop.

Place-names containing the terms *smallholding* and *cottages* are comparatively frequent, giving the impression of a clustered rather than a dispersed community and, in the 20th century, although there is settlement throughout most habitable parts of Caithness, there is a definite impression of concentration on centres of population which afford employment. Many of the isolated moorland crofts are now vacated, their walls crumbling and their names forgotten. Similarly, a large number of topographical names in Scots have been forgotten — a phenomenon which was mentioned earlier with specific reference to Gaelic place-names. It is certainly true that more Gaelic place-names have been lost because there is the additional problem of failure to understand the name, but Scots place-names are equally prone to attrition because the places to which they refer have no part to play in the 20th century lifestyle.

Some of the older Scots topographical names may, in fact, share the problem of Gaelic place-names, i.e. they are linguistically obscure to all but the older Caithness inhabitants and the regrettably limited number of people who have an academic interest in Scots. For instance, in coastal names such as *Craig Hammel* (ND363463), Scots *craig* 'a rock, crag' is widely known but Scots *hummel/hammel* 'used figuratively to describe anything that represents a flat, level appearance' will be known to very few; *Thirle Door* (ND402725) — Scots *thirle* 'a hole or aperture especially in a wall' is used and the tautologous English *door* has probably been added at a later date; *Oswell Speil* (*ND377642) — a highly problematical name that should probably be written *Oswell's Peil* and be derived from Scots *Oswald/Oswell* 'the water-ouzel or "dipper" ' and *peil* which is a Caithness dialect version of English *pool*.

People who enjoy crossword puzzles will understand the pleasure of attempting to decipher these old Scots names but it is not a particularly helpful exercise in terms of forming a picture of place-name usage because it is so highly speculative and even an informed guess cannot be presented as evidence. An obscure Scots place-name in Dunnet Parish could be used as a metaphor for place-name studies as a whole. The name is *Sweerag Well* (*ND261744) and the derivation is from Scots *sweeriewell* which, with the common Caithness diminutive ending *-ag,* becomes *sweerag-well* 'a spring which flows plentifully for a while after rain, but cannot be depended on for a constant stream'. Place-names do afford plentiful information about the settlement history of a county but there are irritating 'dry spells' or gaps in the information and one has to supplement place-name studies from the wells of archaeology, history and other disciplines in order to provide a more complete picture of the past.

Discussion has largely concentrated on place-names created in the past and references to the 20th century have, rightly, suggested a depressing degree of name loss, but there is a more positive note on which to conclude. New place-names *are* being created as required within the confines of a 20th century way of life. So long as there are people in Caithness they will label their environment as a means of rendering it familiar and personal. New houses are being built and given names and, if these houses occur in streets, the streets are given names and so on. Modern name-givers often make use of former place-names in the creation of new names just as, several centuries ago, the Gaels and Scots made use of earlier Scandinavian place-names. Naming is, in fact, very much a continuing process and one is delighted to observe that the creative impulse is still alive and thriving in the 20th century.

The author's book on "Caithness Place-Names" is in preparation.

NOTES

1 Pálsson, H. & Edwards' P., *Orkneyinga Saga,* 1978 The Hogarth Press, London.
2 Marwick, H., *Orkney Farm Names,* 1952 W.R. Mackintosh, Kirkwall.
3 Nicolaisen, W.F.H., *Scottish Place-Names,* 1976 B.T. Batsford Ltd., London.
4 Jackson, K.H., *The Gaelic Notes in the Book of Deer,* 1972 Cambridge.

CHAPTER 12

THE CASTLES of CAITHNESS

The castles of Caithness (Fig. 16), like all Scottish Castles, are the most romantic man-made features of our landscape, dominating all others. The history of the stone-built castle begins during the 12th century with feudalism — the system by which responsibility for local government and ownership of land went hand in hand. In medieval times the authority of the feudal baron (a landowner who held his lands directly by charter from the king) was absolute throughout his barony. He had the power of life and death; he was the sole arbiter of crime and punishment; his pit and gallows were the ultimate sanctions; high treason against the sovereign alone being exempted. The castle, the seat of the feudal baron, was therefore the seat of local power and authority.

THE NORSE CASTLES

During the Norman infiltration of southern Scotland, under the rule of the early kings of the Canmore dynasty, Caithness still lay under the subjection of Norway, ruled by the Norse earls of Orcadia, a province stretching from Shetland to the Dornoch Firth. The earliest Caithness castles — as distinct from the much earlier brochs — were undoubtedly built by the Norse invaders. The architecture of these early Norse structures was in fact closely allied to that of their Norman cousins, although much smaller and less sophisticated. Usually built on a rocky and inaccessible position on a peninsula only large enough to contain the building and its defences, and with a sheer drop to the waves perhaps 30 m (100 ft) below, their keeps three or four storeys high, were small, unvaulted, rectangular in form, with only one room on each floor.

Thurso

Strange to say, however, one of the earliest mentioned Caithness castles was not on a site of this kind but situated well in from the sea, at Ormlie, Thurso. The *Orkneyinga Saga* tells how shortly after 1136, Earl Rognvald, the builder of St Magnus Cathedral, rode from Berriedale with a large retinue and held a conference at Thurso Castle with his co-

THE CASTLES OF CAITHNESS 157

ruler Earl Harold, as a result of which the two earls were reconciled. Again in 1196 it is recorded that William, King of Scots, having gathered a great army, sent it to Thurso, the town of Earl Harold (the Wicked) and destroyed his castle there. Although nothing now remains of the castle (which should not be confused with the much later Thurso East) it is on record that in 1612 it was the seat of Sir John Sinclair of Greenland and Rattar.

Buchollie

The other two main Norse settlements, in addition to Thurso, were Freswick and Wick and they too seem to have been protected and dominated by powerful castles. At Freswick the important castle of Lambaborg is first mentioned as the stronghold of Sweyn Asliefson, the celebrated Norse pirate whose exploits fill many pages of the *Orkneyinga Saga*. He is the ancestor of Caithness Swansons and also of the Gunns through his grandson Gunni. It was the Mowats who, having received a charter of the lands of Freswick from King Robert the Bruce, brought the present name of Buchollie with them from their estate of that name in Aberdeenshire. The Mowats were a Norman family who, having come over with the Conqueror, moved northwards, first to the English-Welsh marches and then into Scotland. The Mowats sold Buchollie in 1661 to the Sinclairs of Rattar.

Buchollie or Lambaborg was built upon a peninsular rock joined by a narrow neck of land which had been cut through by the usual ditch 1.8 m (7 ft) wide and 2.7 m (9 ft) deep. It was obviously spanned originaly by a wooden moveable bridge, the main keep rising from its furthest side. A passage from the doorway facing the land leads right through the keep to a long courtyard beyond, with a range of outbuildings , now very fragmentary, flanking each side of it.

An unusual feature of the architecture is that the walls were built with an external batter. The keep was small measuring some 4.3 m (14 ft) wide by 6 m (20 ft) thick at the base, but narrowing as a result of the batter to about 0.8 m (2.5 ft) at the top. The ground floor and second floor had been vaulted while the intermediate floor was supported on joists. The architecture of the present ruins is clearly of 15th century date, so it must be assumed that the building had been extensively altered during the century of Mowat occupation.

The earlier castle at Lambaborg dates from about 1150. Its builder, Sweyn, was killed during a raid on Dublin in 1171.

Oldwick

Oldwick Castle (Plate 25) near Wick, is a building of great antiquity, going back into the norse occupation era, although unlike the castles of Thurso and Buchollie there is no documentary evidence to support this view. In the sagas there is frequent mention of Wick, apparently a very important place and often visited by the leading personages of the Norse ruling heirarchy, including Earl Rognvald. It must be assumed that they stayed at Oldwick.

Situated on a tongue of land with a steep geo on each side of it, Oldwick is a huge unshapely mass which forms an excellent landmark far out to sea. The roofless keep still stands to a height of three storeys with a possible fourth storey now gone. The castle is a rectangular block of very rude masonry measuring some 7.3 m by 4.9 m (24 ft by 16½ ft) with walls about 2.1 m (7 ft) in thickness at the base, narrowing as they go upwards to form ledges on which the joists of each floor rested. The entrance, as is often the case with early castles, was at first floor level and would have been reached with a portable ladder. The windows were small and narrow, being merely observation loops. There were no chimneys, as these early Norse castles had their only fire reposing on a large flagstone against the wall in the great hall, the smoke simply curling up the wall through holes in each floor, finally to disappear through the roof.

Down the centre of the peninsula, beyond the keep, runs a long narrow lane with fragments of buildings on each side of it. A broad ditch cuts the castle off from the mainland.

In the recorded history of Oldwick we find that in the 14th century it was one of the many strongholds of Sir Reginald de Cheyne, a nobleman of Norman descent whose family had inherited vast estates in Caithness by marriage with an heiress of the Norse line of Earls. Through a daughter it then passed to the Sutherlands of Duffus and then again by marriage to the Oliphants; finally, by purchase, it was acquired by the 5th Earl of Caithness. In Glenorchy's hands by 1676, it was sold by that family to the Dunbars of Hempriggs who recently passed it into the hands of the Department of the Environment.

Forse

On the east coast of Caithness 3.22 km (2 miles) south of Lybster perched on a high rocky peninsula stand the considerable ruins of Forse Castle which was also part of the heritage of Sir Reginald de Cheyne. In situation, architecture and masonry, it so closely resembles Oldwick that its Norse origin cannot be in doubt.

The Keiths inherited Forse through marriage with one of Sir Reginald's daughters in 1350. A daughter of the next generation carried it by marriage to Kenneth, second son of the 5th Earl of Sutherland. Thereafter, no fewer than 17 generations of Sutherlands were lairds of Forse. In 1771, George, 14th of Forse, while losing in law his claim to the Sutherland earldom was adjudged heir-male of the Sutherland line and Chief of the clan Sutherland.

THE CASTLES OF CAITHNESS

Berriedale

Berriedale Castle, another Cheyne stronghold, passed along with Oldwick to the Sutherlands of Duffus and for a long time its lairds were also of Oldwick. Both castles eventually passed to the Oliphants by marriage. Subsequently purchased by the Earl of Caithness, Berriedale fell into the hands of Glenorchy, from whom it passed to a younger son of Sutherland of Forse. Sold in 1775 by that family, it passed to several owners in turn, ultimately to be abandoned.

Castle Gunn

At Bruan, on a forbidding and desolate site on the rocky east coast of Caithness are the fragmentary remains of Castle Gunn, the earliest seat of that clan. There have been different opinions as to who was the founder of that clan, but recent research has been reasonably conclusive that the ancestor was Gun or Gunni, the grandson of Sweyn Asliefson by his son Andres and that Gunni's son Snaekoll was the builder of Castle Gunn. The site was almost inaccesible by land. the only approach seems to have been by a rough stair set in the rock on the edge of a frightful precipice. Measurements of the original keep have been given as 11.28 m by 7 m (37 ft by 23 ft) with walls 91 cm (3 ft) in thickness. Nowadays only fragments of the keep remain.

Of historical records there are none but several interesting legends survive. The best known is the story of the Norse princess who was to be the bigamous wife of a Gunn chief. The ship carrying her to Caithness with a large dowry of gold was deliberately wrecked at the instigation of the chief by luring her on to the rocks close to Castle Gunn. The princess perished with all on board. For a long time afterwards gold could be seen shining in the water. The Norwegian king, incensed by Gunni's treachery, fitted out an expedition which destroyed the castle, killing Gunn and his retainers. Excavation at Castle Gunn towards the end of the last century gives evidence to tradition.

Halberry

Castle Gunn appears to have been superceded by Halberry 1.6 km (1 mile) to the south, There, in the 14th and 15th centuries, successive Gunn chiefs lived in feudal pomp and splendour. The last chief who lived in Halberry was George Gunn, known as the Cronner or Coroner of Caithness. He wore an authorative badge as keeper of the King's peace. During his time a bitter feud developed with the Keiths of Ackergill, culminating in what became known as the massacre at St Tears chapel where the Gunn chief and at least two of his seven sons were killed. The eldest son and heir James was not present and as a result of the massacre he did not return to Halberry. Settling in Kildonan, where according to tradition, his father had a hunting lodge, he was the first of a new line of chiefs known as MacHamishs or sons of James who had Killearnan as their seat.

Halberry stood on a large peninsula behind a ditch 45 m (150 ft) long by 5 m (16 ft) broad. The foundations of the walls still visible are 13 m (44 ft) long by 8.53 m (28 ft) wide.

Brough

On a long rocky promentary near Brough, Dunnet, are the foundations of a castle which by its situation may well be of Norse origin. A trench about 12.19 m (40 ft) wide and 3 m (10 ft) deep had been dug across the neck of protruding rock. a range of buildings had existed but what had been the keep is not now recognisable. Unfortunately nothing is known of the history of the place.

Mestag

Similar origin may be assumed for Castle Mestag on the island of Stroma. Occupying a whole summit of a detached stack about 4.3 m (14 ft) out from the cliff it could only be reached by a drawbridge. A small fragment of walling can still be seen around the doorway. Concerning Castle Mestag history is now completely silent.

Braal

The ancient castle of Braal (Plate 23) is known to be of Norse origin, although not perhaps in its present form. Its architecture provides a striking contrast to the other ancient castles. Beaufifully situated among woods on the banks of the River Thurso at Halkirk, it is the best preserved of the Norse strongholds. It was the principal seat of john, 24th Earl of Caithness (1206–1231), of the old Norse line. It has many characteristics of Oldwick, but is larger and has more sophisticated adornments, although basically it is of the same rectangular form with walls 2.5 m to 3 m (8 ft to 10 ft) thick). Originally known as Brathwell, it was in 1375 granted by Robert II to his son David, along with the Earldom of Caithness which was in abeyance at that time. In 1450, James II bestowed Braal with the Earldom on the High Admiral of Scotland, Sir George Crighton. When Sir George died in 1455 the Earldom was restored to the heir of the ancient line, William Sinclair. The Sinclair earls held Braal until usurption by Glenorchy in 1676. During the period of their ownership it was one of their secondary residences and often used as a place for incarcerating their prisoners. The ruin, as well as the nearby modern castle of Braal, are now held by the Sinclairs of Ulbster, a junior branch of the ancient line.

Dunbeath

Dunbeath Castle (Plate 24) still occupied, is built on the same kind of rocky peninsula so often used by our early castle builders, but its elongated oblong plan and vaulted ground floor places it firmly into the 13th and 14th century. In a castle continuously occupied and thereby often altered to meet changing requirements, it is difficult to assess its character, but certainly a substantial part of it goes back to or before 1428, the earliest recorded date. The advent of vaulting in castellated architecture meant that the danger of fire either from enemy attack or accident was largely eliminated as vaulted ceilings were fireproof. As a result, castle doorways, until then opening into the first floor level, were then brought down to the ground floor. At Dunbeath the ground floor is divided into four apartments with two spiral staircases leading to the upper floors. The measurements at the base are about 19.20 m (63 ft) by 7.62 m (25 ft) with walls 1.52 m (5 ft) in thickness.

The first recorded owner of the castle was Alexander Sutherland, whose daughter Marjory was the second wife of the first earl of the Sinclair family. Dunbeath afterwards passed into the ownership of several well-known Scottish families: to the Crightons, the Innes's of that ilk and the Colquhouns. Finally, in 1529, Alexander Sinclair, second son of William 2nd Earl of Caithness, received a crown charter of the "lands and towers thereof." The last of this family resigned the barony in 1610 in favour of his brother-in-law Lord Forbes, whose son, the Master of Forbes, sold Dunbeath to Sir John Sinclair of the Mey family.

In 1650 Dunbeath was attacked by Montrose. The castle was bravely defended by Lady Sinclair in the absence of her husband, but it finally fell to the beseigers. For a time it was garrisoned by Montrose until relieved after his defeat at Carbisdale, in Sutherland.

Ackergill

With no natural defences Ackergill Tower stands on a low coast close by the shore, although originally it was surrounded by defensive walls and a moat with water flowing in from the sea. Much of the main tower, standing to a height of five storeys, remains unaltered from medieval times, but the roof and battlements were renewed in the middle of the last century. The tower measures 14.6 m by 10.4 m (48 ft by 34 ft) is 20.7 m (68 ft) high with walls 3 m (9 to 10 ft) thick. The two tower floors are vaulted. A straight stair in the thickness of the wall went upwards to the great hall where the finely-panelled roof is twice the height of a normal room and contains a minstrel's gallery half-way up one end wall. The top storeys are laced with mural passages opening into various closets. Underneath the entrance hall is a well 7.31 m (24 ft) deep, still containing water. A short distance from the front of the tower there are 18th century dovecotes.

The lands of Ackergill were part of the heritage of Sir Reginald de Cheyne who died in 1350, but the earliest recorded date mentioning the castle is 1510. There is circumstantial evidence however, that it is older than that with a possible date between 1460 and 1480. From Sir Reginald, Ackergill passed to the Keiths, descendants of one of his daughters. They, in 1612, sold the estate to the 5th Earl of Caithness. It too fell into the hands of Glenorchy in 1676. From Glenorchy's heirs it was acquired by the Dunbars of Hempriggs. They greatly added to and embellished the tower about the middle of the last century, the old keep being finely incorporated without losing its character. Recently, it has been sold to a syndicate for use by business executives.

Dirlot

The most unusual and picturesque position of any of our Caithness castles must be that of Dirlot which is built on top of a high pinnacle of rock rising from flat ground at the edge of a deep pool in the River Thurso just before it enters a rocky gorge some 4.8 km (3 miles) downstream from Loch More. Only fragments now remain of the keep which was small, the interior being only 5.5 m by 3 m (18 ft by 10 ft) with walls 2 m (6½ ft) thick. It probably stood to a height of three storeys. Believed to have been built by Sir Reginald de Cheyne it was afterwards held in turn by the Gunns, Sutherlands and MacKays. The history of Caithness is sprinkled with stirring episodes centred round this 14th century stronghold.

Loch More Castle

Calder in his *History of Caithness* mentions a castle or hunting lodge built by Sir Reginald de Cheyne where the River Thurso flows from Loch More. No vestige of it now remains. Tradition has it that Sir Reginald had invented a contrivance to trap salmon as they emerged from the loch to the river. A bell rang in the castle when a fish passed into the trap. It is believed that the stones from the castle were used to build the bridge over the river at that point.

Achastle

Achastle is a building of the 15th century. The ruins still extant show it to be a large keep with dimensions 21.3 m by 13.1 m (70 ft by 43 ft) and walls 1.67 m (5½ ft) thick. Cordiner, writing in 1788, mentioned two square towers joined by a curtain wall, but these have long vanished. It was superbly situated on a high ridge above the junction of the Langwell and Berriedale rivers. Protected by the steep banks of these rivers on two sides it was further enflanked on the unprotected side by a broad deep ditch.

Achastle is said to have been built by a younger son of an Earl of Sutherland, but no authentic history has survived.

THE CASTLES OF CAITHNESS

Scrabster

The castle of Scrabster, during the whole period of occupation, was the seat of the Bishops of Caithness. Traditionally known as the Bishops' castle, it was built by Gilbert de Moravia, 4th Bishop of Caithness, who was elevated to the See in 1223. There is reason to believe that a Norse "borg" or castle existed on the site before then. In the *Orkneyinga Sage* there is mention that Earl Harold, after landing from Orkney with a strong force, mutilated the Bishop by cutting out his tongue and blinding him. Although the borg was surrendered to the earl, he had the entire garrison killed.

The castle has been partly excavated in recent years, which showed that it had been largely rebuilt in the 15th century.

Knockinnon

Knockinnon Castle, Dunbeath, was the only fortified structure answering to the description of a castle of enciente. This is a style of architecture which had its heyday in the 13th century. In such a castle a great curtain wall surrounded the whole area. Within it the great tower rose usually at the corner furthermost from the fortified gatehouse. Somewhere along the massive wall may have been in separate buildings, the cahpel, bakehouse, kitchens, smithy, stores, retainers' barracks, etc. A typical example of such a structure is Urquhart, Inverness, but the best known is Edinburgh, where the buildings and curtain wall together constitute the castle.

According to tradition the erection of Knockinnon was begun by William, 2nd Earl of Caithness, who having been called away to join in the invasion of England, fell at Flodden and so the castle was never finished. The situation is one of the most commanding and strategic in the county but only the bare foundations of the various buildings and the wall can now be seen.

Girnigoe

The great stronghold of Girnigoe Castle (Plate 26) the most spectacular ruin in the North of Scotland, was the last of our Caithness castles (with the possible exception of Keiss) to be built on a precipitous cliff-top. Erected sometime between 1476 and 1496 by William, 2nd Sinclair Earl, it was at the time completely impregnable. The promentary on which it stands had been cut away from the maninland both at its base and half way along by great ditches. On the edge of the second trench the keep rose to three or four storeys, with one wing behind on the sea side, behind that again was a courtyard with buildings.

In front between the ditches was the outer ward of Girnigoe with a strong gatehouse and a long vaulted pend where a portcullis opened from the main drawbridge. Over, behind, and around these entrance buildings was erected in 1606 the new and very fine architectural addition known as Castle Sinclair. Another drawbridge over the second moat connected the two parts of Girnigoe. The basement of the old keep with its two dungeons, one containing a deep well (now infilled) was vaulted as was the entire ground storey. By contrast, the upper floors were constructed of timber. A stone stair descended to sea level from a chamber some distance behind the castle.

Girnigoe remained the seat of five successive earls, passing with all the Caithness estates to Glenorchy when he usurped the Earldom. Beseiged by the rightful heir about 1690, it was taken and partly destroyed by (for the first time in Caithness) the use of firearms or artillery. Since that time it has been allowed to fall into decay. In recent years the ownership returned to the earls and Girnigoe Castle is listed in Debrett's peerage as the official seat of the Earldom.

L and Z Plan Castles

In the development of the Scottish castle during the 15th and 16th centuries, as firearms came into use, the castle builders added a wing or a "jamb" to a corner of the main keep, and in the wing, fire could be directed along the whole castle front. Later castles were given added and even all-round protection by two wings at diagonal corners so that the castle defenders could cover the approaches in every direction. This was the Z-plan. At the same time the towers were built higher to give extra room and often the "jambs" ending in turrets were of equal height with the main building.

Keiss

Such a castle was Keiss (Plate 27). This tall slim tower was a modified form of the Z-plan owing to the restricted site on which it stood, jutting out slightly towards the sea on the edge of a cliff. The two diagonally opposite towers were small, one containing a spiral stair. Only the basement was vaulted. All the upper floors, the stairway and a large section of a wall, including the entrance which was on the ground floor have now gone.

The castle dates from about the end of the 16th century, although the site might previously have been a fortified one, for tradition has it that a "fortalice of Raddar" stood there in ancient times. Throughout its history the castle was the property of the Earls of Caithness or their branches. George, the 7th Earl, who had put up such a gallant fight for his inheritance against the usurping Glenorchy, lived and died there in 1698. Later it passed to the Sinclairs of Dunbeath, the first laird of that family being Sir William Sinclair who founded the Baptist church in Caithness.

Sir William, who built the new Keiss Castle nearby, finding himself in pecuniary difficulties, sold the estate to the Sinclairs of Ulbster.

Mey

The royal castle of Mey was a typical Z-plan castle of the 16th century. More modern additions down the years have not destroyed its character as the original structure can easily be determined. There is vaulting on the ground floor and also above the main staircase. Jutting towers, corbelled turrets, a great hall 12.2 m by 5.5 m (40 ft by 18 ft), a kitchen fireplace 3.7 m (12½ ft) wide by 1.8 m (6 ft) in depth, numerous gun loops on the ground and first floors, plus the fact that it is stil inhabited, and by a royal personage, makes it the most interesting residence in the north.

Built betwen 1566 and 1772 by George, 4th Earl of Caithness, it was granted by him to his second son William, but on that son's early death he conferred it on the next son George who founded the baronetical family of Sinclair of Mey. In 1789 the Mey family, on the extinction of the senior line, succeeded to the earldom, and the castle became the seat of the Earldom for the next 100 years, until 1889. In that year George, the 15th Earl, having no issue, left the Caithness estates to a stranger, thus separating the castle from the Earldom. The castle is now the northern home of Her Majesty Queen Elizabeth the Queen Mother.

Latheron

A fragment of wall 2.1 m (7 ft) thick on a steep bank of the Latheron burn, a short distance from the public road, marks the site of Latheron castle. The greater part of the building, although ruinous, was standing in 1726. The estate was the possession of the Sinclair family of Latheron, cadets of Mey as early as 1623. Very little is certain about the history of the castle but there are interestng traditions concerning it. For instance, there is a legend that King William (the Lion) stayed there early in the 13th century when he came north with a large army to deal with Earl Harold who was in open rebellion. King William, it was said, exacted a fine of 2000 merks from Harold and occupied Latheron while the money was being collected. It is believed that the castle was completed in 1203 and that three years later the rebellious Earl Harold died there.

Dounreay

On the north coast of Caithness about 6.4 km (4 miles) apart are two late 16th century castles Dounreay and Brims, both of L-plan architecture. Dounreay is considered to be a perfect example of a Scottish laird's castle of that time. The only vaulting is over the stairway which rises from the re-entrant angle around which shot holes pierce the walls.

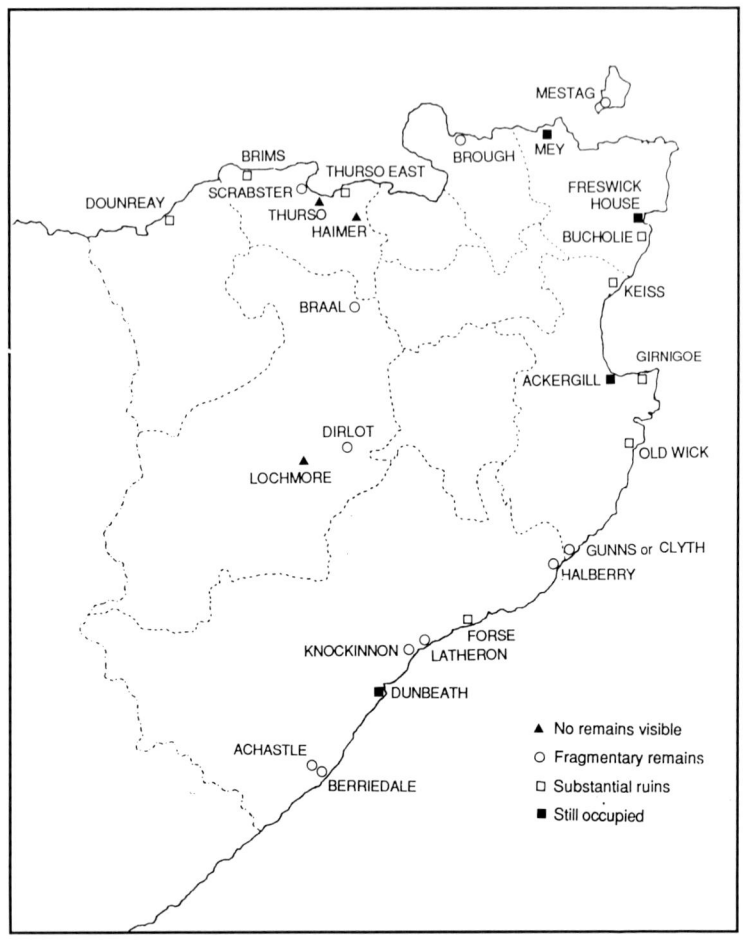

Figure 16. Castles of Caithness

Now roofless and ruinous, there is still much of interest to be seen.

The main block measures 12.19 m by 7.3 m (40 ft by 24 ft) the wing 5.48 m by 4.26 m (18ft by 14ft).

Once church lands, Dounreay passed to the Sinclairs of Dunbeath from Adam, Bishop of Orkney, in 1566. It later belonged in turn to the Earl of Caithness, Lord Forbes and then Lord Reay whose armorial bearings were once embedded in a wall. Cromwell's troops, too, were billeted here. The castle was occupied until 1863, the last tenant being a Mrs Sinclair long remembered in the district as a spectacular figure who drove around in a great coach drawn by two oxen.

Brims

Brims Castle, another Sinclair seat throughout its history, stands on the cliffs where the Brims burn flows into the sea. The keep is rectangular with a "jamb" containing a newel stair attached at one corner. It is three storeys high over a vaulted basement with one room on each floor and walls 1.37 m 4.5 ft) thick at the base. The keep measures overall 7 m by 5.33 m (23 ft by 17.5 ft) with a stair tower 3.20 m (10.5 ft) square. An interesting old arched gateway, with moulding, opens onto a courtyard. The castle, now roofless, had long been used as a farmhouse.

The Sinclairs of Brims who built the castle, were cadets of the Sinclairs of Dunbeath. They sold the estate to John Sinclair of Tannach, a member of the Ulbster family. As his son succeeded to Ulbster, Brims passed to the next brother, the notorious Patrick Sinclair, who it is said murdered his mistress and concealed her body in the castle. He then sold the estate and left the country, but the legend still persists that the ghost of a "white lady" haunts the building.

Thurso East

On a site at Thurso East three castles have risen in as many centuries. the first was built in 1660 by George, 4th Earl of Caithness, who died there in 1676 leaving his estates deeply in debt to Glenorchy. To prevent its ocupation by the latter, George, the heir to the earldom, attacked and destroyed the castle. The Sinclairs of Ulbster who acquired the estate in 1710 built a new castle there. It was demolished about the middle of the last century to make way for a splendid new building which is now roofless and dismantled.

Haimer

Haimer Castle, no longer in existence, was built by Alexander, 9th Earl of Caithness (1705-1765) whose landed patrimony was Murkle. It is said that he moved his place of residence to a more inland site as the notorious pirate Gow, whom he had offended, had bombarded his house there. Haimer proved only just out of range of Gow's guns for it is said that a cannon ball landed at Broynach nearby. A square tower consisting of some eight rooms, the castle was abandoned after its builder's death.

Freswick

Standing on a knoll where the Burn of Freswick almost forms an island as it enters the sea, the house of Freswick is a notable landmark. The date of its erection by William Sinclair of Freswick is given as 1760 but it would appear that parts of it are older*. The two-storey range of buildings attached to the main tower and through which an arched gateway leads into the entrance courtyard is believed to predate the main tower. This range is now roofless. Although obviously a late building the doorway is at first floor level and reached by a wide stone stairway. The house, standing five storeys high, gives a great impression of height and strength. An interesting dovecote, possibly as old as, or older, than the tower itself, stands nearby. Shortly after building Freswick, the Sinclairs purchased Dunbeath Castle and made it their principal seat. Thereafter, Freswick was neglected, becoming initially a seasonal let for shooting tenants and finally the farmhouse of nearby Freswick Mains.

To tell the full story of the castles of Caithness would require many volumes. The families who built and occupied them played a full part in unfolding the history of our county. It is a story of strife and warfare, feuds and forays, intermingled with brave and stirring deeds; patriotism and high ideals are intermixed with bitter jealousies and dark and dreadful crimes. The castles tell a story of the gradual turning to a more peaceful way of living for, existing as they have through all the recorded history of our county, they have seen and show in their stones the transition from one century to the next. They will be with us yet for a very long time to come.

* Captain Gerald Newell of Freswick has stated that the work of the present castle is dated to 1661.

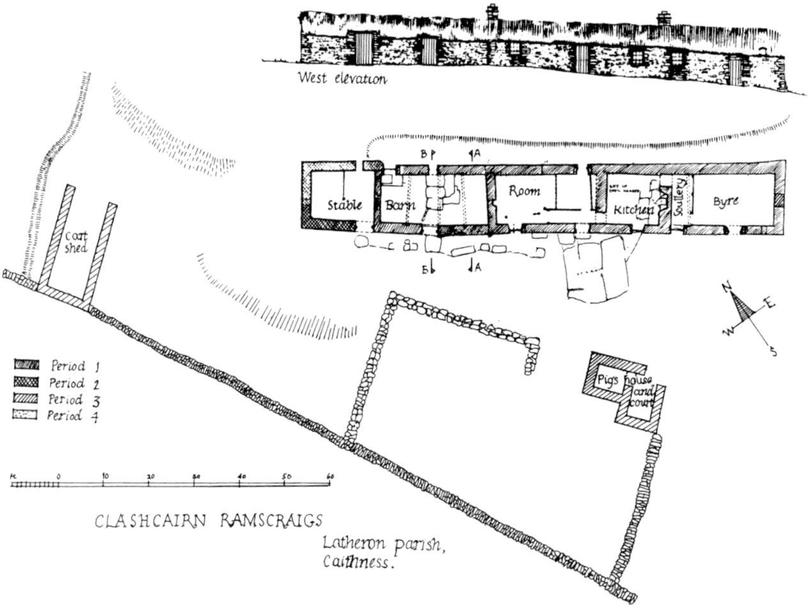

33. Plan of Clashcairn, Ramscraigs, Latheron parish. A cruck framed linear dwelling of 19th or even 20th century date. (RC**).

34. Early 19th century fishery store at Dunbeath harbour. (HBD*).

35. The harbour at Castlehill, Castletown, which had a wide rectangular quay for handling bulky flagstones exported from local quarries. (HBD*).

36. Free church at Achimenach, near Reay, dated 1844. A double aisled church with minister's porch projecting on the left. The manse is to the right, behind the trees. (HBD*).

37. Whaligoe steps, Ulbster. (J. P. Campbell).

38. *Old grain stores* (girnals) at Staxigoe. (J. P. Campbell).

39. *The early 19th century harbour at Keiss.* (J. P. Campbell).

40. (Left) Pictish symbol stone at Sandside House, Reay. (J. P. Campbell).
41. (Right) Memorial commemorating the battle of Altimarlach, near Wick, 1680.

42. The old bridge over the River Forss. (J. P. Campbell).

43. *Stone shelving at the old croft of Achlipster, near Watten.* (J. P. Campbell).

44. *Laid Hay croft museum, Dunbeath.* (J. P. Campbell).

45. *Janet Street, Thurso.* (J. P. Campbell).

46. *Aerial view of Halkirk village with the Thurso River in the background.*
(J. P. Campbell).

47. *Lybster Mains, also known as The Ha'.* (J. P. Campbell).

48. *The old Miller Academy, now the library, Thurso.* (J. P. Campbell).

49. *The old bridge at Halkirk, now demolished.* (J. P. Campbell).

50. *View along Bridge Street, Wick.* (J. P. Campbell).

51. *The 19th century grain mill at Castletown.* (J. P. Campbell).

52. *The picturesque mill at Westerdale.* (J. P. Campbell).

53. (Left) Statue of James T. Calder (Caithness historian) at Wick. (J. P. Campbell).
54. (Right) Statue of Sir John Sinclair, Thurso, with St. Peter's church in the background.
55. Robert Dick's House, Wilson Lane, Thurso.   (J. P. Campbell).

56. The S.S. Sovereign entering Aberdeen harbour. The vessel began regular visits to Wick in 1836. (Aberdeen Art Gallery & Museums).

57. Short-Scion G-ACUU of Aberdeen Airways at Clairdon Airfield c. 1935. The flagstone road led to the hangar. (Mrs Tait).

58. The Prototype Fast Reactor (foreground) and Fast Reactor (sphere), Dounreay. (U.K.A.E.A.).

59. Computerised fibre optic spectrometer in operation in a chemistry laboratory, Dounreay. (U.K.A.E.A.).

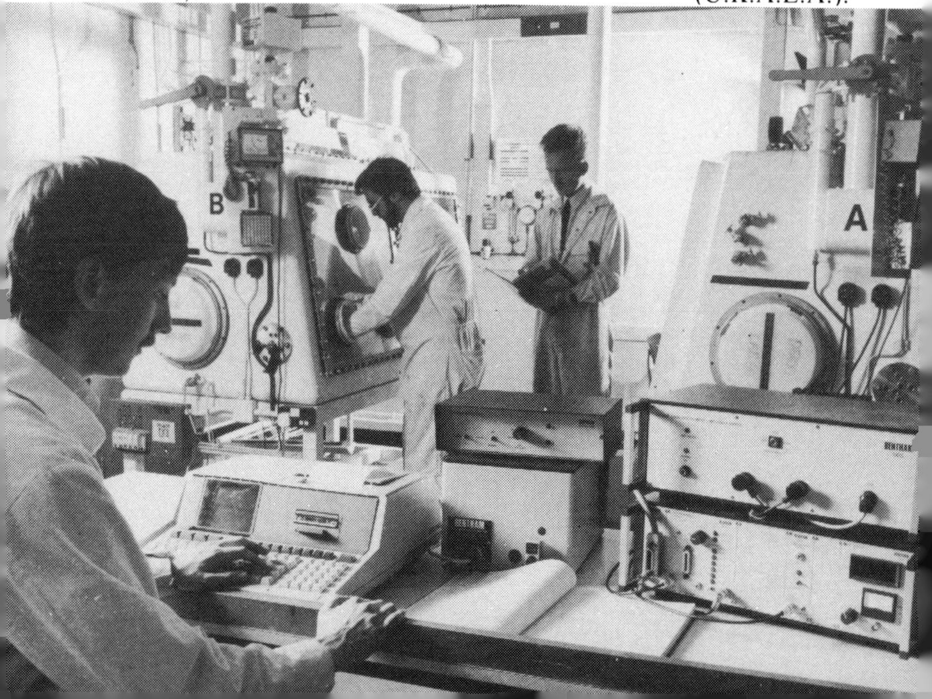

60. *Norfrost Factory, Castletown with Fred the robot flanked by John Lowe (left) and Danny Sutherland.* (J. P. Campbell).

61. *Glass blowers at work in the Glass Factory, Wick.* (J. P. Campbell).

62. *Part of Reay village.* (J. P. Campbell).

63. *Scrabster, lying in the lee of the cliffs.* (J. P. Campbell).

64. *The wooded dell of Berriedale.* (J. P. Campbell).

65. *John O'Groats, showing the last house and the hotel.* (J. P. Campbell).

ORDNANCE SURVEY MAP REFERENCES TO THE CASTLES OF CAITHNESS

Achastle	ND 116227
Ackergill	ND 353547
Berriedale	ND 121224
Braal	ND 136600
Brims	ND 043710
Brough	ND 228741
Buchollie	ND 382658
Dirlot	ND 126487
Dounreay	ND 983670
Dunbeath	ND 158283
Forse	ND 224338
Freswick	ND 376671
Girnigoe	ND 378549
Gunn	ND 308386
Haimer	ND 142672
Halberry	ND 302378
Keiss	ND 357616
Knockinnon	ND 181315
Latheron	ND 199334
Loch More	ND 083461
Mestag	ND 340764
Mey	ND 289739
Oldwick	ND 370489
Scrabster	ND 107692
Thurso East	ND 124689
Thurso (Ormlie)	ND 112681

CHAPTER 13

BUILDINGS IN TOWN AND COUNTRY; THE 18TH AND 19th CENTURIES

Castles and the Baronial Revival

By mid-18th century the medieval castle was outdated, for it was usually sited on an exposed headland, ideal for defence but not necessarily for domestic comfort. Increased wealth after the Union and improved communications generated a desire among the well-to-do for better and more fashionable housing. At Keiss (Plate 27) the early castle on the cliff edge was deserted in favour of a symmetrically-fronted mansion in 1755, its predecessor soon fulfilling the equally fashionable role of romantic ruin. At Brims the c. 1600 tower house was extended two centuries later by the addition of a simple two-storey house, the complex eventually sliding down the social scale to serve as a farmhouse. It is now abandoned as a dwellinghouse but remains the centre-piece of a working farm, surrounded by fields enclosed by excellent dry stone dykes, another stage in the continuous occupation of a site whose built landscape includes a ruined medieval chapel.

Though the castle passed out of fashion as a home in 18th century Caithness, the castellated style soon re-emerged as the chunky turretted mausoleum of Harald's Tower, erected c. 1780 by Sir John Sinclair as a picturesque folly on a site near Thurso where Harald, Earl of Caithness, was reputed to have died in the battle of Clairdon (1196). By the 1850's the baronial revival was in full swing and together with the tartan, the clan and all things Highland, the castle returned to fashion. The 18th century fashionable symmetry of 'new' Keiss Castle was hidden behind an array of turrets, bartizans and crenellations. David Bryce, an Edinburgh architect with an extensive country house practice, who was a well-known exponent of this architectural style, designed the additions to Keiss in 1860, as he had earlier at Ackergill (1851-52) and continued to do so at Latheronwheel House and Stirkoke. His nephew John followed in the same vein with substantial alterations to Dunbeath Castle in 1881, even re-using his uncle's characteristic hoodmoulding over the new principal entrance, flanked by arrow slits and gun loops.

Buildings in this style were also designed by local architects; David Smith's drill hall (1873, and now the Masonic Hall) in Thurso strikes a suitable military note. Thurso Castle is only a gaunt skeleton, but its arched gateway and attendant gate lodge (Plate 28) indicate its former baronial exuberance, with heavy cable moulding, exaggerated corbelling and spiky cusping. The design may have been the work of Donald Leed of Thurso, the estate architect, who was probably also responsible for Lochdhu, a splendid shooting lodge (dating from about 1870) sited on an isolated grouse moor near Altnabreac.

Lairds' houses and mansions

The more substantial landowners retained their ancestral homes, albeit enlarged, altered and updated, but by mid-18th century younger sons and minor landowners were building better houses for themselves than they had formerly been able to enjoy. Improved agriculture and security of tenure gave rise, as elsewhere in Scotland, to a growth of medium and small-sized 'lairds' houses'. Forse House (formerly Nottingham House) described by the Rev. Alexander Pope, the minister of Reay, as 'being an elegant new house' in 1774, is among the larger of these in Caithness, three storeys in height and with a five-windowed symmetrical frontage. Similar, if slightly smaller, are Dale House and Westfield (both in Halkirk parish), Hempriggs and Bilbster (Wick parish). Smaller and with characteristic centre wallhead gablet (a feature not confined to Caithness) are Sandside (dated 1751 but with substantial later additions), and Watten Mains (Plate 29) dated 1763, and Swiney, Gilvoan and Pentland House, 1770, the former Thurso parish manse. All these have regular three or five window fronts with centre entrances; the wallhead gablet is sometimes shaped and decorated with scroll screwputts, capped with an apex chimney stack and may carry a monogrammed datestone. The rubble is sometimes harled, the roof is of graded local stone and internally some have a 'scale and plat' staircase which rises in two flights from ground to first floor, separated by a spine wall.

Simpler, two-storey, three, four and five-bay houses still abound in town and country, indicating the success of improved farming and trade. Ulbster Mains, home of the Sinclairs of Ulbster and the famous Sir John Sinclair, founder and editor of *The Statistical Account* for Scotland in the 1790's, incorporates a fine 17th century chimney mantel from an earlier dwelling; Tannach, West Canisbay and Canisbay Old Manse are but a few of this type, a pattern that continued to be part of the local building tradition well into the 19th century.

Late 18th century Skinnet farmhouse is a charming and unusual essay in rural classicism, the advanced centre pedimented bay matched by similar detailing fronting the lower flanking wings. Either patron or builder recognised the 'Classical Language of Architecture'[1] and applied the simplest of this vocabulary to a plain house with great success. The long rear catslide roof is also unusual.

Olrig House, Castletown, is an architecturally conscious version of these regularly proportioned houses. The three-windowed ashlar (tooled masonry) facade is defined by panelled pilasters and the entrance dignified by a portico. The house, dating from 1830-40, incorporates both earlier and later additions at the rear including an interesting range of service buildings. The idiosyncratic later 19th century Arts and Crafts gate lodge is probably the work of Sir James Gowans of Edinburgh.

Cottages and small farms

The single-storey cottages are very much a feature of the rural Caithness landscape; superficially they resemble one another but closer examination reveals geographical variations, particularly in the south, in Latheron parish and parts of Wick parish. Here the distinctive type is a gable ended and of linear plan form, originally combining domestic and non-domestic accommodation under the single roof, sometimes with a surrounding scatter of ancillary buildings, barn, stable and the like (Plates 33, 44). Some are constructed on sloping sites, the byre at the lower end to facilitate drainage, domestic quarters at the upper part, identified by ridge or end chimney stacks. Many of these dwellings were cruck-framed, the weight of the heavy thatched roof carried by pairs of wooden couples or crucks and transmitted by them directly to the foundations, the rubble walls virtually non-load bearing. Shortage of long lengths of timber necessitated that these cruck trusses were made up of short pieces of wood linked together as exemplified by the tortuously jointed cruck frames in the Laidhay barn. These buildings were thatched and had characteristic rounded ridges; the thatch was held down by a row of stone weights, the 'benlin stanes.' Gables were often of turf, sometimes laid in a herring-bone formation which compacted well.

Besides byre and stable, the barn was also included within the linear structure, at times, with a bowed gable incorporating a grain drying kiln, the damp northern climate requiring that corn be dried before grinding. Barns are also identified by their opposing doors, providing a controllable draught for winnowing, separating the chaff from the grain.

The slightly later, but more general cottage type is of three bays, with a centre entrance flanked by windows, the two-room plan augmented by a small rear chamber. Later 19th century cottages, particularly in the north, have a small gablet above the centre entrance. Slate roofs are more common in the north, for the quarries were sited there.

Besides housing crofters and small farmers, these simple single-storey cottages were home to fishermen, quarriers and those engaged in other trades.

Farm buildings

The earliest surviving farm buildings in Caithness are the dovecotes as they are in other grain growing areas of Scotland. These small buildings, of various shapes and sizes, were the prerogative of the landowner; they were a 'battery' for breeding pigeons for food, the young squabs or 'peesers' furnishing fresh meat early in the spring before lambs and other beasts were ready for slaughter. The circular, tapering 'beehive' type, as at Freswick and Dale House, date from around 1600; two-storey square cotes are at Stemster and on the island of Stroma (dated 1677) and there are mid 18th century 'lecterns,' lean-to buildings with single pitch roofs, at Dunbeath, Forse and Ackergill. They are all lined with stone nesting boxes. However, at Ackergill, there is a pair of very large lecterns in front of the castle; that at the east has 1800 boxes, while its counterpart to the west has none. The latter is fitted with a small mural fireplace and flue, and may have been a hen-house, which was occasionally heated to encourage egg laying. At Canisbay Old Manse the hen boxes are built into the chimney gable of the 'service' cottage, exploiting the domestic heat source!

Also at Canisbay Old Manse, the offices include a kiln barn (no kiln survives), stables and in the garden wall there is a series of nicely rounded bee boles, recesses shaped to accommodate circular straw bee skeps.

Large bottle shaped kilns were a feature on the more substantial Caithness farms; 18th century examples abut the farms at Sibster and Hillhead (both Wick parish). At Brabster the gable of the former castle (probably a tower house) has been incorporated into a tall kiln, which stands in front of the remains of a long, cruck-framed barn. At Sandside the corn drying kiln is built within the handsome rectangular mid 18th century barn, its upper floor being reached by a demi-octagonal stair turret built against the end gable. There is also a dairy, an implement shed and bothies; the gardens are enclosed by a series of high, beautifully constructed walls. Incorporated in the angle of one of these garden walls is a small dovecote, intended for the release of pigeons to marksmen standing in the field outside. This sport is now superseded by the catapult 'trap' and the unfortunate birds by clay 'pigeons.'

Other features of the larger Caithness farm steading include series of fine arched cart bays. Elegant segmental-headed or basket-arched openings of varying height front cart sheds in the larger ranges. There are good examples at Lythmore and Calder Mains, to name but two.

Byres, both large and small, are divided by stone slabs set on end, similar to those which enclose many fields, particularly to the north of the county. Roofing of graded stone slates acquires the characteristic brilliant coating of orange algae when located near the sea. Where large rectangular slabs are used on the roof, these are laid from wallhead to ridge in alternate raised and recessed rows; there is a noteworthy example at Biggins (c. 1860) sited by the roadside at Murkle.

Fine meal mills testify to the richness of the arable land in Caithness as well as to the skills of the masons and mill wrights. John O'Groats mill (rebuilt 1901) is the only mill still in use as such. Enough mills, either empty or converted to residential use, survive to form a group that is the finest of its type in the north, possibly the finest in Scotland. Achingale mill, near Watten, has two wheels, the larger to motivate the machinery and the smaller to drive an automatic stoker feeding chaff to the kiln fire. The graded slated roof, swept long and low at the rear, reveals local materials and skills. At Castletown the large mill (Plate 51) is dated 1818 or 1819 (datestone worn); a pair of c. 1800 mills flank the river at Forss, making a striking and picturesque group.

Coastal buildings and harbours

Grain was exported from the rich farmlands of the north; 18th and 19th century storehouses or girnals (Plate 38) stand by the shore at Staxigoe (which preceded Wick as a harbour) and at Ham. The 'old brewery' in Manson's Lane, Thurso, which appears to date from the early 18th century, may have originally been one of these girnals; it is sited close to the river and an early quay. Though a brewery in 1812, its bulk, regular fenestration, crowstepped gables and simple division of internal space suggests this original role.

Flagstones were exported from Thurso and from Castletown, where there were large quarries. At Castletown the small harbour has a wide triangular quay to facilitate the handling of this bulky commodity (Plate 35).

It is, however, with fishing and in particular the 19th century herring fishing, with which Caithness harbours are associated. Whaligoe, on the east coast, is the least convenient and the most extraordinary of these havens (Plate 37). It is a small inlet at the foot of steep cliffs where the boats were hoisted out of the water onto a platform, from where the catch was carried up flights of steps, over three hundred in all, that snake their way up the cliffside. The Rev. Alexander Pope commented of this landing place in 1774 that it was 'surprising . . . a stranger without seeing, would hardly believe.'

The greatest development of the Caithness harbours belongs to the early 19th century. Thomas Telford travelled along the coast in 1790 noting sites worthy of improving, and within the next 50 years good harbours had been constructed at Lybster, Wick, Keiss and Sandside, to name but a few. The development of these harbours has been excellently covered elsewhere[2]; they were built under the patronage of the British Fisheries Society or by local resources. Quays and piers were soundly made, the area exposed to the open sea faced with vertically coursed masonry which minimised the pressure of the lifting swell. A particularly good example is at Sandside where the harbour was built by Major Innes c. 1830. Here, as at Keiss, Dunbeath (Plate 34) and Lybster, there are rectangular two and three storey fishing stores.

Icehouses, connected with salmon rather than herring fishing, are at Dunbeath, Thurso, Keiss, Scrabster, Castletown and Berriedale. These are large semi-subterranean stone vaults with turfed roofs, in which ice was stored for many months and used to keep salmon fresh during transport to urban markets in the south.

The safety of those 'who go down to the sea in ships and occupy their business in great waters' was assisted by the building of lighthouses at Dunnet (1831), Noss Head (1842), Holborn Head (1862), Clyth (1916) and Duncansby Head (1924), all these designed by engineer members of the Stevenson dynasty serving the Commissioners of Northern Lights. Of early lifeboat stations, only that at Ackergill Shore remains, dating from c. 1880. This was built after the particularly tragic shipwreck of the 'Emilie' in 1876 in Sinclair Bay, causing considerable loss of life. The abandoned lifeboat house retains its original red pottery roundels, depicting a lifeboat manned by oarsmen and the initials RNLBI entwined with oak leaves.

At Berriedale, two tall rubble beacons stand one in front of the other on the cliffside, one crenellated and the other with stumpy angle pinnacles. These are leading lights, and if aligned one in front of the other by a boat coming into Berriedale from the sea, guide the craft to the safe channel.

Towns and villages

Thurso is an early settlement, though little evidence of medieval or post-medieval building survives, except the roofless St. Peter's church and the stair turret dated 1687 at 16/18 Shore Street. A fine 17th century chimneypiece has been re-used in the house at 8 Barrock Street (1832). The contrast between the old and new towns of Thurso is noticeable in their planning and layout, the winding High Street of the old town compared with the formal grid pattern of the new town planned by Sir John Sinclair of Ulbster (c. 1800) and constructed in conformity with that design in the ensuing 50 years (Plate 32). Janet Street (c. 1810) faces the river and is lined with elegant houses flanked by lower service wings, each house with a stable backing the rear garden (Plate 45). This street would be a credit to any town or city and may surprise many who visit Thurso from the south. One must recall, however, that at the time of building, Thurso was the principal mainland town on the Pentland Firth and the urban hub of the maritime highway of the north. Campbell Street, with its alternately advanced and recessed three bay houses, is worthy of note; there are seemly rows of dwellings lining the streets, punctuated by public buildings. The large Gothic St. Peter's church (William Burn, 1832) dominates Princes Street and the square in front; the tetrastyle portico of the Miller Academy (W. Scott, 1859) terminates Sinclair Street and the spires of Thurso West church (David Smith, 1859) and St. Andrew's church (J. Russell Mackenzie, 1870) both former Free Churches, rise above the roofscape. The imposing Bank of Scotland (J. M. Dick Peddie, 1897, the former British Linen Bank) graces Olrig Street and Victorian civic pride is reflected in the ornate Gothic facade of the town hall in the High Street (J. Russell Mackenzie, 1870; officially opened in 1871).

Wick, too, has old and new towns, the new-named Pulteneytown designed by Thomas Telford in 1807 for the British Fisheries Society and developed thereafter. The centrepiece of Pulteneytown is Argyle Square, sited above the bay, enclosed by rectangular two-storey houses. Breadalbane Crescent (1861) is a restrained, almost austere terrace, the houses faced with long sections of dark tooled stone, many with paved curing yards and stable ranges to the rear. The harbour frontage was filled with similar yards and cooperages, all now utilised for other purposes; one in Bank Row is the Wick Heritage Centre, housing a fine fisheries museum. As with the arched cart bays in the farm steadings, the masonry arches framing the entrances to this building and in the centre courtyard are of excellent quality workmanship with regular coursing and keystones.

The expansion of Wick and its commercial growth during the 19th century is reflected in her public and banking architecture, mostly concentrated in Bridge Street and High Street. The Italianate town hall (1828) is matched in style by the Sheriff Court (David Rhind, 1862-6, replacing an earlier court house). The Arts and Crafts style Carnegie Library in Sinclair Terrace graces its corner site with dignity (Leadbetter and Fairley, 1895–8) while the Post Office just off the High Street in Market Place (W. T. Oldrieve, 1912) exemplifies the Scottish vernacular revival. The earliest bank is the classical Royal Bank of Scotland (c. 1830) fronting the river; this is followed by the Venetian Renaissance Clydesdale (J. Russell Mackenzie, 1875, former Aberdeen Town and County Bank) with ornate pilastered street frontage embellished with carving, the classical Aberdeen granite faced former North of Scotland Bank (A. Marshall Mackenzie, 1885, now Woolworths) and the

BUILDINGS IN TOWN AND COUNTRY

reconstructed Bank of Scotland (John Keppie and Henderson, 1935, the former British Linen Bank).

Wick Parish church was re-built on the site of an earlier building (part of which was subsequently incorporated in a burial enclosure), to a design by John Henry of Edinburgh (1820–30). Other churches of note in Wick are the Wick Martyrs' Memorial Church (1839) and the Roman Catholic church of St. Joachim (1835). This last was erected in gratitude to Father Walter Lovi, parish priest at Keith and Braemar, who ministered to the itinerant fishermen and female herring gutters crowding into Wick during the herring fishing season, in special recognition of his services to his flock during a cholera epidemic earlier in the decade. Correspondence between Bishop James Kyle of the Northern District and Father Walter Lovi reveals that the latter and his priestly colleagues travelled north as and when required; it also notes that Lovi was his own fund raiser and master-of-works for his chapel at Wick which was built to a design by William Robertson, an architect in Elgin.

Villages and small towns grew up near harbours as fishing expanded. The broad main street of Lybster is lined with substantial two-storey houses built during the first half of the 19th century as the harbour in the bay below became busier and generated more work for people, curing, gutting and other allied activities. In the main street of the village stands the now disused St. Mary's church (1836), a chapel of ease for the use of worshippers for whom Latheron parish church was too far distant. This church is a plain rectangular building, its plainness relieved by simple Gothic windows with delicate intersecting tracery in the upper lights of the sashes and a bellcote at the gable apex.

Rural Churches

The vast size of many Highland parishes and the difficulty posed by distance to parishioners wishing to attend public worship at Latheron and many other places, gave rise to the financing and building of relief churches by Parliament in the 1820's. Making use of the administrative framework already existing within the Parliamentary Commission for Highland Roads and Bridges and the services of the principal engineer and architect to that Commission, Thomas Telford, 42 churches with their manses were constructed in outlying areas. Two of these are in Caithness: at Berriedale, where the landowner, James Horne of Langwell, gave the land for church and manse in 1826, his generosity perpetuated on an inscribed plaque set above the church door, and at Keiss. Both churches are of standard Telford T-Plan 'Parliamentary' design, though both have suffered later alterations and internal re-casting. Both have manses, also of a standard Telford pattern.

On the Causeymire, in a lonely moorland place where the

boundaries of Wick, Watten and Latheron meet, there is a small T-plan church, now quite abandoned. Over the door a plaque proclaims that it was 'Built by Superscription Anno Domini 1842.' It too was intended to serve scattered crofters who would seldom have been able to attend their respective parish churches.

A further burst of ecclesiastical building occurred after the 'Disruption' of 1843, when the Free Church separated from the 'Auld Kirk.' It is difficult in the late 1980's to appreciate the feelings generated by this break-away movement, the division of the parish, the dispossession of the minister who 'came out' and of his homeless family who had to leave their manse. Enormous efforts were made to construct new churches and manses, the size of many rural Caithness Free churches indicate the numerical strength of their following. Reay Free Church, at Achimenach near Shebster (Plate 36) built well away from the village centre but in mid 19th century surrounded by a greater population than now, is a large double gabled, double aisled church of a style peculiar to Caithness (see also old Halkirk Free Church). It was finished in 1844, within a year of the congregation 'coming out,' with manse and school to complete the complex. At Dunnet, another substantial double aisled Free Church was also completed by 1844, but the congregation could only afford a felt roof. However, by 1849, just five years later, the roof had been slated.

The most characteristic and individual of the Caithness churches are the simple, whitewashed rubble stone parish churches at Reay, Dunnet (Plate 19) and Canisbay (Plate 22) on the north coast, each with a tower serving as a beacon for seamen and the faithful alike. At Reay the church was built on its present situation in 1739, moved from a earlier site identified by the small burial ground in the centre of the village. It was remodelled in 1909 and 1933, but its original character has not been greatly changed, even by the insertion (1933) of a large Gothic window in the west gable. Its plain square tower is crowned with a slated pyramidal roof; inside it has retained the original 1739 panelled pulpit in its traditional position in the centre of the south wall and there is still a long central communion table.

Dunnet and Canisbay are both of medieval origin with later additions. Both have saddle back roofs to their squat towers — at Canisbay crowned with apex ball finials and dated 1720; both have had additions and alterations over the years, but have retained their Presbyterian layout grouped around the central pulpit. Despite, the addition of a north aisle at Dunnet in 1837 to accommodate the increased congregation, Timothy Pont (minister from 1601–10 but better known as one of Scotland's earliest cartographers) would undoubtedly recognise his former charge.

[1] Summerson, John, *The Classical Language of Architecture* (London, 1963).
[2] Dunlop, Jean, 'Pulteneytown and the Planned Villages of Caithness,' ed. John R. Baldwin, *Caithness, a Cultural Crossroads* (Edinburgh, 1982), pp. 130–60.

CHAPTER 14

COMMUNICATIONS

Previous chapters have shown that there has been a steady flow of people, goods and ideas in and out of the county since prehistoric times. Geographical features like hill passes, river crossings and soft 'dubh lochs', have moulded a network of routes which later travellers have continued to use with little variation. Telford's map, for example, showed two older tracks intertwined with his own road line, all the way from the Ord to Wick.

Tracks and Roads

Early tracks were little better than wear marks on the ground; yet, they were main highways of their day and should not be dismissed too lightly. Where possible they followed the firmer high ground, while over wet moorland the easiest route was along the well-drained banks of the burns. When boggy areas could not be avoided causeways were laid. One to the south of Spittal is thought to have been made by Cromwell's soldiers (c. 1650). This spot was already known as 'The Myre Calsay,' so it would appear that the troopers were repairing or extending an existing feature. Turf roads were also recorded in Canisbay in 1725, where:
"there is scarce any travelling by horse except by bridges made of turf and heath, which must be changed once in two or three years."
About the same time, the road over the Ord:
"by the pains of Sir James Sinclair of Dunbeath, is made so broad, that three horses can conveniently ride it abreast."
The best example of such a track ran south-west from Thurso towards Kinbrace. Intermittent traces of it can still be found on the ground and these can be joined together using J. Thomson's map of 1822, which recorded the track when it was still being used as a drove road. There are indications that part of the network could be of a medieval date, as many of the early chapel sites lie at cross-roads or fords along the way.
Perhaps the most comprehensive picture of these early roads is to be gleaned from Bishop Forbes' journey round the county in 1762. He rode

"the Water of Helmsdale by a very rough ford" and thought that the route over the Ord was "one of the finest roads in the world, being so broad, yt. in most places two Coaches might pass one another." He paused at Ousdale Inn to take tea and after a few miles of rough road, crossed the Berriedale and the Dunbeath Waters by very rough fords. To negotiate the Causey-Mire he changed guides and still got bogged down in the soft ground. The party then revived themselves with a dram at Achkeepster Inn before pressing on to ride "the water of Thurso by one of the best Fords close to the town." When the Bishop left Thurso he was accompanied by Mr and Mrs Campbell in a two-wheeled chaise and they travelled over natural carpet all the way to Lochend in Dunnet. The same companions escorted him to Lyth "Still in good Road" but from Lyth to the Castle of Mey he required a guide through the moss although there was a "very pleasant and firm road" near the Castle. From John O'Groats the journey to Freswick was "from moss to moss." The old road from Freswick to Keiss followed the cliff top and can still be found in places. From there the Bishop had an easy journey over the sandy links to Wick via Noss Head. He set out southwards from Wick "once more to travel through Mosses."

In the succeeding years many miles of roads were lined out by the Statute Labour force, which was reluctantly manned by landowners and tenants legally obliged to work for six days each year. The minister of Watten in 1792 wrote, "our roads . . . have been lined out . . . by the statute labour. By these means we have a more plain and direct tract, during the dry season of the year . . . for travellers, as well as riders and carts. But . . . they become so soft after rain . . . that in many places during winter and spring the best horses are not fit to drag a cart with safety."

An example of this type of "lined out" road can be found on the moorland to the south of the Stone Lud in the parish of Bower (ND 220614). It was part of the old Thurso to Wick road (c. 1828) and consists of two parallel ditches about 6 m (20 ft) apart; with an unimproved surface between them. About 1772 Sir John Sinclair assembled some 1200 men and made up the road from Latheron to Braehungie. A few years later with a similar number of labourers he improved a stretch of road to the south of Spittal. The experience led Sir John, in 1793, to arrange for the Statute Labour service to be commuted to an annual monetary payment. This raised about £550 per annum at a time when a mile of road could be laid for £50 to £60 and a single arch bridge could be built for between £50 and £100. Most of this money was spent on the main routes, much to the annoyance of landlords and tenantry of the more remote districts who received little in return for the compulsory payments.

In contrast to roadmaking, bridges required the services of skilled masons and were relatively expensive to build. Special, one-off, taxes were levied to finance their construction. The oldest bridge in the county, according to local tradition, is the single-arch stone bridge at the John O'Groats meal mill, said to have been erected by Cromwellian soldiers c. 1650. Wick certainly had a wooden bridge as early as 1665 and there may have been other wooden bridges which have disappeared without trace. The bridge in front of Freswick House was already in use when it received a passing mention in 1725 and this makes it the oldest dateable bridge in the county. The same writer recorded a bridge at the junction of the Langwell and Berriedale rivers, which had gone by the time Bishop Forbes crossed the rivers in 1762.

With some help from the local gentry, building continued steadily throughout the county: a three-arch bridge at Halkirk in 1731 (Plate 49) and two single arches at Gills in 1755. The bridge at Wick was re-built in 1776, with wooden planks on eleven pillars, while at the east end of Loch Watten the name Bridgend appears on a map of the same date. On the river Forss, the old bridge (Plate 42) was erected a few years before 1791 and the earliest bridge over the Reisgill burn is probably of a similar age. Because of the width of the river and the strength of the flash floods, Thurso had to wait until 1800 before the first road bridge was built near the town. Latheronwheel harbour bridge could not have been many years old when it was by-passed by Telford's Parliamentary road.

Between 1811 and 1818 Telford laid a continuous strip of high quality road, bridging every stream and river from the Ord to Wick and on to Thurso via Watten. This was the final section of his great Parliamentary road from Inverness to the Pentland Firth and is still the backbone of the modern A9. Until 1874 tolls were collected for the upkeep of the road and slightly modified Toll Houses can be found at Thurso and Watten. As soon as the road was finished the stagecoach run was extended to Thurso. It replaced the mail riders and runners who had provided a postal service since at least 1706. The first self-propelled vehicle to use the road was the Earl of Caithness' three-wheeled steam carriage which made the journey from Inverness to Wick in November 1860.

The County Authorities were quick to follow Telford's example and before 1840 many of the 'County' roads had been completed, or were well underway, laying the foundation to the excellent road system of the present day.

Seaways

Long before the Viking era, Roman and other Dark Age voyages had been recorded in these northern waters, but it was not until 1540 that Alexander Lindsay compiled his 'Rutter' which gave concise instructions to mariners sailing round the coast. Of the currents in the Pentland Firth he noted:

"In the middes of Pethland Fyrth beuixt Dungisbe and Orknay ther is a great daunger causit by neppe tydis whiche is called the Boir. To avoid the daunger ye sall mak your cours from Dungisbe northwest till you come north to est from Stroma. At the north end of Stroma is a greater daunger called the Swelle which is the meeting of iiii or v contrary tides with great circulationne of water causing a deip hurlepoole in the middes, dangerous for all shipps both great and small."

Farm produce generated considerable coastal traffic. Thomas Tucker noted in 1655 that Thurso and Wick sent a good store of beef, hides and tallow to the coast. In addition, large quantities (1000 tons in 1695) of grain and meal which had been collected as rent, were exported. Local ships were not used in this trade, for Tucker also reported that Thurso, at this time, had only one vessel of 30 tons, while Wick had apparently none.

About 1744 the chart of the north coast was greatly improved by Alexander Bryce who surveyed the coastline and added copious notes on the harbours and hazards along the way. For sailing between the mainland and Stroma, he said:

"To clear the Men of Mey steer midway between St. John's Head and Stroma, till you can see the roof of Mey Castle when thus far you're out of all danger and may pursue your westward course."

On the currents in the middle of the Firth he was even more optimistic,

"If ship or boat should fail and not be able to get out for want of wind, they may safely allow themselves to be carried up and down till the strength of the tide be spent,"

and

"a stranger wou'd think it impossible to escape being dashed against a Rock, yet these tides will shoot you off almost every rock and Head in the Pentland firth."

Nevertheless, most sailing ships' captains preferred to take on someone with knowledge of this notorious stretch of water. Skilled pilots could be found at Sandside, Brims, Stroma, Freswick and Aukengill. If the weather was bad or the ship was short-handed these pilots were occasionally carried to distant ports and not infrequently used the name of their destination as a byname for the remainder of their lives.

Trade increased greatly from the 1780s to 1860. In addition to agricultural produce, cured herring, kelp and flagstone were all exported in trading smacks and schooners, which returned with salt, coal, timber and small goods. In the 18th century large numbers of young unbroken horses were sent annually from Reay to Orkney and a corresponding number of mature beasts were returned to Skarfskerry and Dunnet.

Skarfskerry Ferry House was drawn by the illustrator William Daniell in 1818 as he waited to cross to South Walls. The ferry terminal in Caithness has changed from time to time. John O'Groats traditionally had a ferry in the 16th century and it was in nearby Sannick Bay that Montrose landed his ill-fated army on 2nd April 1650. However, early maps (1776) show the road terminating at Huna and this was certainly the initial mail route to Orkney. In 1856 the mail contract was taken by the first steam ferry which ran from Stromness to Scrabster. The vessel, appropriately christened the 'Royal Mail', had been built by John Stanger in Stromness and engined on the Tyne. The combination of a powered ferry connecting with the stagecoach, and latterly the railway, quickly established Scrabster/Stromness as the principal crossing of the Firth.

Between 1971 and 1973 the speedboat 'Pentland Atom' re-established a passenger ferry at John O'Groats. She was followed by the larger 'Pentland Spray', superceded in 1976 by the 'Souters Lass,' which ran until 1987 when the 'Pentland Venture' took over.

Steam power had first appeared in 1828 when the 'Velocity' made a trial visit to Wick. She was followed by the 'SS Sovereign' (Plate 56) running weekly from Leith to Aberdeen, Wick, Kirkwall and Lerwick during the summer of 1836. These summer visits were quickly extended throughout the year. A number of steamers made seasonal runs carrying migrant labourers and supplies for the fishing fleet. The connections established at this time with Stornoway and other west coast ports were continued into the 1930s by small trading vessels like the 'Castle Varich,' the 'Dunvedin' and the 'Balone Castle.' They plied from Thurso to villages along the north coast and occasionally as far as Ullapool carrying bulky or heavy items, in this pre-lorry era. Indeed, coal was delivered regularly by the 'Argentum' to small harbours such as Stroma and Reay as well as Scrabster, Thurso and Wick.

Until just before the Second World War, the schooner 'Viking' and the fore and aft rigged 'Althea,' among others, continued a long-established link with Scandinavia, delivering timber from Sundsvall in Sweden to the wood-yards of Wick and Thurso.

Railways

The Caithness Railway Act of 1866 proposed a railway line from Wick to Thurso via Castletown, to be followed at a later date with a second line which would connect with the Sutherland Railway. The suggestion raised considerable debate but little financial support.

By 1870 the Sutherland railway had reached Helmsdale and, in Caithness, most people envisaged that it would continue up the east coast to Wick. However, the railway engineers quickly realised that there was no easy way round the Ord. As early as 1864 Joseph Mitchell had proposed the present inland route up the river Helmsdale and across the moor towards Halkirk with branch lines to Wick and Thurso. Thurso gained substantially more than Wick from this arrangement which gave both towns equal rail access to southern markets whereas, up to that point, Wick had the advantage of easier sea communications. Throughout the construction period Wick's enthusiasm for the railway remained lukewarm.

The Duke of Sutherland, with help from Sir Tollemache Sinclair and the Highland Railway, pushed through his own bill for a Sutherland and Caithness Railway. This encroached on the existing Caithness Railway Act but the Duke's proposal won the necessary support. The new company had a proposed capital of £360,000 and decided on a three-pronged attack on the project. The Sutherland railway was extended from Helmsdale to the county border. From Thurso the line was pushed southwards so that construction material could be delivered easily to the northern end of the moorland section where there were no access roads. At the same time the line from Wick to the junction was constructed. Work commenced in March 1872 and the completed railway was officially opened when the first trains left simultaneously from Wick and Thurso at 5.10 a.m. on 28th July, 1874. A few days after opening, the early morning train ran into a rock fall near Altnabreac. The engine and first two coaches were derailed but fortunately no one was hurt. Initially, there were two trains north and south each day and in addition there was a morning, afternoon and evening train making the round trip Thurso, Wick, Thurso.

In 1877 the Highland Railway expanded into the ferry business running the screw steamer 'John O'Groat' from Scrabster to Orkney until 1881, when the ship was sold. Refrigerator railcars were introduced in 1883 to transport fish to London.

When Scapa Flow was first identified as a major fleet anchorage, there were proposals to extend the railway to Gills Bay to take advantage of the shorter sea crossing to Orkney, but the idea was stillborn. The only branch line to be built was the Wick to Lybster light railway which opened in 1903 to serve the fishing and farming communities on the east coast. It was closed in 1944 as a war-time economy measure and never re-opened.

With the decline of the fishing and flagstone industries, passengers have become more important. Diesel engines made their appearance in 1958 and recent proposals to introduce 'Sprinters' will reduce the journey time to Inverness to 3½ hours. This substantial reduction on the original 7½ hours has been achieved by closing many stations and making others request stops. Unmanned level crossings and direct radio contact with the train have also streamlined the system.

Airways

Caithness was introduced to commercial flying by Captain Fresson during a 'barn-storming' trip in 1931 when he piloted his Avro G-EBGZ with two fare-paying passengers from Wick to Kirkwall. This historic flight across the Firth on 22nd August was followed by three more from Wick and ten days later by one from Thurso. The demand for such a service inspired Fresson to found Highland Airways in 1933. Using the Longman, Inverness, as his headquarters he flew daily return trips to Wideford, Kirkwall, calling at Hillhead, Wick, en route. Initially, a round flight was also made between Kirkwall and Thurso. However, due to the poor condition of the landing field near Scrabster this flight was suspended after a few weeks. The main route proved popular and the original four-passenger Monospar was replaced by an eight-seater Dragon. From 8th May until 16th September, 1067 passengers used the service, most of them making the full journey from Inverness to Kirkwall. On the 2nd May, 1934, Highland Airways made a double crossing of the Firth with 15 members of a Wick Select Football team, which became the first team in the British Isles to fly to an away game. Highland Airways notched up another British first on 29th May, 1934, when they were contracted by the Post Office to convey first class mail without surcharge to the public.

The success of Highland Airways led Mr E. L. Gandar Dower of Aberdeen Airways (later Allied Airways Ltd.) to introduce his own regular service (Plate 57) from Dyce to Kirkwall in May 1934, calling at Wick and Thurso (Clairdon). Bitter competition continued between the two companies until 1939 when a licensing court allocated specific routes to each company.

Wick airfield was enlarged during the Second World War and is now the main civilian airport. Wartime airfields were also constructed at Skitten, Castletown, Brims and Dounreay. Dounreay is presently used by the UKAEA for regular charter flights and both Dounreay and Castletown have been used for occasional Air Ambulance emergencies.

Air transport was nationalised in 1945 and both Highland Airways and Allied Airways were absorbed into British European Airways. For a time larger planes were introduced but they proved to be uneconomic on the short northern flights and it became necessary to allow smaller companies like Air Écosse and the present Loganair to operate feeder lines. Air links have been of benefit to the business community but present pricing policies discourage the general public from using the service.

CHAPTER 15

FAMOUS PEOPLE

Many born in Caithness have by their endeavours made their mark in the far corners of the world; conversely, others have come to the county and achieved considerable distinction. The early part of this chapter summarises in chronological order some of the achievements of the eminent people associated in some way with Caithness. The second part gives brief comments on those born in the county who have made contributions worthy of note. Space demands that only a limited biographical selection can be made.

GILBERT MORAY, BISHOP OF CAITHNESS

Gilbert, who was subsequently sanctified, was one of the most outstanding men in the medieval church in Scotland. Born in the late 12th century, he died on the 1st April, 1245.

In the year 1222 he became bishop-designate of Caithness, with the bishopric seat at Halkirk. Under his rule the cathedral church was founded in Dornoch, following the foul murder of Bishop Adam at Braal, Halkirk.

JAN DE GROT

From Jan de Grot, a Dutchman given grants of land in northern Caithness in the 15th century, the place name John O'Groats is derived.

Legend relates that each year Jan had a reunion with his seven sons; during one of these family gatherings the sons quarrelled about who should have precedence at the table. The diplomatic Jan is said to have resolved the dispute by building an eight-sided room which had an eight-sided table.

Tradition has it that the flagpole near John O'Groats hotel marks the site of the Grot family house. Excavations made at the site many years ago revealed a rectangular building, but no octagonal structure was found. However, Aeneas Bayne, writing in 1735, claimed that the eight-sided table had been in existence "until quite recently".

Inside Canisbay church a red slab of sandstone commemorates the Grot family (Plate 12).

TIMOTHY PONT

In the year 1654 the Dutchman Blaeu published his atlas of Scotland, leaving to us an extremely detailed record of the settlement pattern of the country in the late 16th and early 17th centuries. In compiling the atlas, Blaeu relied upon manuscript maps drawn up by Scottish cartographers, among them Timothy Pont (born c. 1560), who was appointed the minister of Dunnet church in 1601. About the same time his brother Zachary was appointed minister at Bower.

Pont, who was an accomplished mathematician and cartographer, was the first to compile an atlas of Scotland, a task he undertook with great diligence, surveying the equivalent of two counties each summer. The originals of his maps are preserved in the National Library, Edinburgh.

RICHARD OSWALD

Richard Oswald, the son of the minister at Dunnet, was born in the parish of Thurso in 1704 and died in 1784. By marrying Mary Ramsay he acquired large estates in North America and the West Indies and because of this connection he was consulted by the British government during its war with the Colonies.

In the published correspondence of Lord Shelburne there is an account of his employment of Richard Oswald to negotiate peace on behalf of Britain with the rebellious Colonies. At that time Oswald was described as a "well-known Scot's merchant in London". The ensuing negotiations were brilliantly conducted by Oswald and concluded with his signing the peace treaty with Benjamin Franklin.

ALEXANDER POPE

Alexander Pope (1706-82), a son of the minister of Loth, Sutherland, became one of many distinguished ministers in Caithness. He was inducted into Reay church in 1734.

Physically a strong man, he was also blessed with enormous energy, an excellent mind and a formidable tongue. To deal with his unruly parishioners Pope supplemented his normally effective tongue with a stout cudgel which he is known to have wielded against those having a dram in the local inn instead of listening to his sermon in the church. A contemporary described him as a man who had "turned a barren wilderness into a fruitful field".

He will also be remembered as the translator from Latin into English of Torfaeus' *Ancient History of Orkney, Caithness and the North*.

FAMOUS PEOPLE

MAJOR-GENERAL AUSTEN ST. CLAIR

He was born in Thurso about the year 1734 and as a young man emigrated to the American colonies where he enlisted in the army. He quickly gained promotion and carried the regimental colours under General Wolfe's command at the battle on the Plains of Abraham.

The culmination of a brilliant military career was his appointment as the trusted advisor of General George Washington. On retirement from the army he achieved distinction in civilian life, being elected President of Congress and Governor of the North-West Territories.

JOHN MORRISON

John Morrison, D. D., was a native of Aberdeenshire who spent much of his life in Caithness, initially as a teacher in schools in Greenland, Dunnet, Halkirk and Thurso and finally as a minister in Canisbay until his death in 1798. He is remembered as the author of some lovely paraphrases, namely, numbers 19, 21, 27, 28, 29, 30 and 35.

He was a diligent collector of local history and legend, some of which was later incorporated in J. T. Calder's publications.

SIR JOHN SINCLAIR

John Sinclair was born in Thurso castle on the 10th May 1754. He was educated at the Universities of Edinburgh, Glasgow and Oxford before being elected Member of Parliament for Caithness in 1780. Within six years the Prime Minister, Pitt, had rewarded him with a baronetcy for his political services.

As President of the Highland Society he took a considerable interest in the relative qualities of sheep and their wool. By his writings and speeches he was an important catalyst to agricultural improvement in his own county and elsewhere in Scotland. Of all his literary involvements the most celebrated was the *First Statistical Account of Scotland,* a wide-ranging parish by parish description of the country for which historians will always be profoundly grateful. As a reward for his many achievements he was made the first President of the Board of Agriculture and, subsequently, a Privy Councillor.

He raised a regiment of 600 men, known as the Rothesay and Caithness Fencibles, of which he was colonel. A statue in Sir John Square (renamed in his honour), Thurso, shows him in the uniform of his regiment (Plate 54). Sir John Square was the focal point of the new town of Thurso which he planned. Another of his planned settlements was Halkirk.

His long life ended on 21st December 1835. A contemporary called him "the most indefatigable man in Britain" and many would acclaim him as the most distinguished son of Caithness.

JAMES BREMNER

James Bremner, eminent harbour builder, ship raiser, ship builder and ingenious inventor, was born at Stain, Keiss on the 25th September 1784 and died at Wick on the 12th August 1856.

He received an apprenticeship in a Greenock shipyard and after making two trans-Atlantic crossings he returned to Wick to establish his own shipbuilding business. During the next 50 years he constructed over 50 vessels as well as designing and building many harbours around the Moray Firth coast.

James Bremner also showed remarkable engineering expertise and ingenuity in the raising of 236 shipwrecks, his greatest triumph being the recovery of S. S. Great Britain which had run aground in Ireland. For his many important papers on wreck-raising and harbour construction he was awarded the Telford medal.

ALEXANDER BAIN

One of a family of thirteen, Alexander Bain was born at Houstry, Dunn, near Watten. Noticing that he had an unusual interest in clocks, his father arranged an apprenticeship for him with a watchmaker in Stafford Place, Wick. To the family's horror, he broke his apprenticeship and went to Edinburgh where he worked for some time before going to London in 1837. There he attended lectures on electricity and wondered how he could apply this miraculous new power in practical ways. He was one of the first, if not the first, to devise a method whereby a number of clocks could be worked electrically from a standard time piece. He was also among the leaders in developing the first printing telegraph. In 1843 came his most important invention, the chemical telegraph, which gave Bain the credit of being the pioneer of high-speed telegraphy.

Bain received some £7000 for his many patents, but the money was frittered away on litigation. In recognition of his outstanding scientific contributions he was awarded a grant by the Royal Society as well as a government pension of £80 a year.

A memorial commemorating Alexander Bain has been erected at Watten just outside the community centre; inside is the beautiful clock made by the distinguished inventor, in 1845.

FAMOUS PEOPLE

ROBERT DICK

Robert Dick was born at Tullibody, in Clackmannan-shire in January 1810 or 1811. His step-mother made his life a misery and instead of going on to higher education he was apprenticed to a baker at the age of thirteen. In 1830 he moved to Thurso, where his father had been made Supervisor of Excise, and stayed there for the rest of his life.

The shy baker, who had set up in business in Wilson's Lane (Plate 55), was soon exploring the Caithness countryside, taking a particular interest in the rocks, fossils, glacial deposits, plants and shells. In pursuit of these scientific interests he walked up to 97 km (60 miles) in a day. In 1834 he re-discovered the Northern holy-grass, a plant which had been thought extinct in Britain. He was soon proving text-books wrong about the fossil content of the local rocks and his correspondence with the great Hugh Miller of Cromarty led the stonemason to revise some of his geological interpretations of the Old Red Sandstone. Even Sir Roderick Murchison, Director-General of the Geographical Survey, had to change deductions he had made concerning the Old Red Sandstone sedimentary formations.

Unfortunately, business problems and ailing health meant that he spent his later years in privation and had to sell his precious fossils to exist. Prematurely aged, he died in his mid fifties. The townspeople of Thurso, at last alert to the intellectural stature and achievements of the man, gave him a huge public funeral and erected an obelisk in Thurso churchyard to his memory. His other memorial is the remarkable collection of plants, shells and fossils that he left behind.

JAMES TRAILL

James Traill (see also Chapter 10) was born at the manse of Dunnet in 1758 and died in 1843 at Castlehill House. He attended Marischal College, Aberdeen and studied law at Edinburgh University. In 1788 he became Sheriff-depute of Caithness.

He appears to have been the first landowner in Caithness to institute large-scale agricultural improvements and had plantations established, along with many new buildings, roads and harbours on his land in Olrig parish. James Traill will be best remembered, however, as the man who initiated the flagstone industry. Soon the tiny harbour he built at Castlehill was busy with ships carrying flagstone not only to many parts of Britain but to the far corners of the world.

ALEXANDER HENRY RHIND

Henry Rhind, the son of a well-known banker and proprietor of Sibster farm, Josiah Rhind, was born in Wick on the 26th July 1833. He was tutored in Wick by the future professor of Oriental languages at the University of Aberdeen and at the age of fifteen went to Edinburgh University where he studied natural history and natural philosophy.

In 1851 he began his archaeological investigations by opening up the cairns of Yarrows and, later, a broch at Kettleburn, near Wick.

At the age of twenty evidence of pulmonary weakness was all too apparent and in a search of health he went to Egypt where he began researches in the tombs of Thebes. His health never really recovered, but he did manage to write a variety of papers on antiquarian matters. He died on the 3rd July 1863, still not aged 30. A bright star had shone all too briefly.

His bequests reflected his interests: money was left to found scholarships to Edinburgh University; a large capital sum went to the Society of Antiquaries in Edinburgh and from Sibster estate money was used to found a lectureship in archaeology.

JOHN FINLAYSON (or FINLAISON)

He was born in Thurso in 1783 and died in London in 1860. At the age of fifteen he was removed from school and apprenticed to a "writer" in Thurso. After completing a four year apprenticeship he was appointed factor to Sir Benjamin Dunbar (later Lord Duffus) at Ackergill. After a brief stay, he moved to Edinburgh and soon obtained an appointment in the Admiralty. His administrative achievements led to his appointment in 1821 to the office of Government Actuary. He was also involved, in 1837, with the establishment of the registration of births, deaths and marriages and frequently gave evidence to Royal Commissioners. In 1851 he retired from his position as actuary of the National Debt and Government Calculator.

JAMES T. CALDER

James Traill Calder was born in the parish of Dunnet in 1794 and died in Orkney in 1864. He was a schoolmaster at Canisbay where he was an enthusiastic teacher and poet, publishing his verses in the volume *Poems from John O'Groats*. He is best known for his monumental *Sketch of the Civil and Traditional History of Caithness*, which he concluded with these words: "To the county, I feel naturally a strong attachment. It is the place of my nativity; it is the residence of all my best and dearest friends, and it contains within its bosom the ashes of my kindred."

At the instigation of writer John Horne a statue was raised at Wick in the year 1900 to commemorate the "Historian of Caithness" (Plate 53).

FAMOUS PEOPLE

WILLIAM MILLER

William Miller was born in Thurso in 1838 and died in 1923. After a brilliant university career he went to work in Madras. Within four years his run-down school was taking students to degree level. In 1877 the school became Madras Christian College and Miller was described as, "one of the greatest missionaries Scotland ever sent to India". Many honours were conferred on him and a large crowd gathered to watch the unveiling of a statue to him in Madras in 1901.

WILLIAM SMITH

William Smith was born at Pennyland House, Thurso in 1854 and died in 1914. As a young lad he went to work in Glasgow and entered his uncle's business. His leisure time was devoted to church affairs and he also served with the Lanark Volunteers. Perhaps the combination of military training and deep religious commitment produced the idea to form a "Boys' Brigade".

In 1883 the inaugural meeting was held at North Woodside Hall, Glasgow. After a slow start the movement grew rapidly and spread throughout Britain and overseas. Such was the work involved that Smith gave up his employment to become full-time Brigade Secretary. In 1909 the name of William Smith appeared in the Honours' List, with a knighthood for his services to youth.

GENERAL HORNE

Henry Sinclair Horne was born in 1861 and died in 1928. He took up a military career at which he was brilliantly successful. In 1914 he left for France as a Brigadier-General earning a reputation as a resourceful commander. In 1915 Lord Kitchener selected Horne to accompany him to the Near East as his chief military adviser.

In September 1916 General Horne was appointed to the command of the First Army in France. During an advance he used his troops in a dual role: covering the forward movement of his infantry and dealing with hostilities along the flank. This artillery strategy became known as the "creeping barrage".

After the conclusion of hostilities, Horne received the grateful thanks of the nation with a large sum of money (£30,000) and the K.C.M.G.

JOHN HORNE

John Horne, born in Louisburgh, Wick in 1861, became the writer that could most readily be identified with Caithness. He died in 1934.

He set his heart on the Baptist ministry and was for many years a Pastor, but constant poor health caused him to resign and concentrate on writing, chiefly about his homeland.

His many readable publications include *Caithness Originals, A Canny Countryside, Round the Old Home* and *The County of Caithness*, a splendid comprehensive volume which was produced under his editorship in 1907.

In addition to his books he produced a large number of poems (perhaps the best known is "Div Ye Mind") and one act plays.

VISCOUNT THURSO

Archibald Sinclair was born in 1890 and died in 1970. He was educated at Eton and Sandhurst and joined the army in 1910. As a major he was, for a time, second in command to Winston Churchill. On the death of his grandfather in 1912, he succeeded to the baronetcy.

In 1922 he became Member of Parliament for Caithness and Sutherland until his defeat in the 1945 election. During his years in the House of Commons, Sir Archibald held many high offices:

1930-31	Liberal Chief Whip
1931-32	Secretary of State for Scotland
1935-45	Leader of the Parliamentary Liberal Party
1940-45	Secretary of State for Air

In the Honours' List of 1952 Sir Archibald Sinclair became Viscount Sinclair of Ulbster. This honour was the culmination of a long and distinguished political career, a feature of which was his lengthy association, in war and peace, with Winston Churchill.

BRIGADIER JOCK CAMPBELL

"Big Jock" Campbell was born in Thurso in 1894. He was commissioned in 1915 and was awarded the M.C. In the Second World War he was again involved in action, winning a D.S.O. and bar. In 1941 he was awarded the highest military honour the nation can bestow, the Victoria Cross, for "his magnificent example and his utter disregard of personal danger..... His brilliant leadership was the direct cause of the very heavy casualties inflicted on the enemy." Tragically, a month after his decoration he was killed in a motor accident.

FAMOUS PEOPLE

NEIL MILLER GUNN

Neil Gunn was born at Dunbeath in 1891 and died in 1973. He attended the local school where he excelled in English and mathematics. Rather than go to higher education he joined the civil service and eventually became an officer of the customs and excise. Three years after this appointment his first novel *The Grey Coast* appeared in 1926. Five years later came one of his best-loved novels, *Morning Tide*. Other favourites quickly followed: *Butcher's Broom* in 1934, *Highland River* in 1937 and *The Silver Darlings* in 1941. *Highland River*, a highly personal novel, won him the James Tait Black Memorial Prize for Literature.

In the 1980s there has been a marked and welcome revival of interest in Neil Gunn's works; perhaps, at last, he is being given his rightful place among the doyens of Scottish writers.

IAN MACKAY

Ian was born John Mackay in Wick in 1898. He attended the local High School and left it at the age of 14 with a legendary reputation for scholarship and an insatiable appetite for books. In this pursuit he was encouraged by an industrious mother who spent most of her meagre savings on building up a library that ultimately reached 3000 volumes.

During the 1914-18 War he made his first contributions to journalism by sending despatches from the trenches to the *John O'Groat Journal* and the now defunct *Northern Ensign*.

After the war he obtained a post on the *Piano Maker*, published by a fellow Wicker, Herbert Sinclair. In 1934 he joined the *News Chronicle* as its industrial correspondent and soon made friends with the most senior members of the TUC and Labour Party. For many years he was a well-known figure at their party conferences where his conversation and speeches were listened to with rapt attention.

His written word was no less evocative than the spoken and his regular column in the *Chronicle* rapidly became one of the most anticipated pieces of journalism in Britain. He had an encyclopaedic memory, a rare power of communication, a zest for life and a warmth that glows through his essays.

When he was prematurely struck down at the age of 54 a stream of letters from all over the world poured in to his home and office in a tribute to a man the letter writers had never known, but whose gifted pen had made him a visitor to all their homes.

DR. JOSEPH ANDERSON (1832-1916), a one-time editor of the *John O'Groat Journal*, excavated many archaeological sites in Caithness and wrote extensively on prehistoric topics. He became the Director of the National Museum of Antiquities in Edinburgh.

ROBERT BROWN who was born at Camster, near Lybster, became an eminent botanist, author and scientific editor. Mount Brown in Canada was named after him. His two sons (both Professors) had brilliant academic careers.

JOHN ELDER was born in Caithness in the first half of the 16th century. His learning, particularly geographical knowledge, brought him into the court circles of Henry VIII. Unfortunately, the map of Scotland which he compiled has been lost.

ALEXANDER BEGG (1825-1905) was born at Houstry, Watten. He became a famous journalist and newspaper proprietor in Canada.

DR ALEXANDER GUNN (1844-1914), who was born in Lybster became a famous surgeon. He assisted Lord Lister in his researches into the use of antiseptics.

SIR JOHN GUNN (1837-1918), came from Achlipster, near Watten. He made his wealth from shipping before becoming a Liberal MP for Cardiff. He was knighted in 1898.

CAPT. JOHN HENDERSON (1759-1828), of Thurso was an eminent agricultural and statistical authority. Among his publications was *A General View of Agriculture of Caithness* which was produced in 1812.

JOHN HENDERSON (1800-1883), of Thurso was an authority on Caithness genealogy. He published his *Caithness Family History* in 1884.

PROF. WILLIAM HENDERSON (1810-72), was born in Thurso. He became a Professor of General Pathology at the University of Edinburgh and was a pioneer in the study of homeopathy.

REV. JOHN MACDONALD (1799-1849), was born at Reay. He became famous throughout the Highlands as a Gaelic scholar and preacher getting the title "The Apostle of the North".

PROF. JOHN M. MACKAY (1856-1931), was Professor of History at the University of Liverpool. He devoted much of his career to building up the new University system of Senate and Faculty.

FAMOUS PEOPLE

JOHN NICOLSON (1843-1934), who was born at Canisbay, lived most of his life at Nybster. He did important work in the cataloguing, recording and excavating of antiquities.

JOHN RAE (1845-1915), of Wick, was one of the best-known economists of his time. He was the biographer of the renowned economist Adam Smith.

SIR JOHN ROSS (1834-1927), who was born at Gerston, Halkirk, became a captain of industry in New Zealand and was knighted in 1922. He bequeathed the Ross Institute in Halkirk.

DANE SINCLAIR, a native of Wick parish, was the inventor of the automatic telephone switchboard.

SIR WILLIAM SINCLAIR (c. 1700-1767), was founder of the Baptist Church in Keiss, the first in Scotland. He also published a collection of some sixty hymns of his own composition.

CHAPTER 16

TALES AND LEGENDS

INTRODUCTION: A rich store of tale and legend stayed unrecorded for many years until Henrietta Munro's two publications revived public interest in them. Details of these and other sources used for this contribution (which has examples from each parish) are given at the end of the chapter.

LATHERON

The Fairy Mound of Bruan (G. Sutherland).

There is a considerable folklore associating the fairies with prehistoric mounds or tullochs. One such tale concerns the substantial remains of Bruan broch, located at the roadside, opposite the church.

As two men, carrying a keg of whisky for the New Year celebrations, were passing the broch, they heard the sound of stirring bagpipe music coming from the ancient mound. To their astonishment the tulloch was open and a number of tiny people, all dressed in green, were dancing to the music. One of the men eagerly joined them, but the other, a more cautious fellow, stayed outside. He waited a long weary time for his friend to reappear and, losing patience, opened the door and shouted to his companion who replied, "I have not got a dance yet." Eventually he departed, alone, and the following day called at his friend's house to see if he had returned. To his great concern, he had not come home.

So the worried companion returned to the broch which was by now sealed up again. Remembering the old belief that the same dancing scene might be re-enacted, he returned to the spot exactly a year later and found his friend who refused to leave saying, "I have not got a dance yet". But before he could have a dance, his companion seized him and dragged him outside. He could not believe he had been away for a year, as it seemed like a few minutes. It was only when he reached home and saw how his young child had grown, that he realised how quickly time had passed in the land of the fairies.

The Need Fire (J. Horne).

About the mid 19th century a "black death" broke out among the cattle at Houstry, near Dunbeath. A public meeting of the inhabitants decided that the *need fire* (teine eigin) would have to be lit. The order was passed round the district that every fire was to be extinguished. When this was done the men met on a small island and tried to get fire by rubbing sticks together. After considerable effort, they failed to make a fire. This aroused their suspicions and so a search was made. Sure enough, an old maid who had no cattle had fire hidden under her ashes. Her fire was duly extinguished, the men returned to work, their fire came to life and the cattle plague disappeared.

WICK

The rugged district inland from Ulbster is remarkably rich in prehistoric remains. Among these significant monuments is the fort of Garrywhin, where this tale of illicit whisky making unfolds.

Garrywhin (G. Sutherland).

A man and his son who lived near the Garrywhin fort earned their living by making and selling unique brands of whisky and ale. As they had no arable land to grow barley people puzzled as to how they obtained the necessary raw material for making their eagerly-sought beverages, which appeared to have an exquisite heathery flavour. Tradition had it that they stored their ingredients in a cave whose entrance was known only to them. Eventually, public curiosity and jealousy of their success led to a group of people deciding to compel father or son to betray their commercial secrets. To their questioning the old man replied: "If I tell you, my son will kill me, but if you kill my son, I'll think over the matter." They did so and then the old man said: "Now, kill me." They did and so the secret of making heather whisky and heather ale died with them.

A very similar story is told in Latheron parish with the location at Rangag broch.

Leac an Or [The Ledge of Gold] (G. Sutherland.)

A Gunn chief, who lived in his stronghold on the Ulbster coast, went to Denmark to find a wife. Tradition has it that he married a wealthy Danish princess, but, surprisingly, returned to Caithness without her. In due course a ship carrying the princess and her valuables arrived at the Ulbster coast in the dead of night and headed for the agreed signal fire which the evil Gunn had lit above the treacherous peninsula at Rowberry Head. The ship crashed on the protruding rocks and disappeared under the waves, leaving no survivors; mysteriously, after the tragedy, a pot of gold was discovered on a ledge of rock near where the ship had foundered.... Legend has it that the princess was buried under the Ulbster stone (now in Thurso Museum).

When the Clan Gunn discovered the appalling treachery of their chief they deposed him and drove him out of Halberry castle. He took refuge among the broken country inland from Thrumster in an area which was named Toftgun, after him.

CANISBAY

'E SILKIE MAN: This story was first written by the Rev. David Houston in 1909.

Donald and Peter Rugg lived with their sisters Kirsty and Sarah on a croft at Duncansby. One bonnie autumn day the brothers decided to work the land while sister Kirsty, an attractive young girl, took her crubban (wicker basket) and set off for the shore to gather bait. While she worked collecting limpets a thick blanket of fog suddenly fell, making it almost impossible to see. After waiting hours for Kirsty to reappear her anxious brothers went to the shore, searching and shouting for her. All in vain.

Three years went by.... One morning the brothers were fishing the handlines when a fog, thick as broth, engulfed them. They sailed on for hours, completely lost. At last they sighted a narrow geo, sailed into it and eventually made their way into a cave and there sitting on the shore beyond the cave was a young woman rocking a cradle. To their surprise a silkie suddenly appeared, glowered at them and vanished round a corner to reappear minutes later as a human. He informed the astonished brothers that he and Kirsty were married and that it was indeed their sister rocking the cradle. The silkie's only complaint was that he had not been given a dowry: Kirsty's red cow would have done.

While waiting for the fog to lift, the brothers stayed for a few days in the silkie's homeland, which was the Deil's punch bowl, a great gloup on the west side of Stroma. When the fog rolled away the silkie man agreed to accompany them to the mainland, but suddenly he vanished overboard as they neared Robert's Haven. Just as he did so, the red cow (Kirsty's dowry) which had been grazing near the sea jumped over the rocks into the swirling tide of the Pentland Firth. Neither silkie, Kirsty nor the red cow were ever seen again.

TALES AND LEGENDS

The Mermaid (G. Sutherland).

A young fisherman, while at the shore, saw a beautiful mermaid and instantly fell in love with her. He hid behind a rock so that she would not see him; from there he watched her remove the sealskin that covered half her body and place it under a boulder near where he was hiding. The fisherman took possession of the sealskin and invited the divested mermaid home with him. Soon they married and had several children.

One day while the fisherman was at sea, the children, who were playing in the barn, discovered a strange skin which they brought to their mother. On seeing it, she uttered a cry of joy, seized it and dashed towards the shore. The children saw her put on her long-lost covering and disappear into the sea. Neither husband nor children ever saw her again.

DUNNET

St. John's Loch (J. Horne)

Centuries ago there must have been a number of holy wells and perhaps holy lochs in the county, but now very little is known about them. Miraculous cures, for example, were attributed to the waters of St. John's Loch, Dunnet. To acquire a cure it was necessary for the sufferer to walk round the loch, bathe in it, throw a piece of silver into its depths and be away from its shores by sunrise. The commonly held belief was that anybody who attempted to take away a silver coin thrown into the loch also acquired the disease of the cured person.

The Mermaids of Dwarwick Head [H. Munro (1)].

In Chapel Geo in Dwarwick Head lived a beautiful mermaid who became the lover of a handsome man that stayed on a nearby croft. So besotted was she of her lover that she showered on him countless gifts of gold and precious stones. Unknown to the enamoured mermaid her faithless lover had bestowed all her presents on his mortal girlfriends.

One day when the mermaid was cavorting among the breakers she recognised her lover walking along Dunnet beach with a girl; around the girl's neck was a beautiful gold necklace which the mermaid had recently given to her earthling. That very evening, when he came to tryst with the mermaid, she invited him to her innermost cave, where he had never been before. There she showed her astonished lover an enormous collection of treasure. Transfixed, he gazed wide-eyed around the cave and as he did so the mermaid began to sing a soothing lullaby. Soon he was fast asleep. He awoke to find himself tightly bound in chains.* To this day, in stormy weather, you can still hear his moans from the depths of the cave on Dwarwick Head.

*Another version has it that the mermaid departed from the cave leaving no exit for the doomed lover.

OLRIG

The Piper of Windy Ha (J. T. Calder).

A hillock in the parish of Olrig, called Sysa, has long been associated with witches and fairies.... Many years ago a shy young man, Peter Waters, having driven his cattle to the common, halted for a drink at the well of Sysa. It being a warm balmy June day he soon fell asleep and awoke to find a beautiful young woman, dressed in green, standing beside him.

"Don't be afraid of me, Peter, as I have come to help you. Here are two objects, a book and bagpipes. Choose the former and you'll be the most popular preacher in the North; choose the latter and you'll be the greatest piper." Being an enthusiast for music he chose the bagpipes and was astonished that when he blew them they played marvellously of their own accord.

"There is one condition attached to this gift: this day in seven years, at the very same hour of the evening you must meet me by this very same spot." Peter rashly swore on his honour to accept the conditions. He then hurried home in a state of great excitement and astonished his parents with his miraculous piping. His fame as a musician spread rapidly and soon he was making a small fortune playing at social occasions.

The seven years rolled by and true to his promise Peter went to the well of Sysa. What happened at the second meeting? Legend is silent. But Peter was never seen again.

The Silkie Girl (?).

A couple in Olrig who had been married many years had no children. One night the man had a dream in which he was told to walk the length of Dunnet beach every morning before sunrise, for one year and one day. This he dutifully did and on his very last walk he found a baby girl wrapped in a sealskin.

She grew up to be an unusual child who always vanished from home, with her sealskin, at the anniversary of her finding on Dunnet Sands. On one occasion in the old kirk of Olrig she started to laugh during the sermon, claiming that she could see the Devil sitting in the rafters. Not surprisingly, the girl was banished from the church.

While in her teens she married a local man, but, sadly, died the following year in childbirth. Following her death the minister relented and allowed her to be buried in the kirkyard. The headstone of her grave in the old kirkyard of Olrig takes the form of a small rectangular depression which, legend claims, is never dry.

THURSO

The Witch and the Whisky (J. Horne).

A man, who lived near Thurso, was busy making a supply of whisky for the New Year. To his great annoyance he had problems with the fermentation. He noticed, however, that during such occasions a strange cat came in, sat on the edge of the tub, dipped her paw into the wash and then licked it. Suspicions aroused, he concluded that it must be a witch. So, he seized a scythe and cut off one of the cat's paws, which dropped into the tub. When the tub was emptied, a human hand was found.

On enquiry it was discovered that an old woman had suddenly taken to bed with a heavily bandaged hand. The supposed "witch" was actually cited before a commission of ministers and officials in Thurso.

The Scrabster Witches (G. Sutherland).

A Margaret Olson, who was evicted from her cottage at Burnside held a grudge against Alexander Fraser the factor and William Montgomery, the tenant who replaced her. She invited a few of her fellow witches from the Scrabster area to join her in harassing Montgomery and his family. So, they invaded his house in the form of cats, devoured his meat and drank all his excellent home-brewed ale. Montgomery and a friend decided to put an end to these feline intrusions: armed with a sword, axe and dirk they began their war against the cats on Friday 28th November 1718. That evening they successfully maimed two cats and thereafter a woman who had the reputation of being a witch took to her bed. Some months later a Margaret Gilbertson "dropped a black and putrified" leg, which was brought as evidence to the Sheriff-Depute. She was arrested and put in prison.

On examination she confessed that along with others, in the form of cats, she had gone into Montgomery's house. Following her confession a number of people were arrested. All denied the accusation that they were acting in league with the devil. The investigators examined the body of Margaret Olson searching for the devil's marks. They did find marks on her shoulder and then drove a needle almost to the eye into one of them. Margaret Olson never flinched.

REAY

King o' the Caithness Smugglers (D. Mackay).

There were many active smugglers and poachers in Caithness but few could hold a candle to George Fraser, who lived in the Broubster area. He constantly kept the excisemen on their toes as he operated (at least for a period) eleven illicit stills.

Not far from George's but and ben lay the mission church in Shurrery, empty since the Rev. Finlay Cook left the established church with his flock in the Disruption of 1843. The abandoned church proved an ideal place for his "barley bree". More than once he took the excisemen to the church door, hinting that contraband alcohol was nearby, but they never ventured into the church.

On another occasion, having accepted a £5 "bribe" he informed the zealous officers where malt for whisky-making was hidden. On disintegrating a peat stack they found some musty barley (long abandoned as it was useless for distilling), which they triumphantly despatched into the burn.

Hounded one day by a gauger (exciseman) Fraser hastened over the hill and waded into Loch Tormaid where he deposited his incriminating still.

Craig More and Craig Liath [H. Munro (1)].

Two prominent knolls at Reay, cut into the dark diorite rock, are Craig Mor and Craig Liath.

Donald Mackay, an exceptional wizard by any standards, was told by the Queen of the Fairies where he might find a special magic box; she added a grim warning that on no account must it be opened. Being a reckless fellow, Donald opened the box and thousands of fairies swarmed out shouting, "Work! Work!". Donald told them to go and make heather ropes, a task they completed in minutes. Again the fairies exclaimed, "Work! Work!".

He then set them to work draining the small loch of Clash Breac near Broubster. They worked long and hard, throwing up two mounds of earth, Craig Mor and Craig Liath. An old cailleach suddenly appeared and exclaimed to the fairies, "In the name of God, what are you doing?". On hearing the Deity's name, the fairies vanished. Their unfinished work is the deep ravine near the loch. Close to the ravine is a standing stone: the fossil skull of the cailleach whose head Donald split when she interrupted the fairies.

Ultimately Donald tired of the energetic fairies, so he asked them to make a bridge of sand across the Pentland Firth. The stormy seas of the Pentland Firth are the result of the ropes always breaking.

TALES AND LEGENDS

HALKIRK

The Dirlot Treasure (G. Sutherland).

    A Dirlot legend tells of a valuable treasure sunk in the Thurso River in a deep pool by a steep-walled gorge close to the ruinous remains of the old castle. A number of attempts have been made by powerful swimmers to reach the treasure, but none of them ever surfaced alive. All that ever came to public view following a treasure hunt was some of the internal organs of the swimmers; nobody has yet set eyes on the treasure, which is jealously guarded by the fearsome water horse.

Wrong Measure (G. Sutherland).

    A Halkirk miller died and shortly after he would frequently reappear as a ghost before members of his family. Always he walked to "the ben end" of the house. One evening, his son followed him, shining a large torch. The ghost then pointed to corn measures which were stored under a bed and requested his son to burn them as they were false measures. The son carried out the instructions and the restless ghost was seen no more.

Rendering Invisible (?).

    A one-time tenant of Dalmore was known as Donal' Breac. Among his many activities he distilled "the mountain dew". As he had been caught twice by the excisemen, he pondered ways of evading them in the future.

    Eventually he decided to walk to Braemore to visit a practitioner of the black art. His visit was not in vain; he left Braemore with the capacity to make things invisible. The exciseman was no longer a terror to Donal' who could go from Dalmore into Thurso with a cask on each side of his horse and remain undetected.... It is most unfortunate that this art has been lost!

WATTEN

The Robber of Backlas (J. T. Calder).

    David Marshall (originally a Sutherland from Kildonan), a tall man of extraordinary strength, became a famous bandit in the Robin Hood mould: he stole from the rich but was generous to the poor. In fact he was so trusted by the cottars and crofters that he held their money for them at markets. Yet, such was his daring that he had twice broken into Keiss castle and once into the stronghold of Dunbeath. Eventually the laird of Keiss, who had suffered humiliation and loss of money to Marshall, travelled to the robber's hideout in the dark and surprised him. He was arrested, taken to Wick, jailed, then publicly whipped and banished from Caithness to his home county of Sutherland, where his outlaw activites so incensed the authorities that they had him transported to America.

Another variation of the Marshall saga is that he and an accomplice, named Donald Miller, were tried before the local sheriff and condemned to be executed. Marshall, who had his sentence suspended, was sent to Edinburgh for trial, but managed to escape while they were passing through Sutherland. Miller was less fortunate; he was hanged in Thurso, reputedly the last person in the county to have suffered this fate.

BOWER

Dr. Richard Merchison (J. T. Calder).

Caithness had had its share of eccentric — and interfering — ministers. Into both categories fell the Rev. Dr. Richard Merchiston of Bower, a member of the Reformed church and zealously anti-Catholic. In the year 1613 he was pursuing his religious crusade through the parish of Wick and entered the Royal Burgh, where he discovered a stone statue of the town's patron saint, St. Fergus. To the astonishment and deep shock of many people the crusading cleric smashed the image.

A number of Wickers threatened vengeance and pursued him as he returned to Bower. They caught hold of him and drowned him in Wick river; legend says that St. Fergus was seen sitting astride the parson, holding his head under the water!

TALES AND LEGENDS
REFERENCES

J. T. Calder	History of Caithness	Wick	1887
J. Horne	County of Caithness	Wick	1907
D. Houston	'E Silkie Man (reprint)	Thurso	N.D.
H. Lindsay	Folklore of Dunbeath	Dunbeath Preservation Trust	1985
D. Mackay	This was my Glen	Thurso	1965
H. Munro (1)	Legends of the Pentland Firth	Thurso	1977
H. Munro (2)	More Legends of the Pentland Firth	Thurso	1979
G. Sutherland	Folklore Gleanings and Character Sketches	Wick	1937

CHAPTER 17

DIALECT

When considering Caithness dialect through the ages it is necessary to look briefly at the beginnings of the English language and how it in turn influenced the early Scottish tongue. In the 5th and 6th centuries the Angles, a Teutonic tribe speaking a Germanic language, invaded and settled along the east coast of Britain from roughly the Humber to the Forth. They in turn were conquered by the Danes but the old Anglian speech remained and the language that came to be spoken in the Lothian area of Scotland was directly descended from this Anglian tongue. Even up to the 16th century the Scots called their language 'Inglis', which was the northern form of the early language of the Angles.

The original Scots came from the north of Ireland and eventually conquered the lands north of the line of the Forth and Clyde. In 843 AD, their king, Kenneth Macalpin, became the acknowledged ruler of the Picts and Scots and the language of this united kingdom became Gaelic, the language of the Picts (whatever it was) being totally obliterated. This combined kingdom then over-ran the Welsh speaking kingdom of Strathclyde and around 970 AD Kenneth III, King of Scots, took over the Lothians. Now the really significant aspect of this conquest was that amongst the conditions of acceptance was the stipulation that the province would continue to use its own laws, customs and Anglian speech. This led to a Scottish (i.e. Gaelic) king adopting the language and customs of his English speaking subjects, an event which was to have a profound influence on the future language of Scotland and in turn that of Caithness.

By the time of the Scots' occupation of the Lothians, the Norse settlement of Caithness (or at least the northern part) was well established. With settled occupation the Norse language soon spread over the area and continued in use for some four hundred years. Even when Scandinavian domination of the region had ended it was only natural that Norse words would survive into the succeeding Scottish language and their influence has enriched our dialect down to the present day.

DIALECT

About the same time as this early Viking colonisation, i.e. about the middle of the 9th century, the Gaelic speaking Celts were establishing themselves and their language (a form of Irish Gaelic) in the southern and western part of what is now Caithness. With the eventual waning of Norse power in the region the Gaelic language made some inroads into the southern areas of earlier Norse dominance but it is safe to assume that neither Norse nor Gaelic ever separately dominated the whole of Caithness and at best there was only sporadic frontier cross-over. A Gaelic Renaissance in the 19th century following the Sutherland clearances and the development of the herring industry led to a renewed influence of Gaelic speech and tradition, particularly in the parish of Latheron, but this was short-lived.

During the centuries when Gaelic and Norse became established as languages in Caithness, the old Anglian tongue of the Lothians (later to be called Scottis) became the language of the Scottish Court in Edinburgh and of the University of St Andrews. This language with the extension of power of the Scottish kings spread by the end of the 13th century along the coast to the Moray Firth and thence into Caithness where in time it was superimposed upon the Norse and Gaelic tongues.

The dialect of Caithness, therefore, comes directly from these three sources. As a dialect it has features that are distinct and peculiar to Caithness, but it is not a form of speech that is common to every part of the county. There are varied spellings, meanings and pronunciations, some even within a few miles of each other. For example we have the anecdote of the Weikar who observed that "'E Loibster cheels speak afa funny, 'ey caal 'e peiper' 'the peepar!'".

In earlier times the demarcation line between the Norse and Gaelic influence was roughly from Clyth Ness to Forss, Reay, but this has become somewhat obscured over the past hundred years. Nevertheless, even today the speech of a native of the southern part of the parish of Latheron will be considered as being 'a bittie heilan' by his counterpart in Canisbay. The purist might even argue that the true area of Norse-influenced dialect is north of a line from Keiss to Dunnet.

It is quite wrong to think that Caithness dialect is a debased form of standard English or made up of words which are simply mispronounced English. The Scottish element of the dialect is derived from a dialect of the Germanic language as is standard English and an example of three simple words will illustrate how each became "dialect" and standard English.

Old English	Caithness/Scots	Modern English
Mus	Moose	Mouse
Hus	Hoose	House
Cu	Coo	Cow

As the Old English 'u' was pronounced 'oo' as in 'food' the above demonstrates that in this example Caithness dialect is a more accurate pronunciation of the original English than is modern standard English.

The pronunciation of the Caithness dialect is in some areas unique and in all cases distinctive. One of the most obvious peculiarities is where the soft 'j' and 'g' become 'ch' at the beginning of a word as for example. 'Cheorge geid Chean a char o' cham' for 'George gave Jean a jar of jam'. There is also the schoolboy classic of 'In past Cheorge Green Thou leadest me' in reciting a line of the 23rd Psalm. The noun termination 'et' becomes 'ad' as can 'ot' and 'it' so that we have 'Markad', 'Packad' and 'Rabbad' for 'Market', 'Packet' and 'Rabbit' and it was a delight recently to hear a Caithness exile refer repeatedly to the snooker professional John Parrott as 'Parrad'. With proper names the same change occurs and 'Janet Dunnet' becomes 'Chinnad Dinnad' and the pronoun 'it' becomes 'id' or 'hid'. Nouns ending in 'ock' become 'ag' so that 'bannock', 'hillock' and the lowland Scots 'puddock' become 'bannag', 'hillag' and 'puddag' respectively. In the use of the diminutive a 'd' may be inserted before the 'ag' to give 'Chondag' and 'Willdag' for 'Johnnie and Willie'. The broad 'a' as in the English 'fall' does not occur and we have 'paa', 'taak' and 'waak' for 'paw' 'talk' and 'walk'. The 'i' in words like 'time' and 'line' becomes the diphthongised 'oi' to result in 'toime' and 'loine' while similarly the 'o' in 'dog', 'fog' and 'cold' becomes 'ow' to give 'dowg', 'fowg' and 'cowld'. The present participle 'ing' becomes 'an' in words such as 'rainan' (raining) 'sleepan' (sleeping) and 'lookan' (looking). The initial 'th' is dropped in words of one syllable such as 'the', 'they', 'there', 'them', 'that', 'this', 'then' and the initial 'wh' becomes 'f' to give 'far' for 'where', 'faa' for 'who', 'fat' or 'fit' for 'what', 'fan' for 'when' and 'Faligoe' for 'Whaligoe', but this latter pronunciation is now only used by the very oldest of the population. There is still, however, widespread use of the dipthong 'ey' as a substitute for 'ai', and 'ea' as in pail (peyl), and meat (meyt) as is the sound 'ee' in 'reeg' (rig), 'peeg' (pig) and 'geeg' (gig). The double vowel 'ee' can still be occasionally found as a substitute for 'oo' as in 'feet' for 'foot', 'feel' for 'fool' and 'peel' for 'pool', but the latter two examples are now less frequently heard.

The characteristically rolling Scottish 'r' is not a feature of Caithness pronunciation but the 'r' is often pronounced with the inverted point of the tongue as in the call 'mither wir faither hes herreen' and is known as the trailing 'r' while the verb 'beware' is pronounced 'bewayur' and the surname 'Wares' is pronounced even by its owner as 'Wayurs'. A few words beginning with 'ch' may still be pronounced as 'sh' e.g. 'sheir' for 'cheir' (chair) in the Canisbay area along with 'vreck' for 'wreck', 'vrang' for 'wrong' and 'in the', 'on the', 'at the' and 'of the' reduced to 'e. Still in common use in the county is the 'oe' sound before 'r', so that 'born', 'worn' and 'torn' are pronounced 'boern', 'woern' and 'toern'. A dialect sound that is probably unique to Caithness is the use of 'w' before certain vowels to give the sound 'pwient', 'pwiepe' and 'bwiey' for 'pint', 'pipe' and 'boy'. In certain words ending in 'se' the termination becomes 'sh' so that for 'hearse', 'horse' and 'worse' we have 'heersh' 'horsh' and 'worsh'.

A very marked feature of northern Caithness speech is where the double vowel 'oo' is pronounced 'eu', where for example, 'look at the book' becomes 'leuk at 'e beuk'. The 'i' sound in words like 'lift' and 'gift' is pronounced flat to give 'leift' and 'geift' while along the Latheron coast the 'u' sound as in 'duck' and 'tub' becomes 'i' to give 'dick' and 'tib' a form of pronunciation influenced by the Gaelic tradition of that parish.

With such a rich dialect heritage we may therefore ask what has caused its erosion over the last hundred years and in recent decades its rapid decline. The answer is the very factors which brought it into being — dominance of outside influences.

One of the earliest influences was the translation of the King James version of the Bible. As the Reformed Church did not have a version in the Scottish tongue this resulted in an understanding of English being necessary to read, or at least appreciate, the Bible at a time when religion held great sway over every level of society and when even to get married one had to be able to recite the Lord's Prayer, The Creed and the Ten Commandments (in the English of the Authorised Version). The Union of the Parliaments was a further turning point when the educated upper sections of Caithness society began to write and speak standard English and to send their families to English speaking schools. Similarly, with the rise and spread of education in every Caithness parish, the language of the playground was dialect while the language of the classroom was English.

The Gaelic speaking part of the county (as elsewhere in Gaeldom) suffered similarly, with pupils being punished for reverting to their natural language and Gaelic being looked upon with contempt. The result was confusion and a sense of inferiority which created a compulsion to learn "proper" English. Neil Gunn deals with this problem in the passage of *The Silver Darlings* where Finn (a Gaelic speaker with some school English) goes to the Doctor in Wick and is met at the door by the Doctor's maid who asks, "'Fats 'e name?' 'Finn', he answered. 'Far d' ye come fae?' 'Yes it's a long way', replied Finn. She gave a little laugh. Finn reddened, body and mind in an agony..... But his real terror was lack of English".

Just as Finn felt at a disadvantage in the presence of dialect-speaking Wick folk, so also have Caithnessians in turn felt ill at ease about speaking their native tongue in the presence of people from "'e Sooth". They will compromise their dialect to make themselves understood, to any

Glaswegian or Cockney who would not for one moment think of modifying his own form of English. This apologetic attitude has as much as anything contributed to the decline of the Caithness tongue. Just as significant is our lack of a written tradition of the dialect. Our only major works in dialect form are those of John Horne and even he wrote in a watered-down version, possibly deliberately so, in order to appeal to, or be understood by, a wider audience.

Mass communication has been the ultimate death-knell for Caithness dialect (as well as other forms) from the advent of cheaper newspapers and the railway in the last century to the communication satellite and video of the present day. Over the past hundred years dialect has been in decline, old words disappearing with the passing of each generation and no new words being introduced. Not even the great herring days produced much that was new in the way of dialect and while words like 'bark' 'skow' and 'scummer' were in regular currency, outside influences of language and trade must have had a diluting effect on the pure native speech. Indeed, the only word which readily comes to mind as having possibly been coined since the turn of the 20th century is 'dowpag' for the butt-end of a cigarette. We have no dialect words for current domestic tasks such as defrosting a chicken or switching on the microwave oven and because of this we must regretfully conclude that our dialect is no longer an active language. The very fact that this chapter is written in English in order to be understood, is surely telling comment.

We can now but hope that some of the very factors which contributed to its decline may be the means of its salvation and that through the medium of video and tape-recorder our dialect and mode of speech may be saved for posterity so that future generations of Caithness 'shither' may for all time have a record of this special part of their heritage.

GLOSSARY

While several thousand Caithness dialect words still exist, only a limited selection of those which have been in use since the second world war are included here. Natives of the county will have to make allowances for words which may not be hard currency in dialect terms but which are considered of interest to the non-dialect reader. Similarly, inhabitants of other parts of the country are asked to show tolerance with words which are not exclusive to Caithness but have been included because they are still in regular use in the county.

A: the pronoun "I".
Aal: old (northern Caithness usage).
Aans: beard of barley or bere.
Ablach: an ungainly, clumsy person.
Acht: to own or to be parents of. "Fa achts ye?" — "Who are your parents?".
Aig: to work eagerly at something. Aigan: eagerly active.
Aikle: a molar tooth.
Ailiss: a hot blazing — "A roastan ailiss o' a fire".
Ains: owns. "Fa ains 'at dowg?".
Aise: ashes.
Alunt: alight.
Amadan: a foolish or stupid person. From the Gaelic meaning "a fool".
Ammel: the swingletree of a horsedrawn implement.
Antle: to continually complain. "She antled on".
Antran: occasional. "An antran ein".
Ask: a cow's chain or binding in a byre.
Attry: ill-natured or quarrelsome.
Awmry: a plate rack on top of the kitchen dresser.
Awpie: a guillemot.
Baak: (1) a beam of wood often used for roosting hens.
(2) the first two combined furrows in ploughing.
Backie: the stake of an animal's tether.
Bard: a scolding woman.
Bare-Feeted Broth: broth made with little or no meat.
Bark: to tan herring nets. To knock one's shins painfully.
Barm: to rage noisily.
Bauchle: originally a worn-out shoe but now applied to an old worn-out person.
Beest: the curd-like dish made from heating the first milk after a cow has calved.
Begood: began. " 'E nicht hed begood til fall". (Mainly Stroma usage).
Beilan: suppurating.
Belly: to weep loudly; particularly of children.
Benleen: a stone hung from the net or simmans, which held down the thatch on a roof.
Beyce: cattle. "Go an tek in 'e beyce".
Bick: a female dog.
Bink: a horizontal flagstone placed on top of two supporting flagstones to form a shelf for the storage of water in pails; a ledge in a cliff or hillside.
Birze: to squeeze or press. cf 'Burze'.
Blackchock: the blackbird.
Blackgrun: the land to be ploughed after the turnips have been removed.
Blaidies (Healan): a poultice made from plant leaves.

Blearach: defective sight; strained peering.
Bleems: taatie bleems-potato haulms.
Bleeter: a sharp, passing shower.
Blinner: to blink; short-sighted; see obscurely. Also a blinding shower of snow or clouds of smoke, dust etc...
Blockie: a small cod.
Blown Milk: creamy milk frothed up by beating rapidly with a whisk made from hair of a cow's tail.
Bo: a child's word for a louse.
Bodach-Back: the outside peat in a bank which has been exposed to weather.
Boemes: clouds of smoke. " 'E weet peits chist smoored and gave off boemes o' smok'".
Boke: to retch.
Boltie Lairag: the corn bunting.
Bool: a large round stone.
Boorach: a mess; an untidy result.
Boorag: a turf or peat from near the surface of moss, usually placed at the back of a peat fire.
Booran: bellowing of cattle impatiently awaiting food.
Borag: a bradawl.
Boust: to bounce back and forth off a wall or walls "He cem hom' fill an' went boustan doon 'e lobby".
Bowg: stomach, belly, with reference to children.
Bowtree: the elder tree.
Brain: to stun by a blow.
Brander: girdle with bars. A grid-iron.
Branks: the wooden parts of a cow's halter when tethered outside.
Branelstickle: the stickleback.
Brat: a rough apron, made from hessian sacking.
Breenge: a clumsy, violent rush forward. " 'E stirk breenged through 'e wifie's gairdeen".
Breether: first shoots of green corn.
Brither-Bairn: cousin; Brither-Sin: nephew. Brither-Dochter: niece.
Brochan: oat-meal gruel, or thin porridge.
Brotag, Hairy Brotag: caterpillar of the tiger-moth.
Browg: bradawl.
Buggleen: straw on the bottom of a boat to prevent animals from slipping (Stroma word).
Buist: a paint brand on a clipped sheep. When referring to humans; "Hev ye got hees buist?" — "Do you know who he is?"
Burze, Burzan: to overflow; overflowing (of dry material) " 'E coern wiz burzan oot 'e pok when he tried til tie id". cf Birze.
Butts: mates, pals.
Bous: a sulky mouth. "Look at 'e bous on 'e bairn".
Bwee: a buoy.
Byornar: out of the ordinary.
Ca: the sound of the sea.
Ca'a: a path or road left between fields to give access to common pasture.
Caff: chaff.
Caff-Seck: a mattress filled with chaff.
Caibie: a hen's stomach.
Calach: the cockerel.
Camsterious: frisky as a young horse or a young boy. Boisterous.
Carpads: carpet slippers.
Carran: spurrey (spergula arvensis).
Carrieshang: a noisy confrontation of words.

GLOSSARY

Carvey: caraway seed.
Ceese: the cross section of a peat bank (hard 'c') "He wis cuttan thirteen peits till 'e ceese".
Chalouse: guess, surmise.
Checkiebeet: the stonechat.
Checkie Forty Feet: the centipede.
Cheef: very friendly; a close relationship.
Cheeg: a sudden pull; to jerk.
Cheoch: tough.
Claggan: a stiff lump of anything, especially wet earth.
Claagered: smeared.
Claik: a malicious gossip.
Clapshot: potato and turnip mashed together.
Clester: to smear.
Clink: a heavy fall.
Clipe: to scratch with the finger-nails or claws. Having a sharp tongue. A telltale.
Cliver: a term used to encourage a child to do something. "Cliver then an' let me hear ye singan".
Clocher: to clear the throat noisily.
Clock: a black beetle.
Clockan (hen): a broody hen.
Clods; Cloddies: small pieces of peat.
Clookan: huddling for warmth. " 'E wifag wis clookan ower 'e fire".
Clos: the enclosed farmyard.
Closad: the bedroom closet in a croft house.
Clougs: large stones on the sea shore (Stroma word).
Clure: to dent; smash in.
Coachie: soft and spongy, like a withered turnip.
Coerdie blow: a blow to the bicep as a form of school playground retribution.
Cole: a small haystack built in the field from ground level.
Coom: dust from grain when first passed through the mill in the process of 'shillan'.
Corrag: the fore-finger.
Cown: to weep.
Crack: entertaining, invigorating conversation, often about local occurrences.
Crackins: oatmeal fried in fat until well brown.
Creepie: a three-legged stool.
Creetar: a slightly patronising word as applied to someone who is disadvantaged or has fallen on hard times. " 'At poor creetar hes notheen bit social security til keep her goan".
Croach: to make a throat-clearing noise in the throat as with a severe cold.
Croil: a broken-down person, animal or thing. "Ats a richt croil". Also "cryle".
Cromags: the points of all the fingers and the thumb brought together in the act of lifting salt, etc.
Crounkled: crumpled.
Cuddeen: a coalfish.
Cudge: a small room; a very small cottage.
Culk: a large lump of material. "Aboot half o' 'e beef wis chist culks o' fat".
Cundy: a covered drain; a conduit.
Curr: a touch, to move with a touch. To move a sleeping child so as not to disturb.
Cut: a mood, often unpleasant. "He's in bad cut 'e day".
Cyarr: to antle (cf) with menace in the voice.
Daad: a lump of soft substance. "Pit a daad o' greese on 'iss exle".
Daivered: fatigued as with walking against the wind; confused. "Ids a richt daiveran' win 'e day".
Dayset: the end of the evening twilight.
Denshach: fussy, particular about food.

Deugind: obstinate; stubborn; wilful.
Deukie: a duck.
Diad: enough for one meal. "A'll give ye a diad o' ma new taaties".
Dird: a fuss, to show off.
Dirl: "Go at 'e dirl". to drive at noisy speed.
Dirlan: (1) resounding with noise. "Ma heid wis dirlan wi 'e noise fae 'e disco".
  (2) to sting. "His han' wis dirlan wi 'e tawse".
Dirlar: a chamber pot.
Divad: turf for covering a roof or potato pit.
Dode: a slow person, in both thought and action.
Doiter: to stroll indolently.
Doonlay: the rented cultivation of a croft. An infirm crofter or widow would sub-let their croft to a neighbour who would have the "doonlay" for working to his own account.
Dort: to sulk; not on speaking terms
Dossan: the forelock left after a short haircut.
Dowed: fish partially dried; in the drying process. Also the state of cut weeds or thinned turnips which have wilted in the sun.
Dowpag: the end of a smoked cigarette. A schoolboy might plead of an adult "Geis yer dowpag when ye're feenished smokan".
Dozend: stupid.
Dreich: dreary, (of wet weather).
Drooked: soaked to the skin. "He's hom' lek a drooked hen".
Dwan: swoon.
Eem: a rising misty vapour; fine spray from the sea shore.
Eigg: an egg.
Eisewaa: the inside wallhead of a building.
Eishan: offspring; stock; "Yon's a bad eishan".
Elt: to mix meal and water to form a dough. A Carrie-Elt is a thick badly baked oatcake. A Muckle-Elt is a stout clumsy woman. Also the phrase "'E bairn wis chist eltered in gutters".
Faap: the curlew.
Fae: from.
Fael: a square-cut turf.
Faigs: used to stress a point "By Faigs....".
Fann: a large snow-wreath.
Fanoor: whenever.
Far-Drauchted: subtle (of remark); also long-headed; long sighted. Someone whose mind is ahead of everyone else.
Fat-e-caa'd: what's its name?
Fatna: what sort of a?
Feice: the face. "Couldna keep feice" — fell down on the job.
Fellabrek: the stubble ground for ploughing for turnip sowing.
Feochled: tired, worn out.
Ferrantickles: freckles.
Fiarter: a term of disrespect. "A foosum fiarter".
Firlad: a quarter boll of meal, flour etc..
Fitch: to move, "Get a fitch on ye an'mek 'e meit".
Flachter: a heart-shaped spade for taking the top turf off a peat bank.
Flek: a gate or wooden divider.
Flipe: (1) to work with a brush as in whitewashing.
  (2) a piece of torn skin.
  (3) to turn a sock down to the heel for ease of putting on.
Floss: rushes with the pitch removed, used for making small simmans. Also, rushes cut and left to dry for thatch.
Flyte: to scold. "She's always flytan at her bairns".

GLOSSARY

Fornent: in front of.
Foosum: filthy, foulsome.
Fowgie: dry and spongy. A fowgie neep. A fowgie peit.
Fownk: a bad smell.
Fracht: a burden, usually referring to two pails of water, which would usually be carried with a hoop or square frame as a support.
Fummle: to tumble, to upset. Also a busy housewife might "fummle" her empty teacup (i.e. invert it) in the saucer and re-use without washing later on.
Funseless: sapless, insipid.
Fushionless: sapless. cf 'funseless'.
Futterad: a weasel.
Gaat: a gelded pig.
Gailan': smarting hotly, as of a sore. " 'Iss rent in ma thoom is fair gailan".
Gainer: a gander.
Gandygows: silly pranks, usually childish.
Gangs: hand shears for clipping sheep.
Gansey: a jersey, especially a fisherman's.
Gant: to stammer.
Gaapaz: a fool.
Gee: quite or rather; used to add stress. "Hids a gee weet nicht". (hard 'g').
Geeg: to giggle; to laugh in a suppressed way.
Gees: moods (hard 'g'). "She took a mad gee for tekkan up Yoga".
Geevil: gable (hard 'g').
Geevlag: an earwig (hard 'g').
Geo or goe: a rocky sea inlet.
Gilt: a stack of hay on a rectangular base.
Glaiked: vacant, foolish.
Glide: cross-eyed, squint.
Glounk: the sound of air replacing liquid in a bottle.
Gluff: to scare, frighten. A severe fright.
Gollan: the daisy.
Gomeral: a foolish person.
Gowpen: the two hands cupped together. Gowpenful': as much as these hands will hold.
Gravad: a woollen scarf.
Graylord: a large saithe.
Greip: a manure fork. Also "Greep".
Grice: a young pig.
Groatie Buckie: a small cowrie shell found in the John O'Groats area.
Gromish: to crush (usually a part of the body). " 'E horse tramped on him an' gromished his feet".
Grone: a pig's snout.
Grop: the refuse from straw, oatmeal, etc; now used to describe other waste.
Grounglan: the noise of rumbling water. " 'E burnie's fairly grounglan efter 'e speit".
Grumly: muddy, of liquids.
Gruns: sediment, particularly in the bottom of a milk pail. Recently, a bottle of rather good claret on being decanted raised the remark "'At weine's fill o' gruns!".
Gully: a large knife.
Gundy: toffee; usually home-made.
Gurr: matter in the corner of the eyes.
Gushel: to work messily; to spill (as in a saucer).
Gutteran: messing about at unproductive work. "He's aye gutteran' aboot in at sheddie".
Gutters: mud. "Tek 'e gutters off yir boots afore ye come intil ma' clean kitcheen".
Haal: hold; grip; to stand up to rough usage. "A see 'e bairn can waak til haal". "At fence'll had haal til 'e coorsest beyce".

Haavers: halves. To share something.
Had til'id: hold to it; stand up to it.
Hain: to save. Haining boots were kept for Sunday and special occasions.
Half Yokeen: a mid-morning and mid-afternoon "tea-break" on the croft or farm. The period midway between each "yoking" of a team of horses.
Hallan: flagstone divider between cattle in a byre.
Hammel: kindly, homely.
Han-scroo: a small corn-stack built from ground level in the field to secure the crop during wet weather.
Heathercoo: a clump of rough "woody" heather.
Hees: his. "He's in hees bed".
Heishle: a confused group.
Herry: to rob a nest of its eggs.
Heuchy: itchy.
Hev: have.
Hinderley: a cart loaded too much to the rear of the axle. " 'E lod wis so hinderley id wis lek til coup".
Hiz: us. "Id belongs til hiz".
Hoolipan: walking with rolling gait.
Hop: the ploughman's command to a horse to turn right. 'Hy' is to turn left.
Howgs: young male sheep normally fed for butchering.
Howk: to scoop. "He howked oot 'e neep til mek a halloween's lantran".
Hownk: a hump. " 'E stairved stirk hed a hownk on him lek a camal".
Hurl: a deep, hollow sound. Can apply to a sound in the throat prior to death.
Ile: oil; also the fishing ground between the shore and a current.
Intil: into.
Isk: to be breathless through sobbing. Also breathlessness in a sick child causing concern.
Ither: udder of an animal.
Ivenow: just now, even now.
Keebag: a sour milk cheese.
Keet: the ankle.
Kep: (1) to catch. "Kep 'at peit". The person catching the peat from the "banker" was the "keppar" who passed it to the "spreader".
(2) to intercept animals. "Kep 'at yeows an' turn 'em doon 'e rod".
Kiard: a despicable individual.
Kinch: a twist; the doubling of a rope when fastinging it to anything. "He gied himsel a nesty kinch".
Kithan: a mischievous youngster; an imp.
Laager: to besmear. "Her feice wis aal laagered wi' mekup".
Laikan: leaking.
Lairag: the lark.
Lan'Sea: a sea where heavy waves break on the shore.
Lark: used in the phrase "to tek lark" — to make fun of verbally. "'Ey wir tekken lark behind his back".
Lassagie: a young girl.
Lay: to hand-beat iron to replace wear as with a sok (ploughshare); to beat; a lull between waves.
Lay Off: to talk at great length. "She laid off a lot o' trock".
Layr: a habit (usually bad). Also 'leer'. "Her carry-on'ill gie 'e bairns a bad layr".
Leavan: oatmeal and water mixed for feeding hens.
Leens: low-lying ground often flooded from a nearby burn or river.
Leep: to steep or soak in boiling water. "til leep 'e peeg" — to soak the dead pig in order to shave off the bristles more easily.
Leider: short rope for leading a horse.
Leit: used in the phrase "Never leit!?" — "You don't mean to tell me that?" "You don't say?".

GLOSSARY

Lek: like.
Lekkar: preferable. "Is id no more lekkar her til look efter her bairns than be off every nicht til 'e Bingo".
Len: (1) a sloping position "Len 'e barrel ower til wan side".
(2) to set in a sloping position. "Len at boord against 'e waa".
(3) to lean "If at teks a beegar len id'll faa doon".
Lether: ladder. An Edinburgh cousin who referred to "the ladder" was told by his Lybster cousin, "Don't be speakan' so prood!"
Lift and Lay: a person in a hurry "She wis heidan for 'e village as hard as she could lift an' lay".
Limmer: an opprobrious word applied to a female: Two Lybster youths dressed up as two flashy dames from the "sooth" and paraded up the village. One absent mindedly struck a match on the sole of his shoe to light a fag and an old lady who saw this described "her" as "a bowld limmer".
Line: to take aim and to chase away. " 'E dowg stol 'e beef and wis lined doon 'e rod".
Lintie: the linnet.
Lippan: full to overflowing. " 'E milk wis lippan 'e peyl".
Lock: a lot. Lockie: a small quantity.
Loog: ear.
Loogard: a slap on the ear.
Long: "tekkan long" — longing for. "A'm tekkan long away fae hom". "A'm tekkan long for a new taatie".
Lowe: a flame.
Lowse: to unyoke horses, thus to finish work.
Luntan: on fire.
Lurks: folds in material or fabric that require smoothing out.
Maa: the seagull.
Maak: fish milt, false roe.
Maatie: a small firm herring.
Mallimack: a fulmar.
May Gobs: a cold spell of weather in early May.
Meels: crumbled peat; peat dust.
Meese, Meeze: a fisherman's bearing mark.
Mein: weak, feeble. "Mekkan Mein" — sympathising with.
Mell: heavy hammer used to drive in fence posts.
Meraclas: untidy. "A' gee meraclas wifie".
Minshach: mean, shabby.
Mistimeous: clumsy, untidy, undependable.
Moch: a moth.
Moegans: mittens. Glove with a thumb only.
Moeger: to work in a messy way or in messy conditions.
Moeniment: an insignificant person.
Moogard: a mess.
Mullach: used as a term, almost of comfort among women; also applied to children.
Murt: an animal's whimper when sleeping. "Harken til 'e dowgie murtan".
Naetral: of very pleasant disposition; the opposite of objectionable. "A richt naetral sowl".
Naitie: neat, clever with the hands.
Neb: nose.
Nether: an adder.
Nev: the fist.
Niaff: a witless person.
Noor: never. "A noor seyed a word".
Nor: than. "He's owlder nor me".
Nyattry: grumbling, continually complaining. cf 'attry'.
Nyack: a tinker; also 'Nyuck'.

Nyonyach: just perfect.
Nyurran: an onomatopoeic word to describe the noise made by a bad-tempered small dog. " 'At dowgies always nyurran at yir ankles".
Oakie: the guillemot; also 'Owkie'.
Oast: a place dug out on the shore to hold a boat.
Ochanee: an exclamation, usually of surprise, often on hearing bad news.
Ondocht: a mean, puny creature.
Owld: old. " 'E owld cheel" — a colloquial expression for one's father.
Oxter: armpit.
Oxteran: giving support by linking arms. "She wis oxteran her owld mither up til 'e hill".
Paat: to walk in a heavy, noisy way.
Partan: an edible crab.
Pech: to breathe heavily.
Peedie, Peerie: small.
Peedle: to play truant (From the Thurso area).
Peelag: the porpoise.
Peepag: a sharp sounding reed made by squeezing one end of green corn.
Pells: rags; tatters; dung hanging from an animals's coat.
Peter Reidleigs: the red shank.
Piktarnie: the common tern.
Pingelty: a difficulty; flustered "She's in a richt pingelty".
Pirkles: a halter with iron spikes on it, used to prevent a calf from sucking a cow.
Pirlag: a small lump of sheep's dung.
Pit doon a pleice: if a crofter was infirm or had not the necessary implements he would hire a neighbour to do the cultivation. This occupation was known as "pittan doon pleices".
Pleice: literally "a place" and commonly used to interchange with the word "croft".
Ploog: a pimple.
Plowter: to walk or work in a heavy fashion.
Pluck: the moult. "wir hens hev tekken 'e pluck".
Plucker: a small vicious fish. "As mad's 'e plucker" — To be in an angry mood.
Poll: to cut the hair; a haircut. "He's gettan' a poll for 'e dance".
Pooshan: poison. Used as a intensive word. "Yon's a pooshan moeniment".
Poot: a young bird in the nest.
Preeg: to plead.
Preen: a pin.
Prontag: a crumb of dough in baking.
Proug: to prick "A've prouged ma fingar on 'e whins".
Puddag: a frog.
Pulley-cock: the turkey cock.
Purk: to prick.
Purn: a reel of thread.
Purr: to prick; a prick. "He purred hees finger". "Purrs" — thistles.
Pyowt: a feckless whining person, usually female.
Quate: quiet.
Quey: a heifer.
Rachle: in the phrase 'a rachle o' bon's', a lean emaciated animal.
Rachled: wrestled. "His croftie wis rachled fae 'e mire".
Raik: a person who works with fuss and effort but little care. "A raik o' a worker".
Rake: a small load. "A rake o' peits". To rummage in a drawer.
Ramgoose: the red throated diver.
Rander: to darn heavily in order to reinforce stocking heels.
Rawn: herring roe.
Redder: a comb.
Reend: a cloth or wooden border to anything.
Reet: to turn over clumsily; to root. " 'E peeg wis reetan in 'e mideen".

GLOSSARY

Rilleens: originally old shoes or the strips of hide from which they were made. Now used to describe any old tattered piece of clothing.
Ringan: used as an intensive word. "He's a little ringan' devil".
Risk: light drizzle.
Risp: a few stalks of straw or hay.
Rive: fit to burst from over-eating.
Rod: the road.
Roo: a small heap of peats set up during the second stage of the drying process.
Roog: to tear; to pull.
Rooze: to cure in brine; to swirl herring in salt.
Rounk: a shrivelled person or animal.
Sail: a ride in a cart.
San'-Lairag: the ringed plover.
Sap: a general reference to water. " 'Ere's a richt sap in 'e burnie efter aal 'at rain".
Scaap: poor ground.
Scam: to burn the outside of, to overheat. "She scammed her han on a lowan' peit".
Scarf: the cormorant.
Scloug: a blow on the ear.
Scon: crush flat. "He sconned 'e moose wi 'e spade".
Scoo: a large flat basket.
Scoor: a rattle of hailstones; to wipe down a table; to wander about in the hope of picking something up on the foreshore.
Scooreens: a home-spun cloth, like twill.
Scoort: an armful — "a scoort o' peits".
Scoot: to dart quickly away; to squirt water.
Scootie Allan: the Arctic skua.
Scorrie: a young seagull, under a year old and with brown plumage.
Scowth: scope; room to manoeuvre.
Scrayed: dried up.
Scroban: the gizzard of a hen.
Screech: a small amount. "When he's drownk he hesna a screech o' sense" ('ch' as in 'loch').
Screevlan: the scratching of a dog at the door.
Scroo: a stack of corn, hay etc. on a circular foundation and with a conical top.
Scroit: a crowd of worthless vulgar children. "She hes a scroit o' cheeky bairns".
Scrowg: a lean, hard person or animal.
Scruff: a thin membrane; the healing on top of a cut.
Scuddle: to wander away, usually with speed, to avoid a duty. " 'E dowg went scuddlan off an we hed till drive 'e yeows wirsels".
Scuffle: to scuffle neeps is to remove weeds from the drill of turnips using a horse-drawn "scuffler".
Scummer: a net on the end on a pole which a young boy used to catch herring as they fell back from the hauled net to the water.
Scutteran: darting about.
Sea-Dowg: the dogfish.
Seapie: the oyster catcher.
Sellag: a young coalfish.
Sen: to bless. (Sain: to make the sign of the cross).
Sharrow: bitter to taste.
Sheet: soot.
Sheks: worth; standing. "No greit sheks" — nothing special.
Shelveens: portable extensions to the sides of a horse cart.
Shiel: a peat-cutting spade with which a peat can be cut and placed on top of the bank by the cutter.
Shift: (1) a unit of cultivation rotation. "'E neeplan shift" is the turnip field.
(2) a change of underclothing.

Shither: people, folk.
Shochad: the green plover.
Shochlan: shuffling.
Shon: a bog; soft ground which often looks sound on the surface.
Shookie: a call to a horse.
Shoot: posture. "He hed a richt shoot on him at 'e ploo".
Shot: (1) a sheep's underjaw extending beyond the upper one.
(2) drunk. "He wis weel shot efter 'e lamb seil".
Shottle: a division in a wooden kist.
Show: to give. "Show me 'e hammer", means "give me the hammer". It does not mean "I want to see the hammer".
Shuttlegab: a sheep whose upper jaw protudes beyond the lower.
Silkie: a seal.
Simmans: ropes of twisted straw or heather; also of hay to tie down coles in a field.
Sindry: gone to pieces, asunder. Also 'sinry'.
Skail: to spill; to disperse; to empty; to spread as of peats to dry.
Skeepies: a game of tig. cf 'skibbielickie'.
Skelf: a splinter of wood driven into the finger.
Skellad: a tin vessel with a long handle, mainly used to scoop a drink of water from a croft well or pail.
Skelp: a slap; a chunk; to move quickly on foot.
Skeollag: wild mustard.
Skibbielickie: a children's game; tig. cf 'skeepies'.
Skin-Revach: a piece of hide used as a valve on the plunger of a boat's pump.
Skint: (1) a small drop; (2) to bespatter someone with liquid.
Skifter: a light covering — "a skifter o' snow".
Skite: the spree. "He wis on 'e skite last nicht".
Skirlag: a green blade of grass, green corn etc. blown on its edge to produce a skirling sound.
Skook: to move with a stooping motion; to look round a corner in a half bent position in order to pry on someone.
Skow: anything small and broken such as barrel staves after the barrel is broken. "He smashed 'e dressar intil skow".
Skutch: a quick deft turn or movement often applied to an industrious housewife. "She hed a richt skutch on her at 'e Spring-cleaning".
Skybal: poor soil. "Yons a richt skybal o' a pleice he hes".
Slammag: un undefined piece of something, usually held in the hand. "He hed a slammag o' ot breid an' croodie".
Slant: a puff of wind.
Slap: a gap in a wall or fence.
Slaister: doing a tedious wearisome job often in wet conditions. "He wis slaisteran 'e whole day in 'e neeplan' drain".
Sleitar: the woodlouse.
Slock: to put out, of a fire; to ease, of a thirst.
Slooan: a lazy untidy lump.
Slooder: an idle waster.
Slot: a wooden bar on a barn door.
Slounk: a lazy good-for-nothing lounger.
Smiach: sense, gumption, sagacity ('ch as in 'loch').
Smoorag: a grass bonfire damped down (by children) to provide lots of smoke.
Smyaager: to besmear; to make a mess. " 'E bairn hes smyaagered his new clothes wi' 'at ice creime ye gave him".
Snaik: a slug.
Sneck: the latch of a door.
Sneeteran: sniggering.
Sneevlan: sniffling.
Sneeg: to jerk.

GLOSSARY

Sneoug: snug. "Are ye sneoug?" — a question meaning "Have you got your harvest all in?" i.e. snug in the stackyard.
Snotteran: snuffling.
Soachan: drawing breath with difficulty. Wheezing.
Soern: to go about seeing what one can pick up. Also as of a dog searching to and fro.
Sodgers: ribgrass.
Soorag: wild sorrel.
Sooans: a mixture prepared from the finer husks or 'sids' of the oat.
Spangs: long stides.
Spardan: a henroost, made from a spar of wood.
Spart: to spread dung from a moving cart into drills.
Speet: a stick for carrying fish by passing it through their gills, for example, when hanging up for curing in a kiln.
Spel: to relieve, to take turns at wearisome tasks. At a dance, a youth had become tired of manoeuvring a rather cumbersome girl across the floor. Stopping by a companion he requested "Spel me wi' 'iss ein for a whilie".
Speldag: a fish, split and dried.
Spen: to wean lambs from their mothers.
Speurd: a contemptible person.
Spoot: dart quickly; squirt liquid; razor fish.
Sprool: a cross-piece of wire from which fishing hooks are suspended.
Sprowg: a sparrow.
Squaar: a swathe in mowing.
Square: the farm-yard enclosed on three sides by the steading.
Staig: an unbroken colt.
Stab: a wooden fence post.
Staidle: the foundation of a stack of corn, hay etc. often made with stones.
Steethe: a foundation, usually of a building.
Stirler: the starling.
Stouter: to stagger. "He wis stoutteran hom' wi a good dram".
Stoon: a sudden sharp pain; a whim; a dark mood. "Leive him be, he's in a bad stoon".
Stonechecker: the stonechat.
Straik: a small amount. " 'Ere wis only a straik o' sugar left in 'e bowl".
Stran: gutter along the side of a paved street, or up the middle of a byre.
Stravaig: to wander aimlessly.
Stroop: pipe down the side of a house, draining water from the roof often into a barrel.
Stroosh: to walk with long swaggering steps: "Look at 'e stroosh on him mekkan for 'e pub".
Strump: broken bits of straw.
Styme: the faintest trace of light. " 'A canna see a styme in iss fowg".
Swack: lithe, active.
Sweel: to rinse or wash without being too fussy. "He geid a queek sweel til his feice bit his loogs wir still black".
Sweire: reluctant.
Sweir-stick: a broomstick used in a form of floor wrestling.
Swey: the horizontal fire beam with movable hanging hooks for the pots.
Swilkie: a whirlpool. e.g. 'The Swilkie of Stroma'.
Swinger: a tall thin person usually female (soft 'g').
Swinglar: a sheep with a deformity which causes it to trail its hindquarters.
Sy: a scythe; to scythe.
Syer: a fine strainer usually for milk, in conjunction with a 'syer-cloth' of muslin.
Tant: one's limit. "If he can feenish thinnan 'at park 'o neeps 'afore dayset id'll be his tant".
Targer: a bossy, overbearing woman (soft 'g').

Tarter: the noise of scrambling about. "Fitna tarter 'e bairns are makkan". Also a sharp spoken woman.
Tee-Look: a look-to. "Tek a tee-look til see if 'e coo hes calved".
Teem: to empty. "Teem 'at peyl o' meit intil 'e peeg's troch".
Teet: to take a fly look. "She wis teetan' from behind 'e curteens".
Teethag: toothache.
Teetlag: the meadow pipit.
Teugan: pulling.
Thingment: something or someone whose real name has been forgotten. What's its name? What's his name?
Thrawcrock: a hand cranking tool for making simmans.
Throughither: harassed; distressed. "She's a' throughither wi 'e preparashans for her dochter's wedding".
Tiarchersome: ill-disposed.
Til: to. "Are ye goan til Weik?".
Tochie: a call to a calf.
Trachled: fatigued.
Traik: tiring walk. "Id's a richt traik uptil 'e peit bank".
Threep: to assert forcefully. "He tried til threep doon ma throt that ...".
Treffis: the wooden partition between stalls in a stable.
Trink: a rocky opening below water.
Trock: rubbish, trash.
Troolie: untidily dressed, usually referring to a female.
Trosk: a stupid person, or one with a bit of the clown in him.
Trow: to play truant from school.
Turse: to arrange one's clothes; a stout ungainly woman; to turn up the bottom of trousers; to roll up one's sleeves.
Turr: to remove the top turf from a peatbank, etc...
Turrymurry: in a pickle; an upset.
Tuskar: a peat-cutting spade.
Twilt: quilt.
Twite: to whittle a piece of wood.
Vrocht: worked.
Waal: a long sweeping blow of the arm. "He cem at him wi wan waal 'at knocked him flyan".
Waek: weak.
Wallie: an open well.
Wan: the numeral "one".
Warriebowg: a type of seaweed; the grub of the warblefly; an inhabitant of Huna.
Wait: a mill lade.
Warsie: sick or feeble from want of food.
Wattle: to twist or ravel; an entanglement. " 'Iss binder coerd is a' wattled".
Weicht: weights, deserts — "Y'll get yir weichts" — "You'll get your deserts".
Wheepar-in: the school attendance officer.
Willie-Weet-Feet: the common sandpiper.
Winleen: a bundle of straw, bound by short simmans teased from the ends of the bundle.
Wir: our. "Wirsels" — ourselves.
Wirshad: worsted wool.
Wisk: anything bulky and untidy rolled round the neck. "She hed a wisk o' an owld scarf aboot her heid".
Wraxed: over strained or stretched.
Yirned: sour.
Yowl: to howl.
Yowlie: a native of Aukengill, possibly from the high-pitched voice.

BIBLIOGRAPHY

ALLEN, J.R.	The Early Christian Monuments of Scotland	Edinburgh	1903
ANDERSON, A.O.	Early Sources of Scottish History	Edinburgh	1922
ANDERSON, J. (trans.)	Orkneyinga Saga	Edinburgh reprinted	1873 1977
ANDERSON, J.(ed.)	The Orkneyinga Saga	The Mercat Press (new edition)	1981
ANDERSON, J.	Scotland in Pagan Times. The Iron Age	Edinburgh	1883
ANDERSON, J.	Notes on the Relics of the Viking Period of the Northmen in Scotland	*PSAS, 10* 536-594	1872-4
AULD, A.	Memorials of Caithness Ministers	Edinburgh	1911
BALDWIN, J. (ed.)	Caithness: A Cultural Crossroads	Edinburgh	1982
BATEY, C.E.	Caithness Coastal Survey 1980-82. Dunnet Head to Ousdale.	Occasional Paper No. 3 Dept. of Arch. Durham.	1987
BATEY, C.E.	Freswick Links, Caithness. A Re-appraisal of the Late Norse site in its Context	*British Arch. Reports* Series (BAR) 179, Oxford 2 vols.	1984
BAYNE, A.	A short Geographical Survey of Caithness	MSS Inverness Library	1735
BEATON, D.	Ecclesiastical History of Caithness and Annals of Caithness Parishes	Wick	1909
BEATON, D. (ed.)	Parish Registers of Canisbay (Caithness) 1652-1666	Edinburgh	1914
BEATON, D.	Caithness and Sutherland Miscellany	Wick	1930
BEATON, E.	The Doocots of Caithness	Dundee	1980
BRAMMAN, J. I.	The Early Inhabitants in Omand, D. (Ed.) The Caithness Book	Inverness	1972
BRAND, J.	A Brief Description of Orkney, Zetland, Pightland Firth and Caithness	Edinburgh	1701
BREMNER, D.	Industries of Scotland	Edinburgh	1869

BROWN, G.	Plan of Intended Road from Thurso to Dunbeath (Map)	RHP11610	1797
BROWN, H.	Early Travellers in Scotland	Edinburgh	1973
BROWN, K. M.	Bloodfeud in Scotland 1573-1625	Edinburgh	1986
BROWN, T.	Annals of the Disruption	Edinburgh	1893
BRYCE, A.	A Map of the North Coast of Britain	Edinburgh	c1745
BURL, A.	The Stone Circles of the British Isles	Yale University Press	1976
CAITHNESS FIELD CLUB	Bulletins		
CALDER, C. S. T.	Report on the Excavation of a Broch at Skitten, in the Killimster District of Caithness 1940	PSAS,82 pp.124-5	1947-48
CALDER, J. T.	Civil and Traditional History of Caithness	Murray Wick reprint	1861 1887
CAMPBELL, J. P. & OMAND, D.	A Kaitness Kist	Thurso	1984
CAMPBELL, R.	Notice of the Discovery of Eight Silver Rings of ancient wrist or ankle rings, in cists near Rattar, Dunnet, Caithness.	PSAS,9 422-7	1870-72
CARTER, S., HAIGH, D., NEIL, N. R. J., SMITH, B.	Interim Report on the Structures at Howe, Stromness, Orkney	Glasgow Arch. Jour. 11, pp 61-73	1984
CHILDE, V. G.	Another Late Viking House at Freswick	PSAS,77 pp. 5-17	1942-43
CLEGG, P. V.	A Flying Start to the Day		1986
CORCORAN, J. X. W. P.	The Excavation of Three Chambered Cairns at Loch Calder, Caithness	PSAS,98 1-75	1964-66
CORMACK, A. & A.	Days of Orkney Steam	Kirkwall	1971
CORDINER, C.	Remarkable Ruins of North Britain	London	1780
COWAN, I. B.	The Scottish Reformation	London	1982
CRAMPTON, C. et alia	The Geology of Caithness	Edinburgh	1911
CRAVEN, J. B.	A History of the Episcopal Church in the Diocese of Caithness	Peace	1908
CRAVEN, J. B. (Ed.)	Journal of the Episcopal Visitations of the Right Rev. Robert Forbes M.A.	Kirkwall	1886

BIBLIOGRAPHY

GRAY, J.	Sutherland and Caithness in Saga-Time	Edinburgh	1922
GRIEG, S.	*Viking Antiquities in Scotland* in Shetelig, H. Viking Antiquities of Great Britain and Ireland Part II	Oslo	1940
GRIMBLE, I.	Clans and Chiefs	London	1980
GUNN, M. R.	Clan Gunn	Glasgow	N.D.
GUNN, R.	Alexander Bain of Watten	Caithness Field Club	1976
HALL, J.	Travels in Scotland by an unusual route	London	1807
HART, F. R. & PICK, J. B.	Neil M. Gunn: A Highland Life	London	1981
HAY, G.	The Architecture of Scottish Post-Reformation Churches 1560-1843	Oxford	1957
HEDGES, J. W.	Tomb of the Eagles	London	1984
HEDGES, J. W.	Bu, Gurness and the Brochs of Orkney, Parts, I, II, III	*BAR Rep.* British Series 163 Oxford 12-13	1987
HENDERSON, I.	The Picts	Thomas & Hudson	1967
HENDERSON, J.	Caithness Family History	Douglas	1884
HENDERSON, J.	General View of the Agriculture of the County of Caithness	London	1812
HENSHALL, A.	The Chambered Tombs of Scotland Vols. I & II	Edinburgh	1963 1972
HORNE, J. (Ed.)	County of Caithness	Wick	1907
HORNE, J.	Round the Old Home	Wick	1935
HOUSTON, D.	'E Silkie Man	(Originally Viking Club) Caithness Books	N.D.
HUME, J. R.	The Industrial Archaeology of Scotland	London	1977
HUNTER, J. R.	The Island of Muckle Skerry, Orkney	*PSAS,112* 518-524 (Site 4)	1982
HUTCHISON, I.	The Story of Loganair	Western Isles Pub. Co.Ltd.	1987
JACKSON, K. H.	The Gaelic Notes in the Book of Deer	Cambridge	1972
JONES, A. K. G.,	*Man and the Environment at*	*BAR Internat.*	1983

CRAWFORD, B. E.	The Earldom of Caithness and the Kingdom of Scotland	*Northern Scotland 2* Part 2 97-117	1976-77
CRAWFORD, B. E.	The Earls of Orkney-Caithness and their Relations with Norway and Scotland 1158-1470	Unpub. Ph.D. Thesis, St. Andrews University	1971
CRUDEN, S.	The Scottish Castle	Nelson	1960
CURLE, A. O.	Inventory of Ancient Monuments in the County of Caithness	HMSO	1911
CURLE, A. O.	A Viking Settlement at Freswick, Caithness	*PSAS, 73* 71-110	1938-39
CURLE, A. O.	Notebook held in the National Monuments Record for Scotland, Edinburgh.	Ms 28 (SAS 461) 20-21	
DONALDSON, G.	Northwards by Sea	Edinburgh	1978
DONALDSON, J.	Caithness in the 18th century	Moray Press	1938
DONALDSON, J. (Ed.)	The Mey Letters	Kingsgrove Australia	1984
DUNLOP, J.	Pulteneytown and the Planned Villages of Caithness in Baldwin, J. (Ed.) Caithness: A Cultural Crossroads	Edinburgh	1982
EWING, W.	Annals of the Free Church		1914
FAIRHURST, H.	Excavations at Crosskirk Broch, Caithness	*Soc. of Antiq. Scot.* Monograph Series No. 3 Edinburgh	1984
FORBES, BISHOP	Journal of the Episcopal Visitation of the Dioceses of Ross and Caithness 1762-1770	Kirkwall	1886
FRASER, J.	Chronicles of the Frasers (The Wardlaw Manuscript)	Scottish History Society	1905
FRASER, Sir W.	The Sutherland Book	Edinburgh	1892
FRESSON, E. E.	Air Road to the Isles	David Rendel Ltd.	1967
FOOTE, P. G. & WILSON, D. M.	The Viking Achievement	London	1980
GLASS, N. M.	Caithness and the War 1939-1945	Wick	1948
GRANT, D.	Yarns of the Pentland Firth	Wick	1933
GRANT, D.	Old Thurso	Thurso	1966

BIBLIOGRAPHY

BATEY, C. E., MORRIS, C. D. RACKHAM, D. J.	*Freswick Links, A Late Norse Site in Caithness* in Integrating the Subsistence Economy	Series 181	
KEMP, D. W. (Ed.)	Pococke's Tours in Scotland	Edinburgh	1887
LACAILLE, A. D.	The Stone Age in Scotland	London	1954
LANG, A.	The Highlands of Scotland in 1750	Edinburgh	1898
LAING, S. & HUXLEY, T. H.	Prehistoric Remains of Caithness	Edinburgh	1866
LARNER, C., HYDE LEE, C. & McLACHLAN, H. V.	A Source-Book of Scottish Witchcraft	Glasgow	1977
LIESTOL, A.	*Runes* in Fenton, A. and Palsson H. (Eds.) The Northern and Western Isles in the Viking World. Survival, Continuity and Change 224-238	Edinburgh	1984
LINDSAY, A.	A Rutter of the Scottish Seas Circa 1540	Nat. Maritime Museum No.44	1980
LINDSAY, H.	Folklore of Dunbeath	Dunbeath Preservation Trust	1985
LITHGOW, W.	Travels and Voyages, 1628-29	Edinburgh	1893
LIVINGSTONE, A. AIKMAN, C. W. H., HART, B. S. (Eds.)	A Muster Roll of Prince Charles Edward Stuart's Army 1745-46	Aberdeen	1984
MacECHERN, D.	The Sword of the North	Inverness	1923
MacKENZIE, W. M.	The Medieval Castle in Scotland	Methuen	1927
MACFARLANE, W.	Geographical Collections relating to Scotland. 3 vols.	Edinburgh	1906-08
MACKAY, A.	The Book of Mackay	Wick	1906
MACKAY, A.	History of the Province of Cat	Wick	1914
MACKAY, D.	Memories of Our Parish (Reay)	Dingwall	1925
MACKAY, D.	This Was My Glen	Thurso	1965
MACKAY, R. L.	Clan Mackay: Its Origin, History and Dispersal	Wolverhampton	1977
MANSON, S.	The Coal Ship's Coming	*Scots Mag.*	April 1978
MARWICK H.	Orkney Farm Names	Kirkwall	1952
MASTERS, L. J.	The Excavation and Restoration of the Camster Long Chambered Cairn, Caithness District, 1967-80	Forthcoming	
McCONNELL, D.	The Coming of the Railway	*John O'Groat Journal*	1979
McGIBBON et alia	The Castellated and Domestic Architecture of Scotland from the 12th to the 18th Century	Douglas	1889

McNEILL, P. & NICHOLSON, R. (Eds.)	A Historical Atlas of Scotland	St. Andrews	1975
MERCER, R. J.	Archaeological Field Survey in Northern Scotland 1976-79	Edinburgh	1980
MERCER, R. J.	Archaeological Field Survey in Northern Scotland 1980-81	Edinburgh	1981
MILLER, J.	Caithness	London	1979
MILLER, J.	Caithness and Sutherland	London	1985
MITCHELL, A. & CLARK, J. T. (Ed.)	Geographical Collections made by Walter MacFarlane	S.H.S.	1906-08
MITCHISON, R.	Agricultural Sir John: The Life of Sir John Sinclair of Ulbster 1745-1835	London	1962
MORRISON, A.	Early Man in Britain and Ireland	London	1980
MOWAT, J.	Old Caithness Maps and Map Makers	Wick	1938
MOWAT, J.	A Bibliography of Caithness	Wick	1940
MOWAT, J.	Some Caithness Notables	Wick	1928
MOWAT, W. G.	The Story of Lybster	Wick	1959
MUNRO, H.	Legends of the Pentland Firth	Thurso	1977
MUNRO, H.	More legends of the Pentland Firth	Thurso	1979
NEW STATISTICAL ACCOUNT OF SCOTLAND	Caithness		1841
NICHOLSON, R.	Scotland: The Later Middle Ages	Edinburgh	1974
NICOLAISEN, W. F. H.	Scottish Place Names	London	1976
OLD STATISTICAL ACCOUNT OF SCOTLAND	Compiled by Sir J. Sinclair (Caithness & Sutherland reprint)		1790 1979
OMAND, D. (Ed.)	The Caithness Book	Inverness	1972
OMAND, D.	The Glaciation of Caithness	Unpub. M.Sc. Thesis, University of Strathclyde	1973
OMAND, D. & PORTER, J.	The Caithness Flagstone Industry	Aberdeen	1981
OMAND, D.	*The Making of the Caithness Landscape* in Caithness: A Cultural Crossroads J. Baldwin (Ed.)	Edinburgh	1982
OMAND, D. & PORTER, J.	Halkirk and its Highland Games	Elgin	1977
PALSSON, H. & EDWARDS, P.	Orkneyinga Saga	London	1978

BIBLIOGRAPHY

PEGLER, S.	A Radiocarbon-dated Pollen Diagram from the Loch of Winless, Caithness, North-East Scotland	*New Phytologist* 82, 245-63	1979
PENNANT, T.	A Tour in Scotland in 1769	London	1771
POCOCKE, R.	Tour Through Sutherland and Caithness in 1760	Edinburgh	1888
POLSON, A.	The Book of Ross, Sutherland and Caithness	Dingwall	1932
POPE, A.	Ancient History of Orkney, Caithness and the North by T. Torfaeus (Translated)	Wick	1866
PONT, T.	Map of Caithness		c1600
	Register of the Sasines for Caithness 1646-1780	HMSO	1939
REID, N.	Quick Before the Memory Fades	Highland Printers Ltd.	1975
RENFREW, A. C.	INVESTIGATIONS IN ORKNEY	London	1979
	Report of the Commissioners of inquiry into the condition of the Crofters and Cottars in the Highlands and Islands of Scotland	Napier Commission	1884
RHIND, A. H.	Notice of the Exploration of a 'Pict's House', at Kettleburn, in the County of Caithness	Archaeol. Journal 10 211-223	1853
RITCHIE, W. & MATHER A.	The Beaches of Caithness	Aberdeen	1970
ROBINSON, D.	Investigations into the Aukhorn Peat Mounds, Keiss, Caithness: Pollen, Plant Macrofossil and Charcoal Analysis	New Phytologist 106	1987
ROSS INSTITUTE	Ye Booke of Halkirk		1911
SAGE, D.	Memorabilia Domestica	Wick	1899
SAXON, J.	The Fossil Fishes of Caithness	Thurso	1967
SCOTT, H. (Ed.)	Fasti Ecclesiae Scoticanae	Edinburgh	1928
SCOTTISH DEVELOPMENT DEPARTMENT	Statutory List of Buildings of Special Architectural or Historic Interest, Caithness		1984
SIMPER, R.	Scottish Sail	David & Charles	1974
SIMPSON, A. T. & STEVENSON, S	Historic Wick	Scottish Burgh Survey Glasgow	1983

SIMPSON, D.	Scottish Castles: An Introduction to the Castles of Scotland	HMSO	1959
SINCLAIR, J.	Scenes and Stories of the North of Scotland	Edinburgh	1890
SINCLAIR, Sir J.	General View of the Agriculture of the Northern Counties and Islands of Scotland	London	1795
SINCLAIR, T.	Caithness Events	Wick	1899
SKENE, Sir J. (Ed.)	Regiam Majestatem	Edinburgh	1774
SMILES, S.	Robert Dick, Baker, of Thurso Geologist and Botanist	London	1878
SMITH, D. J.	Action Stations (Vol. 7)	PSL, Cambridge	1983
SMOUT, T. C.	A History of the Scottish People 1560-1830	Glasgow	1969
SOPER, T.	The Shell Book of Beachcombing	David & Charles	1972
ST. CLAIR, R.	The St. Clairs of the Islands	Brett New Zealand	1889
STELL, G.	*Some Small Farms and Cottages in Latheron Parish, Caithness.* in J. Baldwin (Ed.) Caithness: A Cultural Crossroads	Edinburgh	1982
STELL, G. & OMAND, D.	The Caithness Croft	Laidhay	1976
STEPHEN, D.	Gleanings in the North	Haddington	1891
SUMMERSON, J.	The Classical Language of Architecture	London	1963
SUTHERLAND, G.	Folklore Gleanings and Character Sketches from the Far North	Wick	1937
SUTHERLAND, I.	Wick Harbour and the Herring Fishing	Wick	1984
SUTHERLAND, I.	From Herring to Seine Net Fishing on the East Coast of Caithness	Wick	1985
SUTHERLAND, I.	The Wick and Lybster Light Railway	Wick	1987
TALBOT, E.	Scandinavian Fortification in the British Isles	*Scott. Archaeol. Forum*, 6 37-45	1974
TALBOT, E.	A Report on Excavations at Bishop's Castle, Scrabster	*Northern Studies* 2, 37-39	1973
TALBOT, E.	The Ring of Castlehill, Caithness A Viking Fortification?	*PSAS, 108*	1976-77

BIBLIOGRAPHY

TATLOW, P.	Highland Railway Miscellany	Oxford	1985
TAYLOR, A.	The Orkneyinga Saga: A New Translation with introduction and notes	Edinburgh & London	1938
TAYLOR, G. & SKINNER, A.	Maps of roads in Caithness	London	1776
THOM. A. & THOM, A. S.	Megalithic Remains in Britain and Brittany	Oxford	1978
THOM, A.	Megalithic Sites in Britain	Oxford	1967
THOM, A.	Megalithic Lunar Observatories	Oxford	1971
THOMSON, J.	Caithness-shire (Map)	Edinburgh	1822
THOMSON, W. P. L.	History of Orkney	Edinburgh	1987
TRANTER, N.	The Fortified House in Scotland Volume 5	Oliver & Boyd	1963
VALLANCE, H. A.	The Highland Railway	David & Charles	1969
WATSON, G.	Roads and Tracks Through Local History	*Caithness Field Club Bulletin* Vol. 4. No 2-4	1985-86
WAUGH, D.	Caithness Place Names	*Nomina*, 8 15-28	1984
WAUGH, D.	The Place-Names of Canisbay Parish	*Northern Scotland*	forthcoming
WEBSTER, B. (Ed.)	The Acts of David II	Edinburgh	1982
WILSON, D.	Plan of Proposed Road from The Bridge of Wick to the Ord of Caithness (Telford Road)	RHP11653	1807
WORMALD, J.	Court, Kirk and Community	London	1981
WORMALD, J.	Lords and Men in Scotland: Bonds of Manrent 1442-1603	Edinburgh	1985
ZIEGLER, P.	The Black Death	London	1969

INDEX

Abercrombie, Charles 109
Acaveilan 146
Achadh Beathaig 146
Achadh a' Chracairnie 146
Achadh Chairnleith 146
Achadh na Gaodha 146
Achadh Mor 146
Achaeter 146
Achagie 146
Achairn 24, 146
Achairn Moss 21
Achalipster 146
Achalone 146
Achanarras 146
Achanon 146
Acharaskill 146
Achardle 146
Acharole 146
Acharynie 146
Achastle 23, 146
Achastle Castle 162, 169
Achavarn 146
Achavanich . . . . . 43, 45, 146, Plate 9
Achavar 146
Achavrole 146
Achbuiligan 146
Achcomhairle 146
Achforsiescye 146
Achgremach 146
Ach Hacon 146
Achiebegg 146
Achiebraeskiall 146
Achiegullan 146
Achies 146
Achieviegle 146
Achimenach 146
Achimenach Free Church Plate 36
Achimore 146
Achinavish 146
Achingale 146, 174
Achingills 146
Achingoul 146
Achins 146
Achkeepster 143, 146
Achkinloch (L. Stemster) . . . 20, 21, 43
Achlachan 146
Achlibster 143, 146, 149
Achlipster 143
Achnabeinn 146
Achnacly 146
Achnaclyth 146
Achnacoile 146
Achnacraig 146
Achnagoul 146, 150
Achnamoine 146
Achnavast 146
Achorn 22, 146
Achow 146
Achoy 146
Achrasker 146
Achreamie 146
Achreregan 146
Achscoriclate 146
Achscrabster 143, 146
Achsinegar 146
Achsteenclate 146
Achunabust 143, 146, 149
Achvarasdal 146
Achverga 146
Achvidigo 146
Ackergill 86, 88, 110, 111, 170, 173, 192
Ackergill Mains 153
Ackergill Tower 161, 162, 169
Adam (Bishop) . . 71, 74, 81, 137, 187
Aimster 143
Altimarlach 97, 118
Altnabreac 24, 171
Anderson, Joseph . 30, 37, 38, 76, 196
Andrew (Bishop) 79
Arbroath, Declaration of 83
Ascend (Skinnet) 82
Asleifarson, Swein 79, 157, 159
Atomic Energy Authority 14
Auckengill 50, 183, 224
Aulton 43

Backies 90
Backlass 41
Badbea 106, 118
Badlibster 143
Bain, Alexander 140, 190
Balbeg 150
Ballachy 66
Ballone 150
Balnabruich 150
Balnahard 150
Bayne, Aeneas 100, 133, 187

INDEX

Begg, Alexander. 196
Ben-a-Chielt 21
Ben Freiceadain 60
Beinn Ratha 150
Berriedale. . 19, 21, 106, 110, 118, 175
Berriedale Castle . . 119, 156, 159, 169
Berriedale Ness 19
Berriedale River (Water) . . 18, 19, 22, 181
Bilbster (Wick). 41, 143
Blackpark 153
Blaeu. 188
Blingery 149
Boggy Park Croft 153
Borgue. 41
Borrowston Mains. 153
Bower 41, 72, 82, 91, 92, 94, 112, 181, 206
Braal 137
Braal Castle. . . . 71, 72, 137, 160, 169 Plate 23
Brabster 100, 112, 143, 173
Brabsterdorran 143
Brabstermire 143
Braemore 21, 205
Brand, John. 97, 98, 100
Bremner, James . . . 110, 127, 137, 190
Brig o'Trams 19
Brims. 87, 169, 170, 183, 186
Brims Castle 167
Brodie (Captain) 124
Brogger, A. W. 72
Broubster 43,143
Brough. 71, 79, 128
Brough Castle 160, 169
Brounaban 53
Brown, Robert. 196
Bruan 45, 198
Brubster 106, 118, 136, 204
Bryce, Alexander 183
Buaile, Oscar. 47
Buchollie Castle 79, 157, 169
Burn, George. 108
Burnside. 203
Bylbster (Watten) 143

Caithness Glass . . . . 126, Plate 61
Calder 139
Calder, James T.. 88, 189, 192, Plate 53
Calder Loch (Cairns) 130
Calder Mains 153
Campbell (Brigadier) Jock 194
Campbell, Iain Glas. 96
Campbell, Robert. 97
Camster 21, 22, 33, 35, 36, 37, 38, 39, 44, 120, 143, 196
Camster Long Cairn . . . 25, 30, 31, 36, 37, 38, 39, Fig.4, Plate 7
Camster Round . . . . . . 30, 36, Fig.4, Plate 6
Canisbay. 82, 87, 92, 95, 98, 100, 107, 128, 171, 173, 178, 188, 192, 197, 200, 209, 210
Canisbay Church Plate 22
Carbisdale. 95
Carn Mor 18
Carn Na Mairg 53, 54
Castlehill (Bower). 72
Castlehill (Castletown). . . 72, 109, 111, 128, 129, 130, 191, Plate 35
Castletown . . . . 14, 72, 109, 115, 128, 130, 174, 175, 184, 186, Plate 60
Castletown Harbour . . . . Plate 80
Castletown Mill . . . . Plate 51
Catnes, John 96
Catnes, Richard 96
Causewaymire (Causeymire) 21, 24, 102, 177, 181
de Cheyne, Reginald 84, 158, 162
Clairdon 79, 132, 170
Clairdon Airfield . . . . Plate 57
Clashmore 106
Clyth 108, 113, 121, 123
Clyth Burn 21
Clyth Ness. 209
Clyth Roadside Farm 66
Cnoc An Eirannich 18
Cnoc Freiceadain . . . . . 33, 60, Fig.3, Plate 8
Cnoc Na Maranaich. 43
Comlifoot. 138
Cook, Finlay 107
Coghill, Donald 105
Couper, John. 136
Craig Scalabsdale . . . 18, 22, Plates 1, 2
Cranesby 82
Crawford, B. 71
Crichton, George 84
Croft of Achimore. 153
Croft of Northfield 153
Croft of Sibster 153
Cromwell, Oliver 95
Crosskirk . . . . . 50, 52, 54, 62, 74, 82, 134, Plate 20

236 THE NEW CAITHNESS BOOK

Dale House 171, 173
Dalmore 205
Daniell, William 184
Deil's Brig 19
Dick, Robert 133, 190
Dirlot 21, 22, 84, 137, 205
Dirlot Castle 162, 169
Dorrery 20, 41, 44
Dower, F. L. Gandar 186
Dounreay . . . 14, 20, 45, 87, 106, 116, 117, 137, 186, Plates 58, 59
Dounreay Castle 165, 169
Drumhollistan 20, 142
Dunbeath 21, 23, 41, 94, 95, 96, 107, 108, 111, 119, 175, 195, 199
Dunbeath Bay . . . . Plate 24
Dunbeath Castle . . . 23, 161, 169, 170, 205, Plate 24
Dunbeath Fisheries Store . . . . Plate 34
Dunbeath River (Water) . . . 19, 30, 43, 66, 181
Duncansby 24, 71, 98, 200
Duncansby Head 17, 18, 19, 21, 94, 107
Duncansby Stacks . . . . 19, Plate 4
Dunmey (St. John's Point) 66
Dunnet 71, 82, 92, 98, 107, 111, 117, 128, 130, 141, 155, 178, 183, 191, 192, 201, 209
Dunnet Bay 13, 23, 41
Dunnet Church . . . . 128, Plate 19
Dunnet Head 17, 19
Dunbar, Benjamin 192
Dunbar, Patrick 102
Dunbar, William 97
Dunrobin 87, 89, 101

Elder, John 196
Eysteinsdal (See Ousdale)

Fergus, St. 91, 206
Finlayson, John 192
Flendie Clett (Stroma) 71
Flow Country 13
Forbes (Bishop) 180, 182
Forbes, Robert 102
Forse 108, 123, 171
Forss 209
Forss Castle 158, 169
Forss (Old Bridge) . . . . Plate 42
Forss River (Water) 18
Fresson, (Capt) 186

Freswick . . . . . . 24, 25, 69, 70, 71, 75, 80, 173, 183, Plates 17, 18
Freswick Castle 157, 168, 169

Garrywhin 30, 31, 33, 36, 45, 47, 199, Fig.3
Georgemas 41, 138
Gerston 138, 139, 142, 197
Gills 127, 182
Gills Bay 20, 185
Girnigoe 87, 88, 89, 90, 97
Girnigoe Castle (see Sinclair Castle) . . 163, 164, 169, Plate 26
Glenorchy, Campbell of 96
Godrodarson, Rognvald 79
Grant, Donald 132
Greenland Mains 153
Griam, Ben 86
Guidebest 44, 143
Gunn, Alexander 196
Gunn, Castle 159, 169
Gunn, George 86
Gunn, Helen 86
Gunn, Neil 119, 195, 211
Gunn, Sir John 196
Gunnison, Snaekoll 81

Haimer Castle 167, 169
Halberry Castle 159, 169, 200
Halkirk . . . 14, 20, 64, 69, 71, 74, 80, 82, 98, 101, 103, 106, 107, 109, 114, 118, 129, 137, 182, 185, 187, 189, 197, 205, Plate 30
Halkirk (Old Bridge) . . . . Plate 49
Haludal 82
Ham 129, 174
Harald (Earl) . . . 79, 80, 157, 163, 170
Harald, Ungi 79
Harald's Tower 170
Haraldsson, John 82
Harmsworth, Sir Robert 114
Harpsdale 138
Haster 143
Heathfield 153
Heilan Loch 20
Helshettir 148
Hemp Rig 154
Hempriggs 99, 154, 171
Henderson, John 105, 196
Henderson (Capt) John 196
Henderson, William 196
Highland Peat Company 24

INDEX

Hill O'Many Stanes 45
Hill O' Works. 53, 54
Holborn Head 19
Horne, Henry Sinclair 193
Horne, John 192, 194, 199, 212
Horne, James. 177
Houstry 199
Hoveden, Roger de 79
Huna 69, 70, 73, 75, 95, 110,
184, Fig.13
Hunster 143, 148

Ingimster 143

John O'Groats 13, 17, 24, 70, 98,
126, 174, 182, 217, Plate 65
John Nicolson Museum 50, 62
John (Bishop) 79, 80
John (Earl) 81

Keiss 23, 64, 69, 87, 92, 96, 97,
110, 115, 127, 170, 175, 190,
209, Fig.9 (Pictish Stone)
Keiss Castle 164, 169, 170, 205,
Plate 27
Keiss Road Broch 52, 53
Keiss Harbour Mound 48
Keiss Whitegate Mound 48, 69,
100, 108
Kettleburn (Wick). 50, 72, 192
Killimster 105, 143
Kilsson, Kali Rognvald. 79
Knockfin Heights 20
Knockinnon Castle 163, 169

Laidhay 119
Lamborg 79
Langwell. 106, 118
Langwell River (Water) . . . 18, 19, 21,
22, 23, 58
Largs, Battle of. 83
Latheron 40, 41, 58, 64, 82, 83,
90, 98, 101, 103, 107, 113, 115,
120, 121, 123, 138, 178
Latheron Castle 165, 169, 198
Latheron Mains 162
Latheronwheel. . . . 19, 21, 23, 44, 119
Leed, Donald. 171
Leodebest. 143
Liot 41
Loanscorribest 143

Loch Calder (Chambered Tombs) . . . .
29, 35, 40
Loch Dhu 171
Loch More Castle 162, 169
Loch Rangag 41
Loch Scarmclate 20
Loch Scye 18
Lybster. 14, 20, 22, 44, 64, 109,
110, 120, 122, 123, 143, 158, 174,
196, Plate 15
Lybster Mains (The Ha'). . . . 121, 153,
Plate 47
Lyth 181

Mackay, Donald. 88
Mackay, Ian 195
Mackay, John M. 196
Maddadarson, Harald 78, 83, 90
Maddarson, Earl Harold. 132
Maiden Pap. 18, 22
Mestag, Castle 79, 160, 169
Mey. 17, 87, 100, 107
Mey, Castle 165, 169
Mid Clyth 21, 45, 64, Fig.11
Miller, William. 193
Montrose, Marquis of . . . 94, 161, 184
de Moravia, Gilbert (Bishop of
Caithness). . 81, 82, 132, 137, 163, 187
Morriston, John 189
Morven . . . . 18, 22, 23, Plate 1
Murkle. 142, 167
Mybster 41, 143

Na Tri Shean (Chambered Cairn) . . . 35
Neck of Brough 66
Ness of Duncansby 70
Nicolson, J. 50, 197
Nipster. 143
Norfrost . . . . 131, Plate 60
Noss Head. 17
Nybster 143, 197
Nybster Broch Fig.7

Occumster 21, 123, 143
Old Reay . . . . . . 64, Fig.10, Plate 11
Oldwick (Auldwick) Castle 71, 84,
88, 124, 157, 158, 160, 169, Plate 25
Olrig 82, 105, 128, 202, 203
Olrig House. 172
Ord 13, 79, 96, 101, 109, 184

238 THE NEW CAITHNESS BOOK

Ormiegill 30
Oswald, Richard. 188
Ousdale 17, 22, 80, 118
Ousdale Broch . . . . Plate 8
Ousdale Inn. 181

Papigoe 92
Pennant, Thomas 101, 102, 127
Pentland Firth 67, 75, 79, 87, 98, 103, 109, 141, 151, 200, 204
Pentland Skerries 75
Philip's Mains 153
Pont, Robert 92
Pont, Timothy 92, 124, 128, 178, 188
Pont, Zachary 92
Pope, Rev. Alexander . . 171, 174, 188
Pulteney, Sir William 125
Pulteneytown. . . 14, 108, 109, 125, 176

Ramscraigs (Latheron). . . . . . Plate 33
Rattar 106
Reisgill Burn 22
Reaster 106
Reay . . . 20, 23, 40, 41, 64, 71, 73, 75, 82, 91, 98, 118, 134, 135, 136, 150, 183, 184, 196, 204, 209, (see Old Reay)
Reay Free Church 178
Reay, Lord 93, 95, 109
Rhind, A. H. 30, 192
Roadside Farm, Clyth 66
Robert (Bishop) 88
Robertshaven . . . . 70, 75, Fig. 13
Rognvald, Earl. 156, 158
Ronald, Earl 124
Ross, John 138
Roster 148

St. Andrew's Church 176
St. Clair, Henry 84
St. Clair, (Major-General) Austen . 189
St. Clair, William 84
St. John's Point (Dunnet) 66
St. Magnus 82, 83, 139
St. Mary's (Crosskirk) 74, 82
St. Peter's Church (Thurso) 73, 74, 82, 94, 132, 176
Sal-vaich. 18
Sandside Bay . . 13, 23, 73, 136, 175, 183
Sandside House . . . . 60, 171, 173, Plate 40
Sannick Bay. 24, 69

Sarclet . . 19, 20, 23, 109, 124, Plate 31
Scaraben(s) 18, 22, 23
Scarfskerry 128, 183
Scrabster . . . . . 20, 69, 72, 80, 82, 89, 134, 143, 175, 184, 185, 203, Plate 63
Scrabster Castle 163, 169
Seater 69
Sgeir Bhan 151
Sgeir Gut 151
Shaltigoe 116
Shebster 106, 118, 136, 143
Shelligoe. 120
Shielton Moss 21
Shurrery 106, 118, 131, 204
Sibmister 142, 143
Sibster 143, 192
Sinclair, Archibald 194
Sinclair Castle . . . . 164, Plate 26
Sinclair, Dane 197
Sinclair, Earl John. 87
Sinclair, (General) 14
Sinclair, George . . . 88, 93, 96, 97, 114, 126, 132
Sinclair, Herbert. 195
Sinclair, Lord William 87
Sinclair, James (of Brecks) 87
Sinclair, Patrick 109, 121, 122
Sinclair, Sir John (of Ulbster) . . . 14, 98, 104, 105, 106, 109, 114, 120, 121, 129, 132, 133, 157, 170, 171, 175, 181, 189, Plate 54
Sinclair, Sir William 127, 164, 197
Sinclair, Tollemache 114, 132, 185
Sinclair, William (Earl of Orkney) . . . 86
Sinclair's Bay 13
Skinnet. 82, 137
Skinnet Stone. 64
Skirza 15
Skitten 50, 15, 186
Slickly 100
Smean 18, 22
Smerral 21
Smith, William 133, 193
Sordale Hill 30,41
Sovereign S.S. . . . . , Plate 56
Spittal . . . 41, 83, 118, 139, 180, 181
Spittal Quarry 17
Sron, Garbh 18
Staxigoe . . . . . 99, 100, 108, 127, 174, Plate 38
Stemster 97, 112, 143, 173
Stewart, Robert (Bishop of Caithness) . 84, 88, 91, 92

INDEX

Stirkoke 92, 93
Stone Lud 41
Stroma 19, 79, 151, 173, 183, 184, 200, 213, 214, 215, 223
Strupster. 143
Summerdale 93
Summerdale (Battle) 87
Sutherland, Alexander 161
Sutherland, Earl John 89
Swiney 121, 123, 171

Telford, Thomas . . . 108, 109, 110, 122, 124, 174, 176, 177, 180, 182
Things' Va. 72
Thom, A. Prof. 43, 45, 46
Thura Mains 153
Thurdistoft 115
Thrumster 19, 123, 143, 200
Thurso . . . . 18, 29, 30, 64, 71, 73, 74, 79, 80, 82, 86, 87, 90, 91, 92, 93, 94, 98, 99, 100, 109, 110, 112, 113, 115, 116, 124, 130, 156, 170, 175, 176, 184, 185, 186, 189, 193, 203, 220, Plates 14, 32, 45, 54, 55
Thurso (Ormlie) Castle 156, 169
Thurso East Castle . 97, 167, 169, 171, Plate 28
Thurso River . . 18, 19, 22, 48, 53, 142
Tister 143
Traill, James 14, 105, 109, 128, 133, 191
Traill, Margaret 130
Tulach an T'Sionnaich 31, 35
Tulloch of Assery A (Chambered Cairn) 35
Tulloch of Assery B (Chambered Cairn) 35

Ulbster 97, 123, 143
Ulbster Stone . . . . 64, Plate 13
Upper Dounreay 45

Wag of Forse . . . . 53, 58, Plate 16
Watenan 20, 22, 45, 60, 62
Watten . . 18, 44, 91, 98, 103, 105, 118, 139, 178, 182, 190, 196, 205
Watten Loch 20, 21, 48
Watten Mains . . . . 171, Plate 29
Well of the Brethren 64
Wester 143
Westerdale 48, 137
Westerseat (Wick) 72

Westfield 137, 171
Whaligoe . . . . 108, 109, Plate 37
Wick . . . 14, 18, 19, 26, 45, 48, 50, 72, 80, 82, 83, 91, 92, 93, 94, 98, 99, 100, 107, 108, 111, 112, 113, 114, 115, 124, 125, 126, 142, 157, 158, 175, 176, 178, 184, 185, 186, 190, 192, 194, 197, 199, 211
Wick Bay 20
Wick Parish Church 177
Wick River 18, 142
Winless Loch 26

Yarrows . . . 20, 22, 30, 40, 51, 53, 192
Yarrows (South) . . 30, 31, 36, 37, Fig. 3
Yarrows (South) Broch . . . . Fig. 8